SALT FOR THE DRAGON

EAST IS EAST AND WEST IS WEST. ESSON M. GALE, 1926.

SALT
for the
DRAGON

A Personal History of China
1908–1945

ESSON M. GALE

The Michigan State College Press
1953

PRINTED IN THE UNITED STATES
OF AMERICA BY
AMERICAN BOOK–STRATFORD PRESS, INC.

To the little Maid
Of a golden Michigan October

Introduction

WHEN THE MANUSCRIPT of this book was first handed to me
to read, it contained, by way of author's introduction, an
Apologia. And a very diffident *Apologia* it was. It was also
something more than just that. It was a key to the character
of the then, to me, unknown author—simple and yet dignified, kindly, courteous, but withal a strength of character
which was represented by the passion of his love for China.
This, one could read between the lines. But after I had finished reading it, I felt sure that no man with these qualities
should write an apology for the history of his life. His life
has been a full one, dedicated to the service of his own country, the United States, and the country of his adoption, China.
To both of these countries Esson Gale has rendered signal
services. And the theme of this book is his recounting of
those services.

It struck me even more forcibly as I read through the
pages of the manuscript that there was no need for Dr. Gale
to apologize for the quality of his writing. After all, he was
not a professional writer. His job in relation to this book was
to tell in simple terms his personal history of a China that
has gone forever—the story of the charm and beauty of that
vast country, of its strangeness and its goodness, the story of
the Chinese people and the foreigners amongst them during
the first half of the twentieth century.

Esson Gale is, I suppose, the nearest thing to a retired
American colonial administrator in the United States today.
There have been others, of course, but few, if any, have
written their memoirs. This is a great pity, for these men and
their lives, if they would only write them, are the translators

of history. When one thinks of the immense amount of literature contributed on little known countries by retired British colonial administrators, who have spent their years of retirement in writing of far off places, one realizes what a service they have done, not only to their country, but to the world in general. Gale may be likened to these men, and it is to be hoped that in the writing of this book, he has set a precedent that will be followed in the years to come by Americans serving throughout the world today.

Lyle Blair

CONTENTS

I

WHY CHINA?, 1908

The Beginning — Pacific Voyage — Port of Entry — Glamour City

The Beginning

IN THE CHILL of an early Peking dawn, I found myself standing below the Dragon Throne. The Emperor of China was holding an audience, as customary, at daybreak. I held perfectly still, as did the other members of the American envoy's suite, military aides, and diplomatic secretaries grouped solidly behind him. Each of us civilians wore evening dress—tail coat, white shirtfront and tie—and each, feeling rather ridiculous, stiffly held a silk hat in his hand.

The Grand Councillors of the Empire, the Senior and Junior Guardians of the Heir Apparent, the Presidents of the Six Ministries of State, stood in two converging rows so as to face us from either side of the lofty dais of the throne. These great mandarins were either Manchu or Chinese. They wore, indistinguishably, the insignia of high rank, the different-hued buttons on their sable-rimmed official hats, the iridescent peacock feathers falling behind, and the silk embroidered square of fabulous bird or beast on chest and back. The sleeves of their elaborately-figured, stiff brocade court-gowns extended sidewise, "like the half-open wings of a bird." Hands were concealed in the long cuff shaped like a horse's hoof, which symbolized the nomad origin of the conquering Manchu clans. Their feet were encased in black-satin boots, thick white soles against the cold flagstone floor.

The Americans and the mandarins gazed at each other with mutual curiosity. Towering-tall, United States Secretary of War Jacob McGavock Dickinson of Tennessee was reading President Howard Taft's autographed letter to the Emperor of China. In loud tones the Special Envoy pronounced the President's stereotyped phrases, describing the two countries' traditional cordiality and amity. His voice reverberated through the lofty green and gold ceilings of the audience hall. The era of "Dollar Diplomacy" was being ushered in. America henceforth would play a pivotal role in China's international financing.

The Emperor himself and the several American Student Interpreters in

1

the envoy's suite were the only persons of tender age in that august assembly. But even I, as one of the Student Interpreters, surpassed His Majesty by at least two decades. There he sat on the gilt-and-lacquer throne, with his short, baby legs stretched out straight before him. The intricately embroidered satin robe on his diminutive person displayed the awe-inspiring Imperial five-clawed dragon done in gold thread. Underneath, as any Peking child would in cold weather, he wore a thickly wadded winter garment which caused his arms to project stiffly from either side, suggestive of a mechanical toy.

With a hasty side-glance at his precariously seated son, the Regent, Prince Ch'un, rose to deliver an appropriately felicitous reply to the greetings of his Exalted Friend, the President of the Land of the Flowery Flag, across the Ocean of Peace. His words seemed high and thin after the sonorous tones of the heavily-mustached American envoy.

The reading of President Taft's letter was followed by a previously prepared translation by Dr. Charles D. Tenney, the Legation interpreter; the Prince Regent's reply and its rendition in turn into English—these formalities occupied but a few moments.

Bowing intermittently, the Embassy staff, in order of rank, backed themselves slowly out from the Imperial Presence. We could view the gorgeous spectacle presented by this, one of the last Imperial audiences which successive European embassies had described.

Above the Son of Heaven, on his throne, great golden Chinese ideographs blazed forth His august virtue and glory. He was the lineal descendant in the ninth degree of the great Manchu Emperors known to the Occident as K'ang Hsi and Ch'ien Lung. When General Wu San-kwei, the traitorous Warden of the Pass at Shan-hai Kuan, had opened the way in 1644, the Manchu hordes had cantered down upon the rich plains of China from their remote Manchurian home. Garrisons of long-bow "bannermen," stationed in every strategic city, had rapidly dominated the unwieldy Empire, from the Wall of Ten Thousand Leagues in the North to the malaria-infested valleys South of the Mists, on the Burma border.

"Rulers on horseback" to begin with, these unlettered nomads had carried Chinese civilization to the farthermost limits of Eastern Asia. However, generations of soft living had brought decadence upon the Imperial clansmen. The throne of Nurhachu, founder of the race, had come under the control of women, eunuchs, and the sleek-minded Confucian mandarins. The very audience we were attending made it abundantly clear that the Mandate of Heaven was departing from the nerveless grasp of the Manchu house.

At that moment I thought how life's determining decisions are thrust upon one in unexpected form. A former class-mate spent a day with me in the autumn of 1907 at Ann Arbor to see a football game. He disclosed that he was on his way to Japan.

"What," I asked him, "takes you there, of all places?"

2

"A government post," was the enigmatic reply.

"I didn't know any members of your family were in politics," I commented.

"They aren't," said "the Duke," the college *sobriquet* of Edwin L. Neville, who was to become one of our new career diplomats. This name had been applied to him by his historically-minded young associates from the similarity of his family name to that of the famous English noble house.

President Theodore Roosevelt, "the Duke" explained, had been shocked by dislosures of inefficiency and even corruption among some of our American officials in the Far East. This conclusion an Assistant Secretary of State had arrived at after a personal tour of the consular posts of China and Japan. The subsequent Executive Order of June 30, 1906, henceforth had made assignments to the foreign service, save for the exalted posts of Minister or Ambassador, subject to competitive examination. This system of appointment replaced the "lame duck" politician, a type from which the ranks of the "Yankee consul" abroad had been recruited, though with notable exceptions.

Like the young Marco Polo with an uncle at the court of the Great Khan, I too had my father's brother in the Far East. My imagination had been early fired by the letters of my "Uncle Jim," who had gone to the Hermit Kingdom of Korea some decades earlier. He was now coming to be a widely known scholar and writer through his graphic and sympathetic interpretations of the little-known people of the Land of Morning Calm, Chosen.

An already established yearning for distant regions of the earth had been further stimulated in me by a glimpse of Viceroy Li Hung-chang at the annual Canadian National Exhibition at Toronto in the autumn of 1896. China's greatest statesman of the nineteenth century appeared as a tall spare form, in rich brocaded satins, with peacock-feather and highest rank button on his mandarin hat. His long sharp features, with a wisp of grey beard at the chin, represented the very image of those engravings of the great Manchu sovereigns, "Kien Lung" and "Kang Hee," which had embellished the elaborate *folio* accounts of the late seventeenth and early eighteenth century British embassies to China.

Viceroy Li was completing a journey around the world. He had been China's special ambassador at the coronation of Czar Nicholas II at St. Petersburg, and had been settling Russia's bill for securing the withdrawal of Japan from Manchuria after the disastrous Chino-Japanese war of two years earlier. He had signed with Prince Lobanov, Russia's Foreign Minister, the Li-Lobanov treaty granting Russia the right to build the railway across North Manchuria, together with the ice free port of Dalny (later Dairen) and the fortress of Port Arthur.

When Li Hung-chang appeared at Toronto, the curious crowd looked upon him as part of the exhibit arranged by the Fair's management. Un-

3

conscious of this undignified role, Viceroy Li took it that he was being befittingly honored as he was carried onto a wide platform, erected across from the racetrack grandstand. To me, a wide-eyed boy of eleven, the grand mandarin was the incarnation of all the mystery of Far Cathay, even as he swayed precariously in the improvised "sedan chair," under which four stalwart Toronto "bobbies" staggered.

Some ten years later, I spied an unusual group stepping briskly across the Campus of my university at Ann Arbor. I recognized the leader, the venerable James Burrill Angell, President of the University, who had served as envoy of the United States to the Court of Peking in 1880. A dapper Chinese personage in silk gown and red-buttoned skull-cap strode beside the President. It was the Chinese Minister to Washington, the elegant and popular Dr. Wu T'ing-fang, whose salty eloquence first awakened America to the exquisite mind of the Chinese gentleman.

Even as early as this, in the first decade of this century, in the universities and colleges of America, young China was quietly preparing for its later stellar role. At a house-party at the University, a Chinese student, "C. T." Wang we called him, was one of the guests. I noted his alert mind, his mastery of English. I observed closely this representative of a people which was to play so determining a part in my own career, for I was on the point of leaving for China. C. T. Wang became my lifelong friend and ultimately as Ambassador of the Chinese Republic to Washington crowned a distinguished career in the service of his country.

Some years later as I sat in the cosmopolitan lobby of the Wagons-Lits Hotel in the inviolate Legation Quarter of Peking, a young Chinese in Western dress dashed up the steps and through the swinging doors. I recognized my friend "C. T." of Ann Arbor days. He was now the Vice-President of the Senate of the new Provisional National Assembly, exotic organ of popular government which Yuan Shih-k'ai, President of the newly established "Republic," had earlier grudgingly approved. On this day, however, Yuan was giving it a Cromwellian purge of its modern-minded membership. My young friend had scaled the back-wall of the Assembly precincts and had made a record-breaking dash for the safety of the Legation Quarter.

*   *   *

However, in this lure of the Orient which stirred me as the way thither opened, there remained another nostalgic vision. It was of a girl with wide grey eyes and dark flowing curls. She had visited us with her parents and her younger sister for two enchanting weeks during a distant Michigan October. The maples had turned their gorgeous autumn tints and the air was crisp in that exhilarating season of the year along the shores of the Great Lakes. About her clung an aura of one who had beheld the strange places of the earth. Indeed, her early childhood had been spent in a distant corner of Asia, the Hermit Kingdom of Korea.

4

This young person was much given to telling the most remarkable stories. For example, she related to us how she had once been taken at the age of four to visit the King of Korea in his very Palace. She hadn't been afraid for she had chatted with His Majesty in voluble native vernacular. To be sure, she did so without the elaborate honorifics appropriate to such an occasion and personage. Taking his hand, she had wandered with him from one entrancing chamber to another remarking on all those things which concern a very little girl.

Again, lying wakeful on a hot summer's night in a Korean mountain inn, as the family journeyed across the peninsula, she had heard the stealthy tread of a tiger, as it prowled past in search of a stray pig. The pandemonium which ensued in the village made further sleep impossible.

She also told us of confounding a wandering Korean Buddhist monk, who had come upon her playing before the house. Rapidly reciting the multiplication table, she bade him repeat even one of his own *sutras* as glibly.

From the family home well up on the hill-side, she had watched Japanese transports land troops in the harbor of Wonsan on east-coast Korea, in a resumption of those ancient expeditions whereby the Island Empire sought to augment its territories at the expense of China's vassal. In connivance with her small sister, their terrified Chinese cook had been hidden behind the parlour sofa, nourished with wedges of apple-pie until he could make off in the night for the Manchurian border.

Taken across the seas, her schooldays were spent in the capitals of Europe.

All this and more had been so far a cry from my prosaic life as a boy in a small town in Michigan that even Mona Lisa or Beatrice could not have awakened a more exquisite ecstasy in their respective admirers' bosoms. The years had gone by and the vision of the wondrous little maid had not been forgotten. Now she had once more merged herself in the mystery of the Far East.

So wandered my memory.

* * *

After the departure of "the Duke" for Japan, my several young associates on the University faculty discovered me at unseasonable hours immersed in Frank Carpenter's *Geographical Readers,* in elements of arithmetic, in French and German conversation primers. When the year's academic effort was ended, I could boast of a Master's degree in the history of medieval Europe; also of an appointment as a Student Interpreter to the United States Legation at Peking. My appointment was signed by President Theodore Roosevelt, who it had appeared had come to repose "special trust and confidence" in the person of my name. By this I was committed to the study of the Chinese language, excluding all else, for a period of two years. Thereafter I might be employed indefinitely (subject to good behavior!) as a Consular officer of the United States in China.

China, in 1908, was to the American a land vaguely known for the evangelizing work of missionaries and their occasional massacre; and specifically for cash contributions, largely for the alleviation of human distress caused by recurrent famine, pestilence, and flood. What could motivate any right-minded young man to leave the security of a midwestern community for such an uncouth region? In the well-ordered world at home one might aspire to be cashier in a bank; hardware could be sold to farmers at gratifying profits; or one could enter the highly respected professions of law, medicine, or the ministry. A fair living could be made at teaching, or by selling insurance or bonds. If one had a predilection to study some outlandish language, there were about us the remnants of Fenimore Cooper's once proud "red skins." The Chippewa Indians had provided us with many of our local place-names. Were they not descendants of the original settlers of the valley of the Saginaw River, eulogized by the celebrated French philosopher De Tocqueville in a remarkable burst of writing when he beheld its "primitive grandeur" in 1831? Did not the *Tittabawassee* and the *Shiawassee* unite to form that noble stream? Were not our nearby beaches called *O-at-ka* and *We-no-na*? As humble basket-makers now, the original warlike owners still had their habitations at a nearby village named *Kawkawlin*. Of all this rich Amerindian lore so near at hand I was quite unconscious. It was years later that a distinguished ethnologist called my attention to these interesting philological features of the Michigan region.

Why go to China? This, once more, was my memory.

Pacific Voyage

THE STATE DEPARTMENT instructions of June 17, 1908, enjoined me to sail from San Francisco by the 30th instant. My services appeared to be urgently required in the Far East! There followed a hasty round of family good-byes. On the way, volcanic Hawaii revived childhood imaginings of Robinson Crusoe's isle—of golden beaches with waving palm fronds, watered by showers of liquid sunshine.

After this came a thrilling three days within the Mikado's Empire, greatly extending an acquaintance hitherto gained chiefly through Gilbert & Sullivan's melodies, Pièrre Loti's romances, and Puccini's musical scores. We had gladly hailed the land-fall off Yokohama after the tedium of the voyage.

Strange bat-winged *sampans* darted about our steamer, as it moved slowly over the blue water into the harbor. The great white cone of Fujiyama, floating flawless in the mists, seemed to belong to a mountain with summit but without base. Tokyo, city of moated castle walls, displayed above its grey-tiled palace roofs twisted pines centuries old; in a brief excursion north we approached through long avenues of towering crypto-

6

merias—Nikko, sacred in its gilt and vermilion shrines; Kamakura, where "the heathen pray," drew us to its colossal bronze Buddha.

Peter Agustus Jay, in the absence of Ambassador O'Brien United States *chargé d'affaires,* honored us with a dinner.

Later, under proper chaperonage, we had a glimpse of that "city of dreadful night," Tokyo's notorious *Yoshiwara.* Behind wooden barred windows open to the street's public gaze, sat the little bepowdered prisoners with their elaborate coiffures.

All this took place under the informed guidance of my old friend "the Duke," who had preceded me to Japan by almost a year. His quickly acquired use of the notoriously intractable language of *Dai Nippon* commanded our deep respect.

Too soon the time to leave arrived. My young companion from Brown University, Harold Henry, and I embarked on a malodorous little Japanese steamer, to cross the Yellow Sea to the shores beyond. Now at last we were plunging into the unknown. Columbus, as he set sail westward, could not have felt more desolate and alone. All friends were left behind us.

The *Sagami Maru,* a rusty little coaster, plowed steadily through the glassy sea in the overpowering July heat. In the offing lurked the ever-menacing tropical typhoon: "June, *too soon!* July, *stand by!* August, *they must!* September, *remember!* October, *they're over."* So runs the admonitory doggerel of the China coast mariners.

We lolled listlessly on rattan chairs set up on Captain Saito's narrow bridge. This was the only suitable space for his two American passengers. There was ample time to reflect upon our temerity. Depressed by the stifling atmosphere, my mind turned sluggishly upon the placid joys and simple tasks of home. There I would be surrounded by the familiar figures of relatives and friends. Here we looked only into the inscrutable faces of our Japanese captain and his crew.

The ever-recurring *rosu-bifu* (roast beef) was leathery and tasteless. Occidentals, of course, were exclusively carnivorous and must be provided with meat, instead of the steaming rice with a bit of fish and pickle condiment set out for the native passengers. Even the *Asahi beeru* was warm and lacked adequate alcoholic content, anticipating the emasculated brews of a still remote American prohibition era.

The black cloud hanging over us lowered when Captain Saito pointed out a distant shore which he called China. The land appeared as a dark mass on the horizon just discernible above the yellow swell of the roadstead. After anchoring in the roadstead, a steamlaunch took us off, passengers and baggage. There was a sickening shake-up when we crossed the shallow bar. We entered a sluggish river, such as Joseph Conrad might have described, cutting its way tortuously to the sea, between eternally crumbling banks of ochre-colored silt.

Only ignorance of history prevented us from being roused to patriotic emotion here. That heroic aphorism, "Blood is thicker than water," was dramatically repeated at this very spot just half a century before when Commodore Josiah Tattnal, U.S.N., disregarded his neutrality instructions "to abstain from all coercive measures" against the Chinese in their war with England. Instead he sent a boat-load of his American bluejackets to rescue from beneath the withering fire of the Chinese forts a hapless British storming party when their landing craft stuck fast on the mud bar.

Without heroics came *our* debarkation. No Nevada desert town could have been more desolate than this port of entry, Tangku, "in a lost and ancient land."

So this was China.

Where, we muttered, were the nine-storied pagodas, the bastioned city walls, the teeming throngs of "Chinamen" lightly swinging on slender shoulder-poles boxes of fragrant tea? Show us the plump mandarins waving silken fans, the little ladies of Cathay slyly peeping from closed palanquins, and all the other authentic features of the China we had so often surveyed on porcelain vases or in our geography picture-books.

Great was our disillusionment. In the stuffy station restaurant we silently ate a prosaic lunch of roast beef and vegetables, cooked in the English style, "as God made them," and a custard pudding, served by a sloppy waiter.

A waiting train stood on the tracks: English type, brass-bound locomotive, and compartment "carriages."

On the station platform pandemonium had apparently broken loose. Shouting coolies dashed here and there, big muscular fellows. They were not the diminutive, furtive types we were accustomed to see about the Chinese laundries and restaurants back in "the States." This was North China.

On these wind-swept plains, the blood of the northern nomads—Khitan, Kin, Mongol, and Tungusic Manchu—had mingled with the sturdy Yellow River Valley stock of the aboriginal Chinese, in a never-ending succession of incursions within the Great Wall. Their mixed progeny are strong-boned, wheat and millet-eaters, and consumers of prodigious quantities of fiery *kaoliang* spirits. Rice is for the delicate southerners.

As our train rolled across the desolate mudflats of the river delta, we saw in the distance skeleton forms revolving with the wind. On closer approach, they could be seen to display flapping, tattered sails. They turned out to be a species of windmill, which as I came to learn, were employed to draw sea water into shallow ponds through deep canals. The North China sun and wind evaporate the brine and in due course great mounds of shining white salt are heaped up to supply the essential savour for all North China's population.

This was interesting to me, for I was familiar with salt and its production. As a boy I had played under the glistening stalactites hanging beneath the massive timber salt-blocks of my great-uncle's saw-mill on the

8

banks of the Saginaw river. I vaguely recalled reading somewhere that the mandarins used salt as a source of public revenue; it was in Messer Marco Polo's narrative.

Port of Entry

TIENTSIN, the first city of China which we were to see, had, less than a decade before, been the scene of a desperate siege by Chinese troops, reinforced by the fanatical Boxer insurgents. When at length the beleaguering armies were driven off, an international naval column under the British Admiral, Seymour, had pushed out to relieve the hard pressed Legations at Peking. One of the participants in the expedition, the late Rear-Admiral Joseph K. Taussig, U.S.N., graphically related the story to me many years later, as we paced the quarterdeck of the battleship *West Virginia* off San Pedro after fleet battle-practice one balmy evening.

A cadet at the time, young Taussig had been wounded, and had had to be carried on a stretcher on the retreat.

For the first time, a well-equipped but numerically small foreign force learned the lesson so patent to China's later invaders: China's defense lies in vast spaces and inexhaustible manpower. This well-led European force was engulfed in the morasses of the millet fields, while swarms of regulars and guerillas attacked, using every weapon from "big swords" to two-man *jingals* throwing murderous iron slugs. The retreat was precipitate, and only by a narrow margin was the column saved from annihilation.

Personages later to become famous played a part in all these stirring events. A young engineer, drawn from organizing North China's largest coal project, the K'ai-p'ing mines, had his first experience here in a notable career devoted to the relief of suffering humanity. Young Herbert Hoover's courage saved hundreds among the Chinese civilian refugees crowded within the British Concession defences. One of these, T'ang Shao-yi, a life-long friend of Mr. Hoover's, was to become a noted statesman of China. Two junior lieutenants in the British contingent achieved lasting fame in World War I, Admirals Lord Jellicoe and Lord Beatty.

Tientsin, to us, was a drab and dusty place. We found it divided into "concessions"—British, French, German, Japanese, Italian. There was even a Belgian Concession. That enterprising monarch-merchant, King Leopold II, had staked out here in North China, as in the Congo, another bit of alien soil. The laws and mandates of the nations at interest ran exclusively in these separate areas. This was our first acquaintance with the practice of extraterritoriality, briefly termed "extrality." By this the authority of the Chinese government was excluded from these model municipal enclaves, carved out of Chinese sovereign soil but administered exclusively under foreign flags.

Tientsin's macadam streets were flanked by high walls, concealing charming gardens and villas within. Only on the road called after the good Queen Victoria, were there shops displaying foreign goods. Beyond

9

the concessions lay sprawled the Chinese "native city." The Pei-ho—
"North River"—divided the areas with broad bridges connecting them, on
which booths were doing a thriving *al fresco* trade.

Particularly noticeable were the fruit-venders' stands. Here juicy melons
were displayed in cut sections under the hot August sun, gathering both
flies and the dust of the roadway, for the later internal discomfort of in-
cautious consumers. Cholera and the melon season always coincided in
China.

*   *   *

The official quarters of the late distinguished diplomat and scholar,
Edward T. Williams, who represented the United States in that important
centre, we found to be a series of low-set buildings fronted by a courtyard.
We were at once ushered into the Consul-General's drawing room adjacent to his offices, where Mrs. Williams, the gracious hostess of the establishment, served us our first afternoon tea on China's soil.

Other guests were present at the invariable five o'clock ritual of the Far
East. Among them was a grave and dignified figure, Dr. Charles Daniel
Tenney, newly appointed Secretary for Chinese Affairs of the United
States Legation at Peking. We were to know this eminent New England
educator much better as time wore on. It was he who was to induct us
into the mysteries of the Chinese language, both oral and written, beginning without delay the very first morning of our residence at Peking.

A sad-eyed Vice-Consul confirmed our early fears as to the primitive
nature of existence at the Capital city. We were admonished that Tientsin
offered the last chance to secure civilized supplies. Beds, mosquito-nets
(*sine qua non* of North China's summer life), even heating stoves, might
be difficult to procure at Peking.

In the perspiring heat of the moment, possible absence of the last item
left us for the moment cold.

Glamour City

ACCOMPANIED by Chinese Secretary Tenney and our precious purchases, we
entrained the next day for the final three hours of our journey.

Fields of giant sorghum, food of man and beast in North China, waved
for endless miles. There were glimpses of the Grand Canal, now nearing
its terminus from the tribute ricelands of the South. Its broad surface was
alive with houseboats and cargo-junks, propelled by long stern-sculls, or
by sails in all stages of tatterdom. Auxiliary power was furnished by half-
naked trackers, straining at long ropes along the foot-paths on the banks.
Here we saw being transported kerosene, cotton piece-goods, chests of tea,
coarse native paper, jars of rice-wine, and all the variety of staple products ministering to the needs of North China's hinterland.

Bulky commodities, such as coarse carpet-wool and furs, were coming
down stream, soon to end their long journey from the caravan-roads of

Mongolia and farther Asia in the holds of steamers at Tientsin, for shipment to all quarters of the Western world.

In the manner of all "old China hands" our travelling companion and mentor, Dr. Tenney, was a vast repository of information. But little present comfort could be gleaned from the stories of his three decades in the Celestial Empire—tales of gruesome treatment meted out to missionary folk, men and women, in the fateful uprising of 1900 against all Occidentals; stories of frustration and failure of promising enterprises initiated by energetic Westerners in China's "limitless market."

Not more cheerful was the outlook from the railway carriage's windows, when for distraction we turned to view the moving landscape. There we saw naked grave-mounds dotting the countryside. Around the tombs were groves of the funereal "white-bark" pine, a tree reserved especially for cemeteries. Sculptured monoliths mounted upright on gigantic stone tortoises, stood out starkly in front of the more pretentious tombs. Occasionally our horrified eyes met the partly emerging planking of coffins, from which the earth had been washed away by the heavy rains.

Finally, the train glided alongside the towering walls of Peking itself. Entering the outer Chinese City first, we were brought to a halt at the station just below the even higher grey-brick ramparts of the adjoining Tatar City.

It was already dusk and the stagnant heat was insufferable. All about was a penetrating odor. This appeared to be a compound of many smells, some unrecognizable. Some we came to know later as arising from sesamum—peanut—and even castor-oil. These are the various vegetable oils in which the Peking populace fries its supper. Surprisingly enough, the oil last mentioned seems to lose its active principle when subjected to the heat of cooking. In cooler weather, we came to learn, the odors of Peking's eventide are not too unpleasant.

Passing through the "Small Water Gate," an informal entrance into the Legation Quarter from the southern city, we found ourselves in the courtyards of a Chinese temple. This, Dr. Tenney informed us, was the Temple of the Three Mandarins. Here in picturesque buildings, with curving tiled roofs and sharp up-turned gables, grouped about a courtyard, the Secretary for Chinese Affairs had his residence.

After a quick brush-up, dinner was served almost noiselessly in one of the halls by a highly accomplished "boy." We were not too weary to be impressed by this gorgeous figure in a plum-colored silk jacket worn over a long dark-blue gown. On his head was a round "pent roof" straw hat with a flowing red silk tassel. He moved about in cloth-shod feet with the silent tread of a cat. When he was permitted to doff his hat because of the heat, his shaven forehead gave him the bland appearance of the traditional "celestial." Midway back from his forehead began his thick braided queue, prolonged into a black silk tassel.

During the protracted dinner, our preceptor continued an informative

11

table-talk. Despite a "punkah" languidly waving over the table, actuated by a somnolent coolie somewhere outside, it grew ever hotter in the otherwise motionless atmosphere. I drank a glass of light wine, followed by a cup of scalding coffee, and melted into a bath of perspiration. The heat of the long day, the continuous admonitions, what to do, what not to do, stupified me.

The "boy" escorted us at length to our own quarters, the Student Interpreters' Mess, in an adjacent compound. Once in my room, I was in bed in a moment. Hardly had I closed my eyes when through the wall a chorus of shrill yelps and barks brought me wide awake. Even the three-headed Cerberus himself could not have excelled the clamor. Unwilling to face a sleepless night, I rang for the "boy."

Chao, the *Major Domo* of the Student Interpreters' Mess, promptly appeared.

"Go and quiet those wretched dogs," I commanded peremptorily. Chao looked his deep embarrassment.

"I cannot give offense for such a trifle," he protested apologetically. "Those are the palace lion-dogs which the Empress Dowager has presented to the great American Engineer, Master Jameson, who lives in the compound next to this," Chao earnestly explained.

I turned my face to the wall, I had already learned "One arrives in Peking weeping..."—the first half of the saying of a temperamental German diplomat, the same who when the Boxers were reported as about to pierce the Legation defences and murder them all, sat down at the piano and executed Rachmaninoff's Prelude.

I was to appreciate the remainder of the *bon mot* in due course, "... but one leaves in tears."

II

PEKING, 1908–1911

Legation Personalities — Legs of a Mongol Pony — Giants of the Missions — The Covenanted Services — Wards of Uncle Sam — An Outlandish Language — When in Rome — A Cathayan Cycle — Beyond the Barrier — Across the Yalu

Legation Personalities

IN FEW REGIONS of the earth is the death of summer less mourned than in North China. Over the swimming fields of giant sorghum, the hot fetid air, born of the southwest monsoon, is wafted away overnight by a crystal-clear breath from the Mongolian steppes. The world is revivified. Horses, donkeys, mules lift their drooping heads. Once more the deep melodic tone of camel bells is heard, as the shaggy trains file through the city gates from Central Asian caravan trails.

For a homesick fortnight I had lingered at the almost deserted Capital. Had I had the means, I would gladly have purchased a return ticket home. To the heat were added exotic discomforts: stinging sand midgets, and agile fleas which no mosquito net could exclude.

The first cool September breezes from the north quickly brought me to a consciousness of the marvelous setting which would be the scene of my activities for the coming two years.

Only now did I realize why destiny had made me a student of Europe's Middle Ages before projecting me into this land of anachronisms. The gorgeousness of the Tatar Court, full of intriguing women and cringing eunuchs, could not have been surpassed in the palaces of Byzantium. The first movements, furtive and suppressed, were to be noted of an era which was far to surpass Italy's Renaissance.

Peking has ever been the setting of a strange world, evoking as early as the thirteenth century the admiration of Marco Polo and his uncle Maffeo and father Nicolo who spent a good part of thirty years at the court of Kublai Khan.

Successive European embassies,—Russian, Dutch, British,—each were humiliated before the all-powerful Dragon Throne when obliged to perform the "kow-tow," or if recalcitrant, by being summarily dismissed without audience.

13

In 1908, the historic Capital displayed a galaxy of European talent. The Legations were headed by men of distinction. There was M. Korostovetz, envoy of the government of that Czar Nicholas II whose star had been dimmed by the disasters and retreats of the Russo-Japanese war, only a scant three years before. The Czarist Legation was the scene of many brilliant social functions, graced by the statuesque Mme. Korostovetz. Here frequently appeared General Horvath, autocrat of the Czar's residual North Manchurian Empire. A patriarchal beard overspread the broad chest of the Viceroy; his uniform shone with glittering decorations.

Sir John Jordan was His Britannic Majesty's representative. Tall, with white hair and mustache, Sir John was an impressive figure.

I was furnished with a note of introduction from Uncle Jim to his friend of many years, for with his knowledge of the Korean language and his familiar standing at Court, my uncle had frequently served Sir John as official interpreter when the latter had held the post of British Minister-Resident at Seoul. Sir John received me most kindly. My call resulted in unexpected recognition for one of my youthful obscurity—an invitation to a formal luncheon at the British Legation.

As the dominant European Power in China, Britain's financial interests and trading operations were carefully watched over and skillfully shaped. This, however, was accomplished by a Legation personnel seemingly only concerned in tennis matches, racing gymkhanas and endless teas!

France's interest was in the far south, where she maintained her "puppet" royal courts in Indo-China. Nevertheless, the Third Republic's *Chef de Mission* at Peking was an experienced diplomat, the polished Monsieur de Margerie whose *bons mots* passed from tea- to dinner-table throughout Legation society. Monsieur le Ministre frequently danced with fifteen year old Madge Ralli, daughter of Mrs. Lewis Einstein of our own Legation. No mere Student Interpreter could seek a dance with that haughty young lady.

Germany was represented by Graf Rex, ponderous and taciturn. Within his Legation walls, plans continued to be developed for expanding Germany's place in the Far East, with the colony of Tsingtao as its focal point.

The enigmatic Japanese mission was headed by a Mr. Ijuin and by various succeeding career diplomats. They silently appraised inert China, waiting for the day when taking advantage of Europe's preoccupations, the fatal "New Order" in East Asia ordained by the Island Empire's immutable policy could be initiated. Every precedent of diplomatic history established by Occidental Powers was carefully studied. The notorious secret "Cassini Convention"—actual or imagined—whereby Russia was to dominate China, was already the prototype of Japan's coming Twenty One Demands of the World War era.

Many of the lesser Powers had legations at China's capital. The career diplomats in charge such as Count Ahlefelt of the Danish Mission, M. Oudendijk of the Dutch, who later received a knighthood for his services

14

to British interests in Russia during the Revolution, and Baron Cartier de Marchienne of the Belgian, were to find promotion to London and Washington. (De Marchienne was Belgium's Ambassador in London on that fateful May 10, 1940, when he declared to Lord Halifax "We have been invaded savagely although we offered no offense.")

The late Count Carlo Sforza, scion of a cadet branch of the great Milanese family, had his brief tour of service in Peking. Later, as Italy's Foreign Minister, he signed the Treaty of Rapallo with Yugoslavia in 1920. I was to renew my acquaintance with Count Sforza in the United States, as a publicist and writer on European politics, beyond the confines of the land in which his forebears played their brilliant Renaissance roles. At length, after World War II, he once more served his country as foreign minister with brilliant distinction.

My own Chief of Mission, first among his compeers, was the Envoy Extraordinary and Minister Plenipotentiary of the United States, William Woodville Rockhill. A tall, impressive man with large head and booming voice, he was the prototype of our career diplomats.

I would often watch the Minister in his office in the Legation Chancery, seated behind a tall roller-top desk, nervously fingering a chaplet of Tibetan prayer beads. While so engaged his inveterate cigarette was for the moment out of his hand. Some two weeks after one of the student interpreters arrived in Peking, he asked him with characteristic irony, "Do you think you know all about China?" Mrs. Rockhill was noted as a charming hostess, a talent not often given opportunity to display itself, owing to the complete absorption of the Minister in his diplomatic and scholarly activities. We Student Interpreters looked forward eagerly to occasional invitations to Mrs. Rockhill's *soirees*.

Such social anticipations were not always vindicated. Once we received invitations to a Christmas Eve dinner-dance provided for the Legation staff. Twenty male guests appeared in correct evening clothes. Only four ladies were present as possible dancing partners, Mrs. Rockhill, her aged mother, the spinster sister of the Military Attaché, and a lady tourist who by chance had been found unaccounted for at the Wagon-Lits Hotel!

Known generally for his aloofness and acid remarks, the Minister condescended to treat me with unexpected kindness. Away back, possibly sometime in the 1890's, I surmise, he and my Uncle James Gale had become friends during a trans-Pacific voyage to Korea. Their conversation had revolved about the curious similarity in Royal objections, to the introduction of tobacco into England and Korea. Gale had written a sprightly monograph on the arrival of the weed in the latter land. Thus their mutual scolarly interests as Orientalists began, a bond not broken over the years.

Rockhill's career as scholar and diplomat was outstanding. After attending the French military school of St. Cyr, he had early in the 1880's secured an appointment as secretary to the American Legation at Peking, as an opportunity to advance his studies on the Far East. He was one of the first to make a scientific expedition into little-known Tibet. This was in 1891 and 1892. Though he did not penetrate far into that forbidden land, a number of his subsequent scientific papers threw new light upon this obscure part of the world. These took popular form in a book entitled *The Land of the Lamas.*

Recalled to Washington, Rockhill was placed in charge of the Pan-American Bureau by John Hay who wished to avail himself of the diplomat's specialized knowledge. He is largely credited with shaping the American Secretary's Far Eastern policy, including the formulation with British cooperation of the celebrated "Open Door Policy." He was made United States High Commissioner in 1900–01, in the gathering of the representatives of the Powers at Peking to determine the penalties to be inflicted upon China for the mid-summer madness of the Boxer fanatics. He fought strenuously on the side of leniency. His efforts, not entirely successful, scaled down the indemnities which amounted nevertheless to $330,000,000 and were to absorb for a period of forty years the unpledged balance of China's Customs revenues. When the Germans demanded that the guilty Boxer leaders be turned over to the Allies for capital punishment, Rockhill flashed back, "Let the Chinese be their own executioners."

Rockhill was credited with initiating the policy whereby after 1908 the unused surplus of the American portion of the Boxer indemnity was devoted to the education of young Chinese in the United States. Rockhill was thus at least partly responsible for some of the educational transformation of China of the past several decades. His career later included the posts of Ambassador to Russia and to Turkey.

My last meeting with him was in 1913 when he had been placed on the shelf by a new administration which knew not the aging diplomat. At my invitation he addressed a large gathering of Americans. He died within the same year at Honolulu as he was returning to take up a post as adviser to President Yuan Shih-k'ai. William Woodville Rockhill was unquestionably one of the ablest diplomatic officers that the American foreign service produced.

When the Dalai Lama visited Peking in 1909, Rockhill was reminded of his early Tibetan adventure. Mitred *hutuktus,* "Living Buddhas," surrounded the great religious chieftain. He and his followers were accompanied by a picturesque train of two-humped Bactrian camels, which transported their vast quantities of baggage. The cavalcade had been set awandering when the expedition of British Colonel Younghusband invaded the sacred city of Lhassa in 1904.

Rockhill promptly had an audience of His Holiness at the Yellow Temple. Presents of red Lama cloth and bundles of black incense rods, resembling the *fasces* about a Roman Lictor's axe, were sent to the Legation. The question arose: how to requite such generosity? A large egg from a Los Angeles ostrich farm reposed in the Rockhill drawing-room. Delicately placed in a satin-lined box, it was transmitted with all due ceremony to the astonished Tibetan Pontiff.

*　　*　　*

The financial agents of the Powers were gathered at Peking in those days. They were prolonging the "battle of concessions" which characterized European "imperialism" in China at the end of the nineteenth century.

The blind Hillier represented that British financial monopoly, the Hongkong & Shanghai Banking Corporation and its affiliated mercantile agencies. We used to see the sightless banker's frail figure on his Mongol pony, riding with a Chinese groom close along-side. They would thread their way slowly through the crowds of carts, rickshas, wheel-barrows, sedans, and carriages which thronged the picturesque Peking streets.

Herr Cortez, manager of the Deutsch-Asiatische Bank, represented German high finance. He had narrowly escaped death in 1900 with his Minister, Baron von Ketteler, who was shot down by a Chinese soldier while on his way to the Foreign Office. Mazot, astute Parisian financier, headed the Banque de l'Indo-Chine, France's official fiscal agency. The Yokohama Specie Bank, like Tokyo's Legation, remained a mysterious instrument of Japan's policy, instantly demanding participation in whatever international financial arrangements other Banks contracted with the Chinese government. The Russo-Asiatic Bank originally founded to further Russian financial imperialism was quiescent since the setbacks of the Russo-Japanese war.

Legation guards were another evidence of the Boxer siege. Never again were the diplomatic representatives of the Powers and their nationals to be left at the mercy of North China armed mobs. The foreign military establishments added to the colorful life of the Capital. The commandants and their staff officers led a gay and carefree life, for their duties were largely routine and social.

The American Marines were conspicuous as handsome men in smart uniforms. Their comfortable quarters and generous pay were the envy of their mates of other nations, a cause perhaps for the bloody feuds which occasionally flared up in the gayer quarters of the city.

Colonel George Barnett commanded the American Legation Guard. Colonel "Georgie" and his bride, Leila Gordon Barnett who brought to the Commandant's drawing room all the charm of a Maryland blueblood, enjoyed a wide popularity. The Colonel's sterling qualities as an officer, in due course, led to his appointment as Commandant of the U. S. Marine Corps at Washington.

Mrs. Barnett dearly loved romance. News flew that the daughter of the Spanish Minister had been forbidden even the sight of a lovesick Romeo in an adjoining Legation. Mrs. Barnett at once offered her home as asylum to the duenna-ridden maiden. The Signorita soon slipped over to the

17

American Lady Commandant's quarters where a hurried marriage was arranged. Tearful but joyful reconciliations in the Latin manner soon followed.

Lord Kitchener visited Peking in our time. This stern militarist possessed a gentle taste in an unexpected quarter. He was an ardent collector of that most appealing of Chinese aesthetic products, porcelains. This being known, the distinguished general was invited by the Court to select a choice vase from the Imperial collection at the Mukden Palace. The General helped himself to *two* choice vases! When he departed from Peking, all Legation society gathered at the railway station. I shall not forget that last sight of the towering military figure, his rigid features burned a deep red by African suns, standing at attention on the rear platform of his special coach as the train pulled out.

*　　*　　*

Far removed from all the foppery and international intrigue of the Legation Quarter, smouldered the mysterious Manchu Court. Little was known of what went on behind the walls of the Purple Forbidden City. Occidental and Cathayan met only through the most formal channels.

The court officials still wore their deep blue, or dark plum brocade robes with the square insignia of rank on breast and back. This was the *p'u-tzu,* embroidered with fabulous birds for the civil officials, and with appropriately fierce animals for the military. Foreign diplomats were said to be literally mesmesized by the Chinese mandarins wearing these costumes, a fact which was supposed to account for the uniform success of Chinese diplomacy.

Manchu women still tottered along the Peking streets on high stiltlike shoes, but with natural-size feet. Atrophied, bound extremities were prescribed for Chinese women—even those working in the stony fields of North China. Elaborate head-dresses built up on frames added to the natural height of the Manchu ladies. The long straight gown, well slit up the sides, gave them an unusually slender appearance. Oddly enough, this sheathlike dress was to be later revived in fashionable Shanghai circles.

Legs of a Mongol Pony

THE STURDY and swift Mongolian horse provided a large measure of the recreation of Peking's foreign population. We Student Interpreters had our own stables with plenty of grooms and an inheritance of saddlery from our predecessors. Week-ends and holidays, when the daily grind with our garlic-scented "teachers" was momentarily interrupted, were generally devoted to excursions on horseback beyond the city walls. These often took us to the Western Hills some fifteen miles distant across the level plain. Here were charming Buddhist temples, perched on jutting crags, or nestled snugly among clumps of pines in little valleys.

Hospitality in good measure, which included excellent native food, was

18

provided by the monks; we never failed to make ample offerings in copper or silver coin, to the honor of Buddha. To be sure, in these hermitages, meat, wine, and women were taboo. But the "vegetarian" dishes tasted suspiciously of pork and mutton. The venerable abbot took frequent pulls from a pewter flask, adding obviously to the ruddy hue of his not-too-ascetic countenance. On various occasions, when we made unexpected calls, there was a scurrying of light feet and unquestionably feminine giggles to be heard from the direction of the inner courts.

The temples formed our refuge from the intense heat of the walled city of Peking. Our scholastic Chinese could be practically applied in long conversations with learned monk or simple peasant. Nothing could be more romantic than to sit on a temple terrace, flooded with moonlight from the heaven-high North China sky. Here we could look out across the plain to the twinkling lights of the distant Capital. The great Emperor Ch'ien Lung himself over a hundred years before had inscribed his sentiments in poetic form and exquisite calligraphy upon a stone tablet high up on one of the temple terraces,

"Beneath my feet my realm I see . . ."

The diminutive but tireless Tatar mount also provided the principal sports events of the Peking year. The so-called "China pony" is actually bred in Mongolia. He is a perfectly proportioned animal, though standing only about thirteen hands high. With skillful training, he develops speed and good racing qualities. All Legation society congregated in spring and autumn at the Race Course. Also present were those folk who were engaged in such prosaic duties as appertained to the banks, the Customs, and the Postal services, and even some few Occidentals, often of uncertain nationalities, engaged at Peking "in trade" of various sorts. Three days were devoted to a complete absorption in the horse, his speed and betting possibilities.

The foreign envoys and their elaborately gowned consorts insured decorum at these functions. There was an assumption on all sides of being at Ascot, or Longchamps, or Saratoga. Lady Jordan appeared in Victorian "feather boa"; Madame Boppe was exquisitely gowned in the latest Paris fashions brought out *via* the Trans-Siberian railway; Mrs. Barnett had the American woman's *flair* for looking well in anything, wherever she acquired it.

The race-club "tiffins" were cheery affairs—cold viands, and above all English game-pie with marinated beets and plenty of mustard. At Barbier's table champagne would flow like water; his Czarist employers, the Chinese Eastern Railway, gave him a generous entertainment allowance. The Commandant of the Austro-Hungarian guard brought out his Zigane stringed orchestra. Sir Robert Hart's Customs Band always played.

The age-old Chinese love of horses is exemplified on early stone sculptures, as on the second century reliefs of the Wu family tombs. The great T'ang conquerer, T'ai Tsung, has left his favorite chargers, six in all, in immortal bas-reliefs. (Two of them are to be seen in the University of Pennsylvania's museum.) Earthen grave-pieces of moulded clay horses are common enough.

Alongside Peking's north wall, we used to watch the Chinese race their fast pacers, in parallel trenches. For such competitions the Chinese developed their own favored technique. They were interested only in the single-foot gait, not in trotting or galloping. In later years vast throngs of Chinese crowded the race-meets, though the opportunity to gamble made the chief appeal.

But the races at the old Peking *P'ao-ma-cha'ang* were as exclusively European gatherings, save for the grooms, as an Indian *gymkhana* of the Kipling era.

Expeditions, by horse, donkey, and sometimes by train, took us far afield. One of these was expertly directed by the United States Military Attaché at Peking, a young cavalry Captain.

One fine morning we took train for the Nankow pass to where an inner bastion of the Great Wall skirts the Ming Emperors' tombs. Our party consisted of the Captain and his sister, two young American lady guests from Korea, Harold Henry and myself.

The railway ended at a little mountain village where the Captain had sent servants to sweep and garnish the only inn available. The Mandarin of the place promptly made his call upon the American military officer. The official, as he took a chair close up beside the Captain, with perfect Chinese courtesy in addressing a superior, shouted his remarks in ear-splitting tones.

From Nankow our expedition proceeded, the men on horse- or donkey-back, the ladies in sedan chairs, to the inner section of the Great Wall, where it crosses the mountains. From this vantage point one can observe this particular section of the great masonry structure, which dates only from Ming times (A.D. 1368–1644), winding its serpentine way over heights and into valleys across the barren hills.

Necessarily one must preserve a souvenir of a visit to one of the wonders of the world, ranking with the pyramids of Egype, the bronze Colossus at Rhodes, or the famous Pharos which lighted the mariner's way at Alexandria. We accordingly extracted from the wall an enormous grey kiln-baked brick of clay weighing possibly 15 pounds. Consciences were allayed by the thought that our act of vandalism would, after all, impair the defences of the Great Wall but little. A simple calculation would indicate that a very considerable number of such bricks, however huge individually, would be required to be removed by tourists to deplete substantially the thousand mile structure.

Our night was disturbed by the arrival from Mongolia of caravans in the inn's courtyard, with all the noise and confusion incident thereto. So an early rising was indicated for the visit to the Thirteen Tombs of the Ming Emperors. The journey was again made by the ladies in sedan chairs carried by stalwart bearers; this time all the men of the party straddled diminutive and recalcitrant donkeys.

We reached in due course the "Avenue of Stone Men and Animals" which leads to the northern mausolea of the Ming Emperors. First towered up across the head of a narrow valley the enormous entrance gate, an elaborately ornate marble arch. Along the Spirit Way to the Tombs we saw the famous eighteen pairs of huge stone figures representing warriors, mandarins, and priests, each nine feet high. In addition are colossal animals, lions, elephants, camels, horses, and mythical monsters. Each statute is cut from a single block of marble. The elephants are thirteen feet high, fourteen feet long, and seven feet wide. These stone monuments were meant for the protection and needs of the deceased rulers in their after life.

We lingered at the impressive tomb of the Emperor Ch'eng Tsu, (usually known as Yung Lo) a solid vermilion colored brick tower, behind which is the great grave mound. Yung Lo was the third of the Ming Emperors, Prince of Yen, and son of old Chu Yuan-chang, a mendicant Buddhist monk who founded the dynasty. Yung Lo attacked his nephew, the legitimate second Emperor of the new dynasty, in his capital at Nanking. In the subsequent destruction of the city the young Emperor was reported to have been burned to death, though there were reports until long afterward that he had escaped to become a wandering Buddhist monk. Still pursuing the luckless youth throughout the realm and even abroad, to make sure of no competitor for the throne, Yung Lo, triumphant but haunted by the shades of his crime at Nanking, moved the capital to Peking. This was early in the fifteenth century. It was Yung Lo who laid out Peking's present-day massive walls.

The Emperor Yung Lo occupied himself not only in embellishing his new city, but organized a sort of early WPA project, not previously unknown to Chinese rulers. To keep them out of mischief, he set the unemployed Confucianist *literati* to reviving ancient Chinese scholarship, almost forgotten in the preceding rule of the unlettered Mongols. Among these achievements was one of the world's greatest literary compendiums, named after its imperial patron, The Encyclopaedia of Yung Lo. Hundreds of volumes of the great Chinese encyclopaedia still reposed in 1900 in the "Forest of Pens," the *Han Lin Yuan* library of Peking. During the attacks by the Boxers upon the nearby Legations in that year, the Library was burned with all its contents. Evidently some volumes had been previously "borrowed," for parts of the collection have been found in various parts of the world. Dating as they do from the early fifteenth century, they form valuable specimens in the history of the art of bookmaking.

*　　*　　*

The "covered wagon" of North China, the iron-tired "Peking cart" drawn by sleek fat mules, rumbled incessantly over the rough macadamized pavements. Passengers peered out uncomfortably from under their blue

21

cotton canopies. Asses, ponies, and steers tied together by long ropes, strained at heavy two-wheeled wains, loaded with coals or grain, in the ruts of the dirt tracks on either side of the pavement.

Giants of the Missions

A MOVEMENT was beginning for the modernization of China, a movement which would grow in strength and volume to an almost inconceivable *crescendo*. This was being fostered by the missionaries, chiefly American and British, not so much through religious propaganda as by secular teaching. The missionary was to bring about the revolution in China, political in only one of its phases.

Virtually every modern movement for social and moral betterment in China can be ascribed to the activities of missions.

Giants of the missions, the intrepid pioneers, were congregated at the Capital in those days when I first reached Peking. They were a generation fast running its course. There was Dr. W. A. P. Martin, dean of them all, venerable missionary, sinologue, and diplomat, author of numerous books on the lore of Cathay. Tall, spare, and with astonishing vigor for one of his age (eighty-four), he preached an inspiring Thanksgiving-day sermon to those of us who braved a suffocating dust storm to go to church.

Necessarily, many stories clung about this dynamic figure. Once Sir Robert Hart, veteran administrator-in-chief of China's Customs Service, was offered the post of British Minister to China. He was preparing to move into His Majesty's Legation when he heard that the Reverend Dr. Martin would be made his successor.

"Unpack my boxes, for here I stay," commanded the Inspector General of Customs—and there he remained for another generation.

There had been much secret rivalry among those who went through the adventure, to produce the first book to follow the lifting of the Boxer siege at Peking in 1900. Dr. Martin, so it was related, had been observed diligently jotting down notes in the most dangerous spots during the desperate defence. Others were shouldering rifles, wielding trench spades, or ministering to the wounded or the native refugees, crowded within the beleagured British Legation Walls. As soon as exit was possible, the Doctor sped by coastal steamer, trans-Pacific liner, and crosscontinent train to New York where he delivered a bulky manuscript to Fleming H. Revell's publishing house.

His was the first eye-witness account to appear in book form. In all its horror and heroism, he told the world of the six weeks encirclement of the Ministers of the Powers, their staffs, missionaries, native Christians, and others, by fanatical hordes. The Chinese people had been roused to this frenzy through the seizure of their territory by European powers.

"Have you been hunting tigers in China?" gasped his publisher when the gaunt, bearded old man confronted him, with a rifle dramatically slung across his shoulders.

22

"Yes," replied Martin, "Yes, human tigers!"

Martin had not recoiled from the heathen's absorbing philosophy and his delightful literature, as did many of his missionary colleagues who took "the narrow way" of Christian sectarianism. In fact the intellectuals among the missionaries, from the famed Jesuit scientists of the seventeenth and eighteenth centuries onward, were profoundly moved (though for policy's sake they sometimes sought to conceal it) by the breadth and depth of that Chinese culture which had made China the mentor of the Far East.

There was, too, Arthur H. Smith, silver-tongued and with a facile and learned pen. His two classics, *Chinese Characteristics* and *Village Life in China,* were our student manuals on the Chinese social structure. These books exhibited with insight and sympathy the world of the simple Chinese villager and peasant. His *China in Convulsion,* jocularly called "Arthur Smith's Fits," is a graphic narrative of the siege of the Peking Legations with the story of the genesis of the Boxer uprising in 1900.

Missions in China were entering upon their Augustan age. The inherent xenophobia of the Chinese, which had for years expressed itself in anti-foreign movements, had subsided. The bloody massacres of 1900, brought about by the political aggressions of the European Powers, were of the past. The missionary and his good works had come to be accepted eagerly.

From 1908 onward, Chinese students, men and women (mostly Christians and products of the mission schools), crossed the Pacific to secure the benefits of training in America. Within less than three decades, the nationalist revolution of 1926–27 liquidated the last of the Confucianist warlords. Thereafter the foreign (particularly American) educated Chinese came into full authority. In the succeeding ten years, American cultural hegemony in China had been achieved.

S. Wells Williams had been the prototype of the sinologue-diplomat-missionary. His and Martin's careers were largely parallel in character. With unusual intellectual gifts, both delved deep into the language, literature, and philosophy of the Chinese world. From the days of the Rev. Robert Morrison, interpreter attached to Lord Armherst's Embassy to the Court of Peking in 1816, missionaries, trained in the spoken and written language of China, had played an indispensable role in all diplomatic negotiations between the representatives of the Powers and Chinese officialdom. Thus Williams and Martin, earlier, and Edward T. Williams, Charles D. Tenney, T. J. N. Gattrell, with others from missionary circles, rendered invaluable service to their governments as linguists. Some ultimately came to hold diplomatic posts of highest importance. It was we, the Student Interpreters, incipient "sinologues" ourselves, with our Chinese language training, who were in time to displace the missionary linguist and interpreter.

The British government in China was the first to emancipate itself from dependence upon extra-official aid. From the very beginning of Sino-Brit-

23

ish relations the representatives of His Majesty's government appreciated the importance of a knowledge of the language, but not until the beginning of this century did the American government decide on a language-trained personnel to serve in China.

The American army and navy authorities have now recognized the potential worth of officers acquainted with Far Eastern languages. It has been from the fighting services rather than from the civil that American authorship of Chinese texts and studies have come, including several useful handbooks on the spoken language.

There used to prevail a belief among the "Old China Hands" of the China treaty-port communities that a study of things Chinese, including the language, disqualified the mind of the white man for any useful purpose. Their own knowledge of the people among whom they lived was often limited to what they learned from household servants or business associates; and their interest in the land was confined to the folk-lore of the China pony.

The Covenanted Services

SIR ROBERT HART, Inspector General of Customs, familiarly known as "The old I. G.," had played a determining role in the history of China of the preceding half century. Hart originally came out from England as a consular *attaché* at Hongkong. Soon he displaced Horatio Nelson Lay as chief of the newly organized Maritime Customs Service at Shanghai.

Removing to Peking in 1865 young Hart had, with all a Belfast Irishman's shrewdness and adroitness, developed the Customs into a most effective instrument for the collection of China's import and export duties. Then, branching out, he had provided China's coasts and rivers with lighthouses and navigation buoys, and finally he organized her far-flung Postal service. The latter became, in time, an independent organ. France's aspirations in China were satisfied so long as a French national could be "Chief Postal Secretary," almost the equal of Hart in authority.

While British nationals predominated in key positions, the Customs and Postal services were actually operated by an international staff which was representative of most European countries and the United States. In the Customs service, class distinctions were strictly maintained by an "Indoor" and "Outdoor" staff, the former occupying the administrative positions, the latter forming the "examiner" and "tide-surveyor" staff. Until quite late Chinese were relegated to clerical positions. Japanese, in time, entered both services.

Among the Americans to join Sir Robert Hart's organization in earlier years were three young Harvard graduates—Henry F. Merrill, Drew, Spinney, and Hosea Ballou Morse. The first I knew when he was Commissioner of Customs at Shanghai in 1911, and later in his well-earned retirement at Cambridge, Mass. Merrill early demonstrated unusual administrative talent. Sir Robert Hart accordingly projected him into the centre

24

of international intrigue at the feeble court of the King of Korea. Here, in 1885, at the age of twenty-nine he represented the astute Hart, who stood behind Li Hung-chang in his designs to retain Korea in the Chinese political orbit in the face of Russian and Japanese encroachment.

"Remember," wrote Hart to young Merrill, "that your best holding ground is with me in Peking."

This admonition contained a veiled reference to Merrill's predecessor, P. G. von Mollendorf, a German subject, who while representing China's Customs service at Seoul appeared to have fished in the troubled waters of the Korean Capital.

Moving from post to post in the treaty ports of China, Hosea Ballou Morse, another of the Harvard group, became the recognized chronicler of China's international trade and her political relations with the Powers. His well documented volumes, have formed the starting point for many special monographs by later historians. His intimate correspondence with the "I.G." at Peking is at times disclosed in the discreet (but always illuminating) footnotes to his pages. Sir Robert Hart is shown to have inspired almost every move for bettering China in the half century prior to his departure from Peking in 1908.

Stories and anecdotes galore survived him, some illustrative of his shrewdness and good sense, some reflecting the perverseness and pettiness which stand out so conspicuously in the case of many great men.

Among the criticisms advanced against the "I.G." was that of nepotism. Relatives came out from Ireland to assume well-paid posts in the Customs, including a few black sheep. Others were of distinguished service to China, such as his nephew Sir Frederick Maze, Inspector General of Customs during the Nationalist regime. Sir Robert Hart's immediate, but temporary successor, was his wife's brother, Sir Robert Bredon, trained in medicine but for many years a prominent Commissioner of Customs.

The office and residence of the Inspector General of Customs at Peking consisted of a group of connected semi-Chinese bungalows set in a spacious garden. The "I.G.'s" dinners were famous, but his garden parties were more so. For one thing, the latter were enlivened by the performances of the Customs Band—an amazing assemblage of Chinese "artists" performing on a complete assortment of western musical instruments.

Weekly concerts were held upon Peking's lofty city wall. Then Legation Quarter's élite turned out to stroll up and down the forty-foot paved avenue on its top. From here they could peer over the mighty crenelated parapets at the distant yellow-roofed palaces, or far beyond to the purple Western Hills.

As officiating Inspector General of Customs during his aged brother-in-law's absence on furlough, Sir Robert Bredon maintained the traditions of a generous hospitality as previously set by the absent "I.G."

Bredon was a fine, hearty type of Irish gentleman, portly and wearing side-burns in the Earl of Derby style. Each guest felt, as it were, his host's individual interest.

Lady Bredon too was a personage of much charm. In 1908 the French Minister possessed the only motor car in Peking, a brass-trimmed *de Dion Bouton*, with ample arrangements for baggage on top, like a London taxi-cab. But the wife of the officiating "I.G." continued to drive out on fine days in an open "victoria" drawn by a pair of plump Mongolian ponies. Gorgeous livered *mafoos* sat on the box. With lace-parasol and ostrich-plumed hat, Lady Bredon in her carriage was the most colorful sight on Legation Street.

The principle of fairly liberal personal compensation in the Customs had been established as early as the retirement of young Horatio Nelson Lay, who might be termed the first Inspector General of Customs. Lay was an impetuous fellow. In the latter days of the T'aip'ing rebellion in the 1860's, Lay was entrusted by Viceroy Li Hung-chang with a mission to return to England to secure a few gunboats, as possibly the nucleus of a coast-guard patrol. He terrified his employer by bringing out an entire naval flotilla under the command of Captain Osborne of His Majesty's navy and manned by as pretty a parcel of cut-throats as the sweepings of British ports could assemble. In haste the Viceroy ordered the immediate sale and dispersal of this Frankenstein monster which might threaten the safety of the tottering Empire. Lay himself was bidden to go back to his own country, with however a final pay-off of 14,000 pounds sterling.

Sir Robert Hart was allowed a lump sum by the Chinese government for the annual maintenance of the Customs establishment. This he disbursed in salaries and administrative expenses at his own discretion. There were substantial savings which were prudently banked in London, where they accumulated against the future needs of the Service. His associates complained of their Chief's parsimoniousness. Sir Robert Hart and his successors nevertheless developed slowly and cautiously a "covenanted service" after the manner of the British Indian Civil Service, which in time amply compensated its members in security of tenure, in actual salary, with housing accommodations added, periodical home-leaves on pay, and pensions.

These benefits were extended as time went on and formed the basis for the civil service set up in other departments of the Chinese government, especially the Posts and to some extent later the Salt Revenue administration wherein foreign nationals were largely employed. All such arrangements were looked upon with misgivings by the Chinese mandarinate for they were quite at variance with ideas of Chinese official service where "public office was traditionally regarded as personal opportunity." The political philosopher, Mencius, in the fourth century B.C., held to this principle, and so furnished scriptural authority for personal aggrandizement from public funds. Hart's was the "root and branch" policy advocated by that vigorous early British envoy to China, Sir Rutherford Alcock. Probity was to be introduced into public administration, and abuses

26

eradicated. All those Chinese serving within the *imperium in imperio,* as the Customs came to be denominated, shared in these benefits and approved.

Wards of Uncle Sam

THE STUDENT interpreters were dubbed "Wards of Uncle Sam" by a visiting steel magnate from Pittsburgh, a former associate of Andrew Carnegie, after we had entertained him lavishly in the American Student Interpreters Mess. In a mood of extravagance Congress had appropriated sums of $1000, as annual salary, and $225 for tuition for each of the several young men whose qualities of intellect and character had enabled them to pass the examinations in Washington.

With some sixty other aspirants for foreign service appointments, I had succeeded in heading the list with a grade of 86 per cent. The subjects in April, 1908, had been simple arithmetic, commercial geography, single-entry bookkeeping, elementary economics, modern languages, and the rudiments of commercial and international law. None of these, save the languages, had been requisites for my attainment of an M.A. degree in medieval history! Fortunately, a parental interest in languages had projected me for five of my early years into a German school; I had been tutored in French and Latin even before school age.

"May I express a preference for an appointment to China," I had asked the chief examiner in the old State, War and Navy Building. "You may" was the diplomatic reply, "but that does not signify that you will be assigned to that country." Only two of us were allotted to the Peking language posts. My young colleague's health failed him after a brief period at the Capital. The other successful examinees were appointed as Consular Assistants or Vice-Consuls of career to various foreign posts. What Congress did not appreciate in its generosity was the length to which the American dollar's purchasing power could be extended in the marginal economic region of Peking. In the first place we were free of *rent.* After 1900 the Chinese government had penitently ceded certain areas at the Capital with whatever tenements and other appurtenances they might have upon them, as the official quarters of the Legations of the Powers. *Inter alia* the Temple of the Three Mandarins, with all its courts, villas, outhouses, walls, and gateways fell to the American government. Here various attachés of the Minister's staff were lodged.

The choicest section was once inhabited by a Legation Secretary of unlimited private means. He set to work to rehabilitate the existing establishment. These premises consisted of a series of courtyards, each surrounded by Chinese type bungalows. A large central hall was converted into a magnificent dining room. The ceilings were done in green and gold squares representing the coiled Imperial dragon. At each end of the chamber were ornate carved teakwood fireplaces fitted with gigantic mirrors above. The room's supporting pillars were in Chinese vermilion and black. Entrance

27

on either side was through latticed doors. Over these was pasted translucent oiled Chinese paper, as well as over the latticed windows which in addition had small squares of glass. The room was thus well lighted. A magnificently executed bronze God of War stood guard in the outer courtyard.

Some years later we inherited this establishment. Separate one-story buildings were built around paved courts. Here we had our bed-rooms and study-rooms. In the relatively mild Peking climate small coal-stoves were sufficient to heat these rooms. The thick mulberry-bark paper which served as windows, with only occasional small panes of glass, allowed sufficient light to enter and radiated less heat than glass itself. Adjacent out-houses provided kitchens and servants quarters. Each Student had his own "boy" or personal servant, while Chao, the handsome butler, supervised the entire establishment. He was held responsible for all native employees. Beyond, in a separate compound, were the stables, housing our riding ponies, each animal with its groom. For such was the division, and the cheapness of labor.

Our personal servants were paid eight Chinese dollars a month or about $3.20 in American currency. The extremely efficient butler, Chao, drew twice this amount from joint Mess funds.

For relatively lavish meals we each paid the Mess cook Chinese dollars thirty-five (U.S. $14.70) monthly. The contract did not, to be sure, include ketchup, pickles, and some other overseas condiments indispensible to young American palates. The Peking market provided all that the appetite desired, from upland game to sea-food from the coast. The latter included the large prawn which is so deliciously fried by Chinese cooks. During cold weather, oysters came frozen in the shell from Dairen on the Manchurian peninsula. When the "fire bird"—as the turkey is known to the Chinese from its flaming wattle—could not be had, the bustard, the enormous wild turkey of the Mongolian steppes, was to be found in the markets. Its meat is dark, but tender and delicious, and from the time Xenophon mentioned it in his *Anabasis,* it has been favored by epicures.

This and other native delicacies did not preclude our enjoying the more common comestibles, such as beef (secured only from Mohammedan butchers for the ox is regarded as the co-worker of man in agricultural China and is eaten only in emergencies), mutton (North China is the carpet-wool producing region of the world), pork of which we partook sparingly (an invariable part of the Chinese menu), and the ubiquitous chicken. The large white duck, known even in America as the Peking duck, made enormously fat by forced feeding, was the Capital's most celebrated delicacy. Barbecued over a hot fire, it is served native style in sizzling slices rolled up in a pan-cake with the crisp skin attached and with soy-bean sauce and tender green onion shoots. "Earth-beans," as the potato is called by the Chinese, and all the ordinary vegetables, were abundant. "Ping-chi-ling,"—ice cream—was frozen with the questionable ice harvested in winter from the Peking moat. "Pu-ding" (here phonetically rendered, but suggesting appropriately enough in the colloquial, "uncertain") represented the common pudding in its various forms, which appeared regularly on our table. Milk, unless straight from the can, might derive from cow, goat or waterbuffalo. At any rate it had to be boiled, as did all drinking water. Luckily for themselves, the Chinese in a land of bacterial contaminations, never drink water cold. It is taken boiled from the ever handy tea-pot.

Fruits of every description were abundant, especially the mammoth persimmon. When mellowed by the first frosts this golden apple of North China assumes the texture of a custard. It is then entirely free from the astringent qualities which induced General "Stonewall" Jackson to prescribe the persimmon to his famished Confederate veterans in lieu of tightening their belts. Dried and candied fruits were on sale in the Peking sweet-shops, especially the "honey-date," a variety of jujube which when steamed and rolled in powdered sugar is often preferred to the real Syrian date.

The Mess specialized in a celebrated dessert known as Great Wall Pudding. Our *chef* prepared this elaborate confection not only for further titillation of the appetites of already well-filled diners, but for its delectable appearance. First a circular wall like that of a Chinese castle was constructed of *glacé* fruits cemented together by candied sugar. Within the "castle," depths of mashed boiled chestnuts were surmounted by billows of whipped cream. Above all this, golden strands of finely spun sugar spread a misty aura.

The Students Mess "wine-cellar" was availed of by the entire Legation personnel. Well-known wine-merchants, stocked a room with every variety of beer, ale, wine, and liquor. Conveniently checking the stock at the end of each month, they charged the Mess only with such items as had actually been consumed. This went on well enough until a bibulous clerk of the Legation let his account run for a couple of months without settlement and then disappeared, after announcing a brief hunting trip to Mongolia. This person, as Legation typist, had been privy to certain correspondence between Minister Rockhill and the State Department which disclosed that there was no provision for extraditing American citizens committing crimes in China back for trial to that country. Making his way to Singapore, a British colony, he felt himself safe. With the connivance of the port officials, however, he was "Shanghaied" onto an American vessel, and promptly returned to North China. There he answered for his indebtedness to the Mess, as well as for helping himself generously to Legation funds. In session at Tientsin the United States Court for China sentenced him to a five years residence at the Federal prison at St. Quentin.

As there was no "internal revenue tax" on foreign liquors and only a 7½% *ad valorum* import duty, waived in the case of members of the diplomatic corps, even champagne could be had for a modest price. Unforeseen problems arose incident to the administration of the wine-cellar; how much should be charged for individual drinks. A self-appointed committee of two assumed to ascertain, for example, how many glasses a bottle of cognac represented. Assiduously applying themselves by actual experimentation to this calculation they ultimately lost count, and the question was never scientifically determined.

Not only was there wine, but there was music in the Students Mess. Seldom during the day or evening were the piano or the Pathé phonograph silent. Appropriately enough, our travelling companion on the Pacific Mail Liner *Mongolia,* Mrs. W. W. Kimball of the Chicago organ family, had provided us with a number of choice operatic records. Paul Jameson drew from the piano the poignant strains of *Lucia di Lammermoor*. Peking's most accomplished but temperamental pianist, Mrs. Hatch —whose husband was establishing China's first Bureau of Engraving and Printing—was our frequent guest. First Secretary of Legation, Henry P. Fletcher, insensible to the sweet sounds of music, continued an audible conversation during one of the after-dinner renditions of this sensitive artist. The result was disastrous to the *soirée,* until apologies were tearfully accepted.

Nelson Johnson's guitar accompanied him as he sang Kipling's plaintive "Come back to me beloved or I die." And when the auditors of his sweet tenor were about to dissolve in tears of compassion, his nimble fingers would strike up the lively "For she's a cousin of mine"—a theme much developed during the Heron girls' visit at Peking as guests of their "stepcousin." With lights turned low, Willys Peck would narrate in deep, mysterious tones the romantic story of "The girl with the amber eyes"; or in matchless North China vernacular recite a Chinese version of "George Washington and the Cherry Tree," the while mimicking small George and his dignified father in Chinese character.

From the depths of the servants' quarters the plaintive note of flute and three-stringed violin would be borne on the soft warm evening air and a quavering falsetto would startle the stillness. With the Chinese, music lies in the spirit. As in their theatre, no elaborate stage settings are required, so no ingenious and intricate musical instruments have been devised. Despite simplicity in media of execution, the Chinese musical scale comprises overtones unknown to our own. But the less imaginative Western mind requires obvious scenery for the one, and much wood, brass, and catgut for the other. The soul's ears and eyes provide these for the still pre-Elizabethan Chinese.

The fame of our hospitality spread afar. Distinguished visitors came. The Hon. W. L. MacKenzie-King, Canada's leader, looked in on us on one occasion; Frank Carpenter, renowned traveller and geographer, and Francis Millet the artist, soon to close his gentle life in the *Titanic* disaster, sat at our table. Frank Carpenter and I rode temperamental Mongol ponies around the entire circumference of the Peking walls. Frank's seat at dinner that evening was uneasy. Millet, world traveler and *gourmet,* declared that our roast Peking duck was excelled by nothing he had tasted in two hemispheres. Why should it not, we concurred, when served continuously at least since the famous Pien Yi Fang restaurant had been removed from Nanking to Ming Emperor Yung Lo's new Capital at Peking in A.D. 1421! Stanley Hornbeck, later pivotal State Department adviser on Far Eastern, and particularly China's, politics, lunched with us while on a visit at the Capital from his provincial college post in Central China. Kenneth Lataurette, historian at Yale of missions and China's cultural development, likewise sat at our table in those early days.

In later years I never visited Peking without enjoying the hospitality of the old Mess. On one of these occasions in the winter of 1919–20, Witter Bynner, who was in Peking engaged on the task of rendering Chinese poetry into English stanzas, was late for lunch one day. This was because, as he put it, he had been detained listening to Professor John Dewey "saying the things that he should only be thinking!" The great pragmatic teacher was at the time impressing his philosophy upon audiences of Chinese students at Peking, Wu-chang, Changsha, and elsewhere. Bertrand Russell had similarly been engaged for a series of lectures before Chinese university audiences, and Professor Dewey found himself paired with the English philosopher on several platforms.

Ministers and *chargés d'affaires* did not disdain our fare. The Cook's contract stipulated a charge to us of Chinese money fifty cents, or about twenty-one cents in American currency, for each extra guest! Distinguished-looking Henry P. Fletcher, freshened with a few *chukkas* of polo on the Austrian Legation *glaçis* with Freddie Mayers, representative of British high finance, and hastening from a quick game with Senor de Freitas, Portuguese Minister and Doyen of the Diplomatic Corps, at the Peking Club's bridge tables, or Leland Harrison our dapper Harvard Third Secretary, would sometimes come down from the Legation. We raised the cook's *ante* a trifle when so signally honored.

Judge William J. Calhoun, successor to Minister Rockhill, accompanied by his charming wife, reached Peking in the midst of one of North China's fiercest April dust storms. The world was a swirling torment of red impalpable *loess,* blinding, choking. No more inauspicious reception could have been provided for the distinguished Chicagoans. The Legation staff turned out in full complement under *chargé* Henry P. Fletcher's leadership to greet them at the railway station. It was not, however, until the newcomers sat in the mellow candle-light of the Student Interpreters Mess Hall, with a perfectly appointed dinner served them, that the stern features of the new Minister Plenipotentiary relaxed.

By 1908 a future Major General Commandant of the U.S. Marine Corps had already served a two year tour of duty as Captain in the Legation guard. His enthusiasm for Peking and his interest in the Chinese lan-

31

guage brought him a continuance of his assignment as one of the first pair of Marine language officers...Captain Thomas Holcomb was taking his company out to the rifle range. "Come along, Gale, and do a little camp life with us," proposed the Captain. "You've been studying your Chinese too hard lately. Weak minds often give way under pressure!" The food served in the Marine camp kitchen I found better than our own. The regular *per capita* mess allowance converted from American into Chinese money enabled the Marines to feast on the fat of the land, with ample savings for special gorges on Thanksgiving, the Fourth and other holidays.

Rifle practice at the range outside the Peking wall often resulted in ricochet bullets overtopping the high yellow clay butts. Unfortunately the great flagstone-paved Peking-T'ungchou highway, raised several feet above the level of the country, passed not far beyond. From time to time a wayfarer was bowled over. There was a fixed scale of compensation for such casualities, arranged according to man, woman, child, horse, cow or donkey, or by nationality of the responsible troops. The American Marines on the latter basis paid at the top of the schedule, which correspondingly tapered off down through the British, French, etc., to the lowest tariffs of all for the Japanese.

Chao, our Mess major-domo, was omnipresent and ommiscient. He was a fine upstanding type of Northern Chinese, clear of eye and with ruddy complexion, affable and self-respecting. The studied insolence of the "English butler," at least as portrayed by Hollywood, is entirely lacking in even the best of Chinese servants. With long braided queue, a black silk tassel at the end of it, Chao's appearance lent prestige to the formal dinner parties of the Mess. He would officiate garbed in full regalia of plum-colored jacket and blue brocade gown. He had been picked up, a stray waif, by the American troops in 1900. He never knew anything about his parents. Brought up by the men in the Marine Guard, he acquired, instead of the "pidgin English" jargon of the usual servant in foreign employ, a most astonishing American dialect. Once when I inquired the price of tickets to a Chinese theatrical performance, he glibly replied, "10 cents for the 3rd class, 20 cents for 2nd class, but *if you want to be a sport 50 cents!*" His elegant English thus set him far above his fellows. He was ultimately filched from the Student Interpreters to become chief messenger at the Legation Chancery, an incredibly exalted post in the eyes of his fellows.

Chao's only equal was Secretary Henry P. Fletcher's famous Chinese butler, Liu. Fletcher had relinquished his post at Peking as *chargé d' affaires* on promotion as Minister to Chile. He cabled me from Washington "Have Liu meet me in London." Whereupon I set international machinery in motion to hasten the invaluable Liu's departure—passports from the Russian Legation, tickets for the trans-Siberian Railway and thence to England, sums of money in roubles and sterling for expenses *en route*. In due course, Liu departed on his hemispheric journey.

* * *

Naturally we had colleagues in the other legations who were similarly engaged in studying the Chinese language. Most numerous of all were the British student interpreters with whom by reason of language and other cultural affiliations, we felt most at home. We rode together to the Western Hills, we exchanged dinner invitations, we visited in each others' summer temples, and we swapped race-ponies.

To nations and individuals is sometimes allotted a time of free and untrammeled flowering. Too often it is only a legend or a dream of what might have been, imagined in the misery of actualities. But the Student Interpreters had their veritable Golden Age in those old Peking days.

An Outlandish Language

LIFE in the Student Interpreters Mess at Peking in 1908 could not be regarded as all beer and skittles. We were charged with one of the most appalling mental labors that can confront the mind of an Occidental: the task of learning to recognize and read thousands of ideographic Chinese characters and of acquiring a speaking knowledge of the monosyllabic, tone-inflected, oral language. Chinese children are set to memorizing the written character at as early an age as four or five. We student interpreters were all in our twenties when the mind has lost the greater plasticity of childhood. Our temerity in attempting this mnemonic feat was doubtless prompted by the valor of ignorance.

Harold Henry and I were seated beside our native "pundits" by eight o'clock of the morning following our arrival in Peking on that hot night of July 31, 1908. Thereafter, together with our six or seven young American associates in the Mess, we droned after our individual *hsien-sheng,* the "elder-born," as the teacher in China is respectfully addressed, the interminable vocabularies in the four "tones." We practiced with camel-hair brushes, first grotesquely and then with increasing calligraphic neatness, the numberless ideographs that make up the written language. Each of us at first appeared to make phenomenally rapid progress, especially in the spoken language. In a week or two we were out in the fascinating Peking shops bargaining in local *argot, Che-ko to-shao ch'ien?*—"How much is this?"—we could ask the shop-keeper. And, as his reply involved the simple numerals, we had no difficulty in understanding him.

Fellow voyagers across the Pacific, who turned up in Peking a month or so after our arrival, were amazed at our linguistic prowess as we chatted with shop-keepers, and with gate-men as we took our friends on the round of the city's sights. Alas, colloquial Chinese lends itself to the "basic English" principle. A few words will go a very long way with the attentive and quickly responsive Peking shop-keeper or palace guide. Soon the freshness and novelty wore off; the mind became saturated and refused to absorb more. Discouragement set in. More and more frequently the *hsien-sheng* upon his morning arrival for the day's lessons, was addressed with the stereotyped formula, *Ch'ing hsien-sheng ming-t'ien-lai*—"Teacher is

33

respectfully invited to come tomorrow." A period of mental relief and change was clearly indicated. A week-end riding party to the Western Hills provided the antidote.

Our induction into the Chinese spoken language and the literary forms opened up new and hitherto unrealized linguistic vistas. Accustomed only to the languages of Western Europe with their relatively simple phonetic spelling, to us the difficulties of remembering a vast number of ideographs appeared insurmountable. Every idea in China has its individual symbol; the language has as many "characters" as the entire vocabulary itself. The best analogy we have in the Occident to Chinese ideographic writing (that is, representing ideas independent of sound) is perhaps the Arabic numerals. They, like the Chinese characters, suggest meanings, however they are pronounced. One-two-three, has its individual symbol.

In Chinese "horse" is represented by one ideographic symbol, obviously with some resemblance to a primitive pictorial representation of this historic animal. The same pictograph is used by the Chinese, Japanese, and Koreans, but pronounced differently by each of these peoples, as in the case of our Arabic numerals in the Occident. The same characters are pronounced in different ways even among the several varying dialects of the Chinese language. But the symbol itself invariably represents the same idea. Thus the Chinese character, the written medium of China, takes the place among Far Eastern peoples that Latin took in medieval Europe. It is a universally understood written language, the *lingua franca* of the Extreme Orient's hundreds of millions.

Fortunately this literary medium contains inherent aids to memory and understanding. It is not as erratic and irrational in construction as the uninitiated are led to imagine when they observe the apparently meaningless 214 arbitrary signs, beginning with the simple horizontal stroke"—" meaning *one* and proceeding through various combinations of strokes to a maximum of 17 strokes. Each of these simple or radical forms, the "character-mother," represents a thing or an idea. They are combined to form other things or ideas according to certain prescribed rules. The more developed character is then composed of combinations of the basic 214 "radicals."

There are thus two parts to a complex Chinese character, first, the "radical," which indicates the general class of ideas to which the combination conforms; secondly, the "phonetic" element which often, though not invariably, suggests the sound. This sound in Chinese is always a monosyllable. So if a Chinese character has the radical for "water," this is an indication that the thing or idea represented is related to something "fluid"; the other part of the character may be a familiar symbol pronounced generally in a certain way. The combination of the radical for "gold" with a character pronounced "chien" (*jien*), by a phonetic transposition, is pronounced "ch'ien." This is the oral word for "money," and the symbol, formed as described, represents that idea. Such combinations

34

proceed from concrete ideas to abstract concepts, providing a literary medium of extraordinary flexibility and brilliancy. Other examples are "good" made up of a combination of the two separate characters for *son* and *woman;* "fierce," *claws* and *tiger;* "home," after the Irishman's concept, *pig* under a *roof;* a *man* and *two women* produce "eloquent," "specious"; a *man* and *words,* "believe," "faith."

While these devices are definite aids to memory and understanding, the exceptions are many. Innumerable characters are arbitrarily formed, with little or no intrinsic indication of meaning or sound. They require sheer memorizing. Characters in combination take on new and apparently unrelated meanings, as "east-west" means *things,* or may be applied as a term of opprobrium to a *stupid person.* The Chinese written style, too, is terse (as in an economically worded telegram), full of allusions, without capital letters to indicate proper names and without punctuation, as understood in Occidental sentence structure. These features have been largely overcome in modern *pai hua,* a simple popular Chinese written in the oral speech style, with special indications for capitalized proper names and Western punctuation symbols.

Despite the much advertised *pai hua* style, and misleading Occidental notions of "simplified Chinese," most books, newspapers, and formal correspondence preserve practically unchanged the archaic characteristics of early Chinese. "Simplified Chinese" has nothing to do with modifying the structure of the usual character; it means teaching the illiterate a *limited number* of the *most frequently* used characters. A Chinese scholar of the Han dynasty era (B.C. 206–221 A.D.), if miraculously projected into modern Shanghai, could read the characters of the daily newspapers with facility. Written Chinese assumed its final form at that early time and has never been modified since, save for specialized forms of writing. These differ less than our own type fonts do, as for Old English, Gothic, Roman, etc., or in handwriting for "Spencerian," vertical, backhand and other styles.

The spoken language presents its own unique features and difficulties. The words are all monosyllables which reduce the variety of sounds employed to not more than 420. We have the same phenomenon of "homophony" in our language on a small scale in such words as *bear* (as the wild animal or in bare-feet, disclose, etc.)

In speaking Chinese this confusing similarity is overcome by distinguishing between the meanings of identical sounds by means of varying "tones." In the North China dialect these are four or five. Thus, the sound "chi" (*jee*) may be pronounced as an *even,* quickly *rising,* slowly *rising,* or *falling tone.* But there are some 140 different meanings for the one sound "chi," as listed in the ordinary dictionary. So other devices are employed, such as combinations of two monosyllables of approximately the same meaning. *K'an-chien,* literally "look-see," is thus employed as the verb "to see" in the spoken language. A "numerative" or "classifier" is a

35

means of distinguishing between words of the same sound. As we say "three *head* of cattle," they say "three *mouth* cattle," for the words for *ox, perverse, twist, versed in,* and *button* are all pronounced niu ("new") in the same tone. So each word has its own "classifier."

These difficulties do not appear in the ideographic written language where the eye distinguishes between the different characters, whatever the pronunciation. This gives rise to much repetition and "oriental" circumlocution in a Chinese speech or conversation. In fact, it is held in some quarters that to understand a Chinese public speech the auditor must first know what the speaker will say before he begins!

Old style Chinese scholars composed our corps of individual tutors, or "informants"; Teacher Hsing was a "bannerman" Manchu, Hu a Chinese "colonel" of decayed fortunes, and others there were. The unfailing courtesy of the Chinese *literatus,* combined with a practical eye to the retention of his meager pay, led to an amusing, if disconcerting, situation. We sometimes found our teachers unwilling to correct our often ludicrous mistakes; nay, at times they would even repeat our solecisms and misplaced tones for fear of offending the studious but paying guest from afar."

"Colonel" Hu's career had not been without incident. He was the first teacher with a knowledge of English who was permitted to serve the Student Interpretors. At the time of the occupation of Peking by foreign troops in 1900, after the siege of the Legations by the Boxers had been raised, "Colonel" Hu had engaged himself to the American forces as interpreter.

One day at the great Ch'ien Men [Front Gate], of the Tatar City, a high Manchu official, Ch'en Pi, wished to enter with his retinue. Taking advantage of his position of temporary importance, Hu subjected the haughty "Bannerman" to the indignity of a long wait. Some years later when things had quieted down, and the Court was restored to its old authority, "Colonel" Hu mysteriously disappeared. In due course it was learned that the long arm of Ch'en Pi, now restored to power, had reached out and Hu was in gaol for an indefinite period.

Once more the tables were turned. Ch'en Pi was entrusted with the responsibility of rebuilding the same massive Front Gate which had been almost completely demolished in the attack upon Peking in 1900, and which had been the scene of the insult by Hu. No sooner was the task finished and a new and finer gate erected at enormous cost, than Ch'en Pi was cashiered, deprived of all his honors and heavily fined. This was the customary "shake-down" by the Court of a greedy official who had made too much money too ostentatiously.

His old enemy out of the way, "Colonel" Hu soon secured his own liberation. Through his friendship with Dr. Tenney, Chinese Secretary of the American Legation, he obtained an appointment as my teacher. This prosperity resulted shortly in his marriage, which we all attended with due hilarity. The high-light of this ceremony in China occurs when the bride,

36

seated on the nuptial couch in the bedroom, is unveiled for the first time to the gaze of the expectant groom. We crowded into the narrow room to share the groom's joy in the bride's first-disclosed beauty.

A great shout went up. The marriage go-between had swindled the "Colonel." The bride's features were deeply pitted with small-pox scars!

*　　*　　*

Ours then was the monstrous intellectual task, a veritable labor of Hercules, to be accomplished if the "due trust and confidence" reposed in the Student Interpreters by the President of the United States was to be vindicated. Paradoxically enough, the linguistic talent in Western Languages possessed by certain of the students seemed of little avail in the mastery of Chinese. One facile bi-lingual youngster of French-American origin failed to make any progress whatever with the language. He was ultimately transferred from the China Consular area *via* an appointment to Saigon in Indo-China. This post was usually the way out for those possessing no capacity for Chinese. Others with no marked linguistic turn of mind, and with no previous training in languages, frequently excelled. Special mnemonic faculties and a capacity for the control of infinite detail appear to be required for the written language; a sensitive and retentive ear for the oral.

There are examples of persons of little or no formal educational backgrounds who have obtained a thorough knowledge of Chinese. One of these developed an overwhelming curiosity in written Chinese, while employed in a library where he chanced upon some Chinese books. He has since distinguished himself as a translator and bibliographer.

A feature of Chinese is that there is little relationship between the spoken and written languages. Many foreigners in China, especially those whose occupations have taken them for periods of isolation into the interior of the country, have picked up the colloquial from hearing it spoken constantly about them. These persons often remain completely "illiterate" as to the written forms. On the other hand, several noted sinologues such as Stanislas Julien and Edouard Biot, founders of the modern French school of Chinese studies, never visited China, nor perhaps attempted to speak the language.

Consequently there is the temptation to approach written Chinese as a dead language. It must not be forgotten that though China and Japan trace their history back to a remote antiquity, theirs have been continuous and unbroken civilizations to the present. They are among the most vigorous cultural, political and economic entities in the world of today and doubtless of the future. The decadence and exhaustion of the Near East is no part of their heritage. The Western scholar of China and Japan is attended upon, unlike the Egyptologist whose mummies have no breath of life in them, by the direct and living descendants of the Chou, Han and

37

T'ang dynasties and by the children of the Sun God and of Jimmu Tenno of Japan.

Many years ago I determined upon a career in China with actually a knowledge of one Chinese character among the 44,400 as represented in the great eighteenth century *K'ang Hsi* dictionary. Since then a remarkable development has taken place in the opportunities for the study of Chinese and Japanese civilizations, including the languages, in this country. From obscure beginnings at Harvard, Columbia, and the University of California, dozens of institutions of higher learning are providing courses whereby American students have available curricula equal to the provisions for the study of early and modern European cultures.

I sometimes wonder when the Chinese themselves are credited with fantastic "percentages" of illiteracy in their population. I have taken pains to observe closely the reading habits of the lower orders in China: cooks, gardeners, household servants, more latterly, elevator boys and messengers. They invariably are found reading a well-thumbed book. I examine the little volume, often taking it from their hands unexpectedly. What do I usually find? Some entrancing thirteenth-century thriller of warlike prowess or palace intrigue!

Possibly, considerable numbers of the peasantry do not know their written characters. Yet when out on country walks through the smallest villages, I have often heard a concert of shrill childish voices coming from some humble cottage. Peering in, I have discerned a score or more of boys with some girls possibly, busily repeating in all likelihod the text of the *Book of Mencius* (fourth century B.C. philosopher). A shrunken old scholar, bespectacled and thinly bearded, will be found exercising "the teacher's severity" above the din. Text-books have greatly changed in recent times, but the sum and substance of Chinese literary education must remain the memorizing of the age-old curriculum of classic writings, traditionally attributed to Confucius and his disciples. No one can read Chinese intelligently, however well he may know individual characters, unless he is saturated with the style of the early literary masterpieces. Much less can he compose.

When in Rome

IF, instead of Chinese, we Student Interpreters had been engaged in studies of classic Greece or Rome, we assuredly could not have found nowadays a study centre in those ancient empires equal to Peking. Here were all the living monuments of an ancient culture, instead of the pitifully few fragments of a long lost world, exhumed in Roman Forum or Athenian Agora, at vast labor and expense.

At Peking we were in constant contact with the evidences of China's past. Our living quarters were beneath the massive city wall erected, almost a century before Columbus' voyages, by the Emperor Ch'eng Tsu, more familiar as Yung Lo, third of the Ming dynasty. Within our frequent sight, towering above the Palace walls near the artificial "Coal Hill," was the huge *dagoba,* or Tibetan *chorten,* erection of which is attributed to the devout first emperor of the Manchu domination Shun Chih, in 1652. As we rode beyond the northern city wall, our ponies crossed the earthen ramparts which bounded Khanbalig, the City of Kublai Khan. In the temple yard consecrated to the honor of the Great Master Confucious were the stone drums of the Chou period, of at least four centuries before Christ, with their still decipherable legends of royal progresses and hunting expeditions.

A few miles to the west, lay the charming villas of the more recently built Summer Palace. Their graceful curving roofs emulated the First Emperor's celebrated palace, O-Pang-Kung, an almost legendary architectural feat of the 3rd century B.C. which prescribed all later building forms in China. Behind were the ruins of the 18th century palaces, the Yuan Ming Yuan. On the city wall were still a few of the bronze astronomical instruments, many of which had been carried away to Berlin by German troops in the fateful Boxer year. By a strange turn of the wheel-of-fortune, they were to be restored after World War I to their original mountings by the German government.

As we wandered throughout the great city or in its environs, the visible evidences of the esoteric cults of East Asia were made manifest to us in brick and mortar, in lacquer and bronze. In the northeast corner of the city lay the mysterious Lama Temple, where at certain religious festivals its yellow robed priesthood practiced occult shamanistic rites from Tibet and Mongolia, culminating in the terrifying devil-dances. The occasional astonishing resemblances of these Central Asian priesthoods to the early Christian Church were described by that pious traveller, the Abbe Huc, as "a device of the devil to delude honest souls." For in use in the ceremonies in the gloom of the great temple hall were the mitre, the swinging incense-pot, the rosary and other ritualistic paraphernalia familiar in the early Christian church. Doubtless Buddhism, always eclectic, had come into contact with Nestorian priests in Central Asia in the early Christian centuries and had frankly imitated the ritual of this branch of Christianity.

On our way to the Western Hills, we rode past an equally mysterious center, a great Taoist monastery. Here the original tenets of *Tao*—The Way of the "Old Philosopher," quietistic, mystical, actually deriving from the ancient schools of divination, had come to be sadly perverted. Borrowing from the religion of Buddha its theology and ritual, Taoism attempted to produce a national religion in opposition to the foreign-born Indian cult. In order to appeal to the masses, it became largely a search for the "Elixir of Immortality." Taoism, one of the "Three Religions of China," thus ultimately degraded itself into a system of charlatanism, concerned with the exorcism of demons. In and out of the temple gates passed a constant stream of monks. They were clad in dark blue gowns and wore the

39

"top-knot," in contrast to the shaven-headed Buddhists with the three cicatrices of their initiation burned into their shorn polls.

South of the city were the vast enclosures of the Temples of Heaven and of Earth, among groves of hoary cedars. Here the austere religion of primitive China, the worship of heaven and earth, agriculture and the forces of nature, was performed at stated seasons. The Emperor attended, serving as Pontifex Maximus. In our time, at the close of the first decade of the nineteenth century, the Imperial family had become too listless to maintain the observances of these rites. The living Emperor, Kuang Hsü, who was of the same generation as his deceased predecessor, had ascended the throne. This was stricly forbidden, and was an act which had brought deep humiliation upon the reigning family. It was condoned by the intrigues of that wicked, wilful woman, the Dowager Empress Tz'u Hsi, who was now in control. No longer were the sacred temple precincts closely guarded from infidel intruders. A handful of copper coins opened the gates, and our gay riding parties clattered down the grass-grown pavements, or dashed full speed under the gaunt old cedars of the parks, disturbing the herds of black bulls which had once furnished the sacrifices and burnt offerings.

The blue glazed tiles of the pinnacle of the Altar of the Worship of the Year, rising gracefully from the white marble terrace, pierced the azure Peking sky. Within, the ritual vessels, unattended, gathered the red-brown dust blown through the open lattice windows by North China winds. Enormous wooden columns, brought, it was said, from distant Yunnan "South of the Clouds" upheld the soaring tiled roof. Nearby were marble altar platforms reached by parallel pairs of stone stairs separated by huge monoliths carved with dragons and phoenixes disporting themselves among conventional clouds above symbolic waves. In such sacrosanct precincts we Legation folk held our picnics. Heavily laden hampers were brought along by the native servants, who were usually so engrossed in their mundane duties that they scarcely raised their eyes to the monuments of an almost forgotten religious rite of their very own and as ancient as sacred Mount T'ai itself.

Within the city was the Temple to the Great Sage. Here we saw no image of man or god only a slender tablet to the Teacher of Ten Thousand Ages. But on every side, above and below, blazed in golden letters of exquisite calligraphy the prescriptions which moulded decisively the habits and character of the Confucian *literati* of China for twenty-five glorious centuries. Thus was brought about the singular uniformity of Chinese culture, even among the "cotton clothed commoners." "For what those above practice, those below imitate," says a well known Chinese proverb.

Confucius was a self confessed agnostic, but a real lover of antiquity and a conservative. He was a transmitter, not an originator. But a wealth of literature, a glorious art, and a compact social organization which has

40

made the Chinese the most persistent of all races, flowered from the writings transmitted through the ages and attributed to the oral teachings of the Master of Ten Thousand Ages, K'ung Fu-tzu. Shakya Muni, Moses, Jesus Christ, Mohammed did no more in moulding their own vast segments of humanity than this disillusioned, matter-of-fact teacher with his little group of loyal disciples, scorned by princes, and a victim of ruffians and bullies.

Few have ever been privileged to live in Peking without sharing the impressions of a powerful culture which even in the full decadence of the closing years of the Manchu dynasty still continued to exert an overwhelming influence over untold millions of men. Those who have once felt the lure of Peking long to return, and "... they leave in tears."

A Cathayan Cycle—1911

THE BRITISH LEGATION Golf Club was housed in the most exotic *sportspalast* in the world. This was the Yellow Temple, a lamasery of great dimensions, located on the dusty plain north of the city. A gentle tolerance characterizes the Buddhist fraternity. The kindly monks saw no affront to religion in the assignment of one of their smaller out-buildings as a place for storage of the queer-shaped wood-and-metal rods which the erratic foreigners employed in a laborious and evidently objectless pastime. A small ball was hurtled through the air for great distances often at great risk to man or beast... Moreover, despite their rule of abstinence from wine and meat, the monks interposed no objection to a locker containing the fiery "Scotch" and the bubbling soda water with which it was mixed, to revive the weary after their tramp over the plain in pursuit of the ball. *Huntley & Palmer's* biscuits and tinned fish and meats were also on hand as restoratives.

The golf course itself was for most of the year an arid plain, cut up into deep trenches which centuries of iron-tired carts, pulled by straining draught-animals, had worn in the soft friable *loess*. "Old roads, new rivers" is the saying in North China. In the dry season from September to June, the dust from Mongolia is gathered up by the winds. In the swirling yellow haze, fur-rimmed goggles are a necessity for the wayfarer. The wind-dug roads become rushing torrents or deep quagmires in the summer rains. They sink deeper and deeper beneath the surface and finally camel- and wagon-trains are quite swallowed up from sight as they pass along, many feet below the level of the plain. These sunken roads formed unusual hazards as the golf-balls disappeared with costly frequency. Flocks of fat-tailed, coarse-wool sheep eked out a precarious existence on the sparse vegetation which some way or other clung to the surface. These animals, too, were a hazard to the player.

After a strenuous game and the ensuing refreshments in the locker-room, we would often stroll through the temple grounds whose courts were paved with large flag-stones. A colossal image of Buddha, accom-

41

panied by his disciples, stood in the main sanctuary. Bronze and porcelain-enameled altar-sets stood before the deities, while various vegetable-oil lamps shed a dim glow in the dark recesses of the lofty hall. On the black and vermilion pillars were inscribed golden characters, excerpts from the sacred writings, the Buddhist *sutras*. Led by the Lord Abbot wearing a mitre, reminiscent of the crested helmet of a Roman centurion, shaven-headed monks knelt before the great idol on the woven cushions as they droned their *pater nosters*. The temple with its hundreds of monks was a self-contained community with dormitories, reading rooms and refectory. Under the rules, itinerant clerics from nearby Mongolia or far Tibet could claim three days' free board and lodging. In a remote court, we once came upon a room hung with dust-covered sacks. These, we were told, contained the ashes of deceased brothers awaiting return to their eternal homes in central Asia.

In the centre of the temple grounds rose a lofty, white marble monument or *dagoba*. This had been erected a century before to the honor of a Tibetan pontiff, the "Deshoo Lama," who had succumbed to smallpox while on a state visit to the Manchu court. The monument contained hundreds of figures sculptured in high relief, depicting the life of the Buddha. But there had been much vandalism, for many of the figures were now without heads or other projecting parts.

"Who were the perpetrators of such sacrilege?" I asked a young monk.

"What is your honorable country?" was the question by way of reply, as he scrutinized my features sharply.

"My humble country is America," I informed him.

"Ah, this was done by Japanese soldiers in the cyclical year *keng-tzu* (1900)," stated my informant suavely. Doubtless the reply to a similar question by a Japanese visitor would have tactfully disclosed that it had been the impious work of soldiers from Europe and America who had had no respect for Buddha.

Our only mode of reaching the Yellow Temple was on horseback. One fine mid-November afternoon in 1908, we had finished our golf game including the nineteenth hole. Remounting our Mongol ponies we cantered back toward the grey walls of the city. We entered through the gate of "Righteous Victory" through which the degenerate descendants of Kublai Khan had fled back to their native Mongolia before the avenging forces of the monk who restored a native dynasty to China in 1368. Through this historic portal we now found ourselves carried along with hordes of cavalrymen as they poured in on shaggy, diminutive mounts. Within the city itself blue cotton streamers, sign of Imperial mourning, were being hung out over the shop-fronts. The long street we rode along buzzed with excitement—the Empress Dowager, the Old Buddha, "had mounted the Dragon and ascended on high." Soon it was whispered that the ill-fated Emperor, known by his reign title of Kuang Hsü, had accompanied her on this last royal progress. Here were "sad stories of the death of kings." An era was ended. The strong-willed woman who had ruled the Empire, either openly, or from behind the throne, had at last relinquished the power which she had exercised since her bridal day thirty-six years before (1872).

In her last years Yehonala lived most of the time secluded in the fastnesses of the court, or more often in her favorite pleasure dome, the Summer Palace. Here she contented herself with the daily ritual traditionally prescribed for court ladies, as in the Ming painter, Ch'iu Ying's charming portrayals of Han palace scenes. Few if any of us laid eyes on the Old Buddha in these final years. No audiences for foreign envoys were being held. The feeble Emperor Kuang Hsü had become less than a puppet. His momentary energy for reform in the "Hundred Days" of 1898, had drawn down upon him the wrath of the powerful conservatives in the Court. His rash Cantonese mentors were either executed forthwith, or escaped to inspire others to carry on the torch of liberalism for China. Incarcerated on an island in the Palace lagoons, the Emperor had been deposed at the time of the Empress Dowager's *coup d'état* which rescinded the reform edicts and restored absolutism. The reaction against Western influences culminated in the Boxer madness of 1900.

Funerals in China are arranged with quite evident common sense— they are observed a considerable time after the actual demise. This enables grief to be softened by time. The succeeding protracted and elaborate ceremonies may thus take on a subdued spirit of festivity, like the Irish wake, while all the outward semblances of mourning are maintained. It was not until late in the following spring, after prodigious preparation, that the remains of their Imperial Majesties were consigned to the eternal silence of the Eastern and Western Tombs.

To the Peking populace in general and to the Legation Quarter in particular, the Imperial obsequies promised to take on the aspect of a Roman holiday. Not since the lamented passing of the Emperor T'ung Chih in 1875, had the elaborate ceremonial of an Imperial funeral taken place. Within the Palace the flustered members of the Board of Rites, charged with arranging the ceremonies, earnestly conned the classic rituals. Of these there were three. Perhaps, surreptitiously the Board looked up the more readily applicable records of the proceedings at the funerals of sovereigns in recent times.

Official notifications of the Empress Dowager's funeral were in due course received by the Legations. The *cortège* was to pass a certain point where reviewing stands were erected to seat the representatives of the Powers and their suites. At the suggestion of the Chinese foreign office, certain lucky younger Legation attachés were to be designated by their Ministers as ushers. These favored persons, who included the most impressive member of our own Mess, George Hanson, were the objects of much envy. They were instructed to take up their posts at break of day, garbed in full evening dress.

43

Our glamorous anticipations were more than fulfilled. The Imperial funeral procession answered every expectation of barbaric splendor. The great catafalque, containing the Old Buddha's mortal remains, was covered with Imperial yellow satin, richly embroidered in gold and colors. It was borne along by no fewer than one hundred and twenty-eight bearers. The heavy coffin rested on the shoulders of this throng by means of poles linked together in such an intricate and ingenious manner that the weight was equally distributed. Processions of chanting Buddhist, Taoist and Lama priests filed past. From long bronze tubas mournful blasts were drawn. Gongs and cymbals were intermittently struck. The military escorts ranged from crack regiments of Yuan Shih-k'ai's model army, to squads of Mongol cavalry.

The paraphernalia required by Her Majesty in the world of the Yellow Springs was provided in regal abundance—carriages, horses, human servitors, silver ingots, jewels, clothing, embroideries, brocades, utensils, even pavilions. All this would in due course be burned and so return in immaterial form to the other world. Fortunately since the sixth or seventh centuries B.C., the Chinese had abandoned the cruel practice of immolation of living creatures, either human or animal. Thus, humanely enough, the prospective burnt offerings were now represented in living form, such as droves of emaciated horses, limping and spavined. Their pitiable condition was concealed beneath gay trappings of brocades and tapestries. Later the animals would be burned only in paper models. We suspected, too, that the avaricious Palace eunuchs would see to it that inanimate objects of a precious nature, such as rolls of tribute silk, jewels and the like, now exposed in the procession in authentic form, would be quietly exchanged for *ersatz* objects of much lesser worth before the consuming fire was applied.

We viewed the completion of a Cycle of Cathay. Despite the tinseled paper and tawdry show, an historic epoch of pomp and glory was ending. Another of the twenty-five dynasties of the Middle Kingdom was coming to its close. Before the beginning of the Christian era, old Ssu-ma Ch'ien, the Froissart of Chinese chroniclers, had observed on the "frequent rise and inevitable fall of families and dynasties."

Yehonala, Tz'u-Hsi Huang-T'ai-Hou, Grand Empress Dowager, was the last of the Manchu sovereigns to rule as well as to reign. Following the tradition of most women rulers of China, since the wicked Empress Lu of the Han dynasty, Tz'u-Hsi's reign had been marked by numberless crimes. Administrative decadence in full tide had set in. Creature of conservatism and reaction as she was, she was astute enough to recognize the inevitable. After the disastrous attempt of 1900 to drive all foreigners into the sea, she assumed an appearance of conciliation and cooperation with the Western world. This took the form of some gestures of formal social intercourse with the ladies of the Legations. These disingenuous moves won her the adulation of such trusting minds as Katherine Carl, who painted the portrait of the old lady, and later published an account of her intimate days with the Empress Dowager in the Palace. Elizabeth Yü, brevetted Pincess Der Ling, the only voice of the disappearing Manchu race to be heard, had just returned from abroad. She and her sister were the first Chinese (Manchu) women to obtain an education overseas, and were the sole modern-minded members of the Empress' retinue. Their father, Yü Keng, a Manchu diplomat, had resided in Tokyo and Paris as Chinese Minister for a number of years, thus providing his daughters with opportunities for a European education.

I have already described that memorable occasion when the Hon. Jacob McGavock Dickinson of Tennessee, United States Secretary of War, presented an autograph letter from President William Howard Taft to the Princely father of the infant Emperor. The American Minister to China, the Honorable William J. Calhoun of Chicago, introduced the special envoy of "dollar diplomacy." It was upon this occasion that a few of us had our unique view of the Court in all its Tatar splendor. No Hollywood director could have imagined a setting more dramatic or colorful than this gorgeous spectacle of an irretrievable past.

It was at this moment that American bankers had been inspired by Willard Straight's brilliant salesmanship to hurl themselves into the vortex of international finance in China. Larz Anderson's figure loomed among the Special Envoy's suite, though not as tall as the six-and-a-half foot Tennesseean himself. The gold braid on the uniforms of Colonel George Barnett, commandant of the Legation Marine Guard and his aide, Captain Thomas Holcomb, and of Captain James H. Reeves, U. S. Military Attaché, furnished the only touches of color in the American group. The others incongruously wore their sombre black "evening clothes."

How different the appearance must have been when Earl Macartney in 1793 and Lord Amherst in 1816 conducted their gorgeously outfitted embassies to the Manchu court. Their object too had been to facilitate intercourse and trade, an earlier "dollar diplomacy." But both had retired, unsuccessful and humiliated, because they had refused to perform the "nine genuflections" and the "three head knockings" before the Son of Heaven. This was the controversial *"kow-tow"* ceremony required by the Emperor of China of the representatives of all tributary states of which England was regarded as one. Our own Commissioner, John E. Ward, had made a similar refusal in 1858. He declared that as a true southern gentleman "he bent the knee only to God and woman."

Caleb Cushing, the canny first United States Commissioner to China, astutely refused to push the question of a court audience, for this would have involved the *"kow-tow."* Instead, he obtained a very satisfactory treaty through the Imperial commissioners at Canton by the mere threat of proceeding to Peking. He returned to America with personal prestige enhanced. In 1909 we were spared the embarrassments of the court ceremony. The Court had yielded the point to Japanese pressure as far back

45

as 1873; and for European powers in 1891–93, but at the same time retained an Oriental satisfaction in still receiving the envoys of the Powers (except the too-understanding Japanese!) in the hall of audience reserved for tributary states. Finally the century-old controversy was settled on November 12, 1893, when the diplomatic body was received in audience in the Wen-hua-tien, a grand hall of the Imperial palace itself.

Carriages were provided to carry us to the gates of the Forbidden City. Here we entered green-hooded sedan-chairs and were rapidly conveyed down the great avenue through successive gateways to the Throne Hall. The Emperors of China were traditionally early risers and audiences were held "at the crack of dawn." Such service was so wearing on officials whose duties carried them on through the day, that one discouraged courtier put his hard lot in a celebrated poetic lament.

Obliviousness to the needs of a well ordered workday was common among high Chinese officialdom. It reached its climax in the story told of Chang Chih-tung, Viceroy at Wuchang. As he advanced in age and dignity his responsibilities increased correspondingly. He therefore acquired the habit of taking his rest at odd hours during the twenty-four by napping in his chair. Waking at any time of the day or night he would summon his secretary. This unhappy fellow, finding himself thus constantly on duty and unable to enjoy a night's rest, was soon reduced to nervous distraction and begged leave to resign.

*　　　*　　　*

The tangible results of our early-morning diplomatic *démarche* were made evident in due course in the protracted negotiations which resulted in the Reorganization Loan of 1913 for which the entire salt tax of China was pledged as security.

Beyond the Barrier

ONE FROSTY JANUARY morning of 1909 Uncle Jim had me up early. We walked briskly across town along the broad dusty streets, lined with low, thatched-roof shops and houses. The burghers of Seoul, ancient capital of Korea, still wore their horse-hair hats—with "bird-cage" crown just large enough to hold the top-knot—flat round brims, and the whole tied by a string under the chin. This gave them a jaunty, bibulous look, especially when the hat was worn a bit awry. A freshly laundered, wide-skirted coat with full sleeves, and the voluminous pantaloons, completed a costume rightly enough designed as the dignified apparel of a scholar and gentleman. Of course, no one could work in these immaculate white garments. The delicacy of the picture was emphasized by the long, slender tobacco pipe with its minute brass bowl held in one hand and, in warm weather, the graceful silken fan in the other. *Koseki,* "What's-her-name," the hardworking female partner, was personally responsible for the immaculateness of all this finery. We saw her and her neighbors vigorously beating

46

the family washing with wooden paddles on the flat stones of the roadside brook.

Uncle Jim and I proceeded across the city, past the Drum Tower, the monument commemorating Genghis Khan's invasion of Korea in the thirteenth century, and along the broad avenue leading to the Palace Gate. The air was sharp with the smoke of burning pine brush. Stolid bulls, half concealed under mountainous loads of this fuel, staggered along the streets. The Koreans were stoking up the under-floor flues which heat their diminutive rooms, and boiling *pap,* which, together with most of rice-eating Asia, forms the staple of their two or more meals a day. Accompanying the fine white rice, served in burnished brass bowls, would be the invariable *kimchee,* pickled cabbage highly seasoned with red pepper, ginger, a dash of garlic, and sometimes oysters. Around the low-lying city the mountains rose to jagged peaks, their sides alternately yellow patches of disintegrated granite or green with groves of grotesquely formed pines.

At the railway station which was our destination, a not too numerous crowd was discreetly gathering. Uniformed Japanese and Korean police wearing the short swords of their office, were liberally scattered about. In the background a battalion of Japanese infantrymen stood "at ease." The mustard-yellow of their red-trimmed uniforms and caps took up the rising sun's rays. Important looking Japanese civilians, in morning coats, striped trousers, and silk hats, bustled about the station platform. They greeted one another with profound bows and scarcely audible sibilant salutations. Military officers moved from here to there, their long sheathed sabres clattering on the pavement.

We took our places on the platform alongside Dr. Hishida, Columbia trained editor of the English-language *Seoul Press,* and with some of Uncle Jim's other Korean and Japanese friends. The deportment of all parties suddenly stiffened. Officers barked sharp orders, while the infantry battalion came to rigid attention. The *gens d' armes* took positions at strategic points from which to keep eyes in all directions on the crowd. Flourish of trumpets and roll of drums and a cavalcade of gorgeously caparizoned troopers dashed up, followed by a number of closed carriages. Out of them stepped a variety of personages. At once recognizable was His Majesty the Emperor of Korea; several gentlemen-in-waiting followed him, and then a bevy of palace beauties, and finally a short, stocky Japanese with a big head, Mongoloid face and grey stringy beard.

Prince Ito Hirobumi was one of the outstanding statesmen of the late nineteenth and early twentieth century. He was the right-hand man of the Emperor of Japan (whose reign was called Meiji) in the transformation of the Sunrise Kingdom from feudalism to constitutionalism, industrialism and other concomitants of an up-to-date state. His contemporaries were Li Hung-chang of China, Salisbury of England, and Bismark of Germany. Prince Ito was now to accompany the puppet Emperor on a northern

47

progress. Ito continued his journey to Harbin, where he fell at the hands of an assassin.

Whether it was true that he was the victim of his stubborn advocacy of a moderate policy for Korea, in that he opposed its forthright annexation to the Japanese Empire (effectuated the next year), will remain a matter of speculation for historians. At any rate, I had now seen the two greatest statesmen of the Extreme Orient, Earl Li Hung-chang and Prince Ito Hirobumi. The one, conservatively progressive, was unable in his time to move the vast mountain of China's inertia; the other had speeded his small, and therefore more mobile, country on a course of modernization which already had apparently outdistanced his own calculations.

These two doughty warriors of the council table first confronted each other at Tientsin in 1885. They were to draw up an agreement providing mutual and simultaneous introduction of Chinese and Japanese troops into Korea in case of disturbances of the peace in that remote corner of East Asia. For once Li doffed his bluff, chaffing manner. He realized he had met, in the Japanese diplomat, an antagonist worthy of his steel.

It is said that on this occasion Earl Li's constant attendant invented the useful "puff-pipe pause." At a moment when the Viceroy was hard put for an answer to Ito's demands, the adroit attendant thrust the stem of Li's water-pipe between his master's lips and proceeded deliberately to light it for him. Between this attention and the succeeding single puff of tobacco smoke from the minute bowl, Li was able to cogitate an appropriate reply. The device was so effective that Li Hung-chang incorporated it henceforth into his diplomatic technique.

My journey had begun from Peking, traversed new lands and exhibited new scenes. In the increasing cold of late December, North China was blanketed with snow. I had fortified myself with a heavy Irish frieze overcoat, with a cotton-wadded lining and a mulberry-paper interlining. This latter was the idea of old Van, the "bespoke" tailor from Shanghai who was responsible for most of our sartorial achievements at the Peking Mess. The whole was set off with a fur collar dyed black, which, while without question adding to the warmth of the garment, managed mysteriously to transfer part of its sombre hue to the wearer's neck and face.

*   *   *

The Peking-Mukden express train traversed the narrow corridor, between the mountains and the sea, which leads from the North China plain into Manchuria. At this "bottle-neck" I first saw the Great Wall, China's oft-pierced Maginot Line, as it tumbles wildly down from the mountain crags and then timidly crosses the intervening plain to the seashore. Here it was that the misguided Wu San-kuei, the Emperor's Warden of the Marches, Captain-general at the Wall, invited the Manchu hordes into China. The rebel Li Tzu-ch'eng had not only occupied the Capital and driven the Ming Emperor to dispair and suicide; he had secured possession

48

of General Wu's favorite concubine! The dyke once broken, the torrent of Tatar nomads poured through until all the rich Empire was overrun.

Wu San-kuei sullenly accepted office under the conquerors, as puppet Prince Pacificator of the South West. In distant Yunnan, "South of the Clouds" he established what was virtually an independent kingdom of his own. There he nursed his plans of revolt and recovery until death overtook the old warrior, at the moment when the second Manchu Emperor K'ang Hsi was on the point of launching an overwhelming punitive expedition against his recalcitrant vassal.

I was now entering high Tartary, that vast area of North Eastern Asia which early travelers had made vaguely romantic to all Europe. To the Chinese it was the Eastern Three Provinces, according to its more recent administrative reorganization. But in their earlier history it was known simply as "Beyond the Barrier." After the conquest of 1644, the Manchus, a Tungusic people, generally related to Mongols, Koreans, and Chinese, migrated *en bloc* from this their original home to China south of the Great Wall. Manchus in Manchuria in my time had become as rare as Indians in Indiana.

This land, on whose frozen plains the British-built Chinese railway operated as far as Mukden, had been in earliest Chinese records a land of savages. Extant earth works witnessed the evidences of early kingdoms extending to Siberia. The land was successively overrun by nomadic Kins, Khitans, and Mongols, who similarly ravaged North China. Over the centuries, out of North East Asia there had continued to erupt masses of humanity who, locust-like, devoured or destroyed everything before them. In the early Ming period, just before Columbus discovered America, South Manchuria formed the frontier province of the Chinese Empire.

It was in this region that an obscure tribe emerged. In time, it came to be equipped with the essential supernatural ancestor, one Aisin Gioro, conceived immaculately of a virgin mother. A jackdaw had aroused some suspicion by hovering about at the time. He became the tribal bird. The first great Manchu leader, Nurhachu, was born in 1559. He early developed a deep hatred for the Chinese, charging them with the treacherous murder of his grandfather and father. By the time he became nineteen, he had achieved the leadership of the five Manchu tribes, though later he had a severe struggle with the recalcitrant Yeho tribe, from which sprang, in time, the Grand Empress Dowager known by her tribal name Yehonala.

Nurhachu was an able organizer. He formed his tribe into "Four Banners," under the strictest military discipline with an improved technique of battle, supplemented by the far-shooting Manchu long-bow. When ready to give battle to the unwieldy Empire to the South, he declared the "Seven Hates" of the Manchus against the Chinese. Like Philip of Macedon with his designs on the great Persian Empire, Nurhachu did not live to effect the conquest he had prepared for. He died in 1626. With the decadence of the Chinese Ming dynasts, and the aid of the Warden of the

Marches, Wu San-kuei, the Manchu Regent Durgan finally occupied Peking. He turned in the direction of Mukden and loyally proffered the Dragon Throne to the infant, his royal nephew, who became the first Manchu Emperor of China, under the reign title of "Obedient Rule." The Manchu Kingship in China thus began with an infant in 1644 and was to end with an infant in 1912.

The advent of the Manchus began one of those periodical flowerings of Chinese culture under a new racial blood-transfusion. "More royalist than the King," the successive Manchu emperors became the greatest patrons of Chinese letters of all time, and of the art of China in all its forms. Those known to Europeans as K'ang Hsi and Ch'ien Lung, enjoyed phenomenally long reigns. The latter abdicated in the sixtieth year of his reign in 1796 so as not unfilially to exceed that of the former, his revered grandfather who had reigned from 1662 to 1722. They extended the sway of the Chinese empire by brilliant campaigns to an extent not reached since the great Han dynasty, Far Eastern contemporary of the ancient Roman world. They wielded facile pens themselves; and under the Imperial *imprimatur* they caused to be compiled a vast dictionary containing 44,400 words, an encyclopedia in 5,040 volumes, which has a content several times the size of the *Britannica,* and a massive catalogue of twenty centuries and more of Chinese literature.

It has been asserted that by the middle of the Manchu reign the volume of printed books in the Chinese language surpassed the total of the printed books of all other peoples. This may well be the case as printing in China (from wood-blocks or, occasionally, from cast, moveable bronze or wooden type) had been in full vogue for hundreds of years before Gutenberg invented the printing press in Europe. The early Manchu Emperors did however impose an inquisition upon what they regarded as seditious books, or any literature subversive to their dynasty. They encouraged the production of the first porcelain in the southern kilns of Ching-teh-chen. Painting and calligraphy, the artistic formation of the Chinese ideograph, flourished mightily under their patronage. Their famous palaces at Peking, Jehol, and Mukden became the treasuries of vast stores of the aesthetic expression of all China and of all time.

Despite their devotion to art in its most splendid aspects, the early Manchu Emperors were stern disciplinarians. They suppressed revolt mercilessly, as at the bloody sack of Yangchow. They imposed the shaving of the forehead and the wearing of the queue after their own fashion, in order to obliterate distinction between Chinese and Manchu. This was one of the most extraordinary feats of merging of nationalities in the history of conquest. When they had secured control of China by the establishment of their garrisons in all strategic cities in China, they exhibited a remarkable sagacity in sharing the civil government with the Chinese.

Thus, after the initial resistance of a few irredentists, such as the famous Chinese naval commander Koxinga who made Formosa his base, China and the Chinese settled down to almost three centuries of relative peace and phenomenal growth of population. At length the inevitable decadence of the Manchu family, the activities of the anti-dynastic and patriotic secret societies, and growing economic distress led to such widespread popular disturbances as the T'ai-p'ing, Panthay, and Mohammedan rebellions in the middle of the last century. China's swollen population was thereby reduced by many tens of millions by war, massacre, famine and pestilence.

*   *   *

Mukden, chief city of Manchuria, and my mid-way destination to Korea, had long ceased to be the Manchus' capital, save in a symbolic sense, for here were the tombs of the early sovereigns. But it was bidding fair again to be the scene of historic developments. The international intrigue which had centred in Seoul, had now shifted to the Manchurian city. Foreign financial imperialism was stretching out its several hands, to be warmly clasped by the Chinese authorities. Smart American-educated T'ang Shao-yi, as Governor at Mukden, was hatching schemes to interest American and British capital by way of railroad construction. While the Russian Bear had retired to North Manchuria to lick his wounds after his recent encounter with Japan, the Nippon Empire was already formulating plans of consolidation and exploitation of its conquests in South Manchuria. Li Hung-chang's age-old policy of "making friends with distant peoples to check those near at hand" was still the game.

I put up at the American Consulate-General. Situated on a dusty plain, this was a Chinese *kung-kwan,* a group of one-storied, tile-roof buildings surrounded by a high brick wall and with an imposing double gateway. One traveled through the city's unpaved streets in small Russian "droshkies," drawn by half-tamed Manchurian ponies. The diminutive carriage lurched through deep mud-holes or threw up clouds of dust, as the season dictated, and was always in imminent danger of capsizing.

At the season of my arrival, late December, the near-Siberian cold had descended upon the land. All humanity was wrapped in furs, sheep skins or thickest cotton-wadded garments, as means permitted. The ground was frozen iron-hard. The two-wheeled Manchurian cart with its three, four or five draft animals attached, could now negotiate the earth's hard crust. Despite mountain-high loads of grain or salt-sacks, heavy lumps of coal, or fragile earthen wine-jars, there was no danger now, as in summer, of bogging down in bottomless morasses.

Mukden's foreign community were a vigorous group of individualists in a robust climate. They exhibited no traces of that lassitude which inevitably overcomes the European who in the treaty-ports of China-proper suffers the long and enervating heat of the summers. Skating, horseback-riding, tennis, and golf combined to maintain the energy in these men and women of North European origins. The youngsters employed in the great

51

trading firms, such as the oil and tobacco companies, in the course of organizing or inspecting agencies, made lengthy trips into the interior. These involved long days in open carts or on horseback in sub-zero weather, sleeping at night in crowded native inns, alongside carters snoring stentoriously on the brick *k'ang* beds, superheated by hot-air flues. The Mukden Club was the scene of some good honest drinking, an invariable concomitant of life in extreme northerly climates. Neither the "Scotch" or brandy-and-sodas of the Club as consumed by the foreign community, or the fiery "kaoliang" native spirits, had more effect than to heighten the color of fur-trimmed ruddy faces.

One did not need to go to the adjacent tombs of the early Manchu sovereigns for historical evidences around Mukden. Hereabouts was a vast and recent battlefield, far dwarfing Gettysburg's twenty-five square miles of combat. The battle of Mukden, fought by a million men from February 23 to March 10, 1905, along lines extending for one hundred miles, was the greatest battle of modern times to that date. Russia in this and other engagements was defeated on land and sea, but not materially reduced in strength. Four hundred miles to the south, one of the most bitterly fought sieges in history had occurred. Within a few weeks I was to scale 203 Metre Hill at Port Arthur with its wrecked concrete gun emplacements, evidence of the desperate assault of less than five years before. In the pulverized gravel on the summit I kicked up brass bullet-shells and even bits of human bone. Japan was brought by the costly struggle to the end of her financial resources. Only by Theodore Roosevelt's timely mediation was she awarded the victory, which confirmed Japan's position in South Manchuria, but left the northern half still Russian.

It was on the narrow-gauge military railway, thrown down through the mountains by Japanese engineers during the war, that I made my way from Mukden to the Yalu River on the Korean border. What was a two-days' trip for me became a matter of a few hours for tourists by the Seoul express. I had as traveling companions an American agricultural expert employed by the Manchurian government, and a raffish Englishman from Hongkong. The later enjoyed such rugged health and ebullient spirits that a straw "boater" hat and a light "Burberry" raincoat sufficed him against the full rigors of the Manchurian winter. Though it was bitter cold, his Rabelaisian cheerfulness never left him. After relating many racy personal anecdotes, he confided to us that in his early years in the homeland he had been precentor in the local village church. He could recite glibly lengthy portions from the responses.

Our night's stop was at a midway mountain village. Here we were guests of the "Japan-China Hotel," a small caravansary presided over by a scarred Japanese veteran of the war of only four years earlier. Mine host managed to convey to us with justifiable pride that Lord Kitchener had honored him by lodging there a night. This apparently had fired the innkeeper's ambition to expand his mastery of English. The presence of three

English-speaking guests must be fully exploited. As we dined, close up to the warmth of the charcoal fire-pot, our host held up an egg enquiringly. "Rotten," brazenly pronounced the Hongkong Englishman; whereupon the assiduous seeker after foreign vocabularies jotted down in phonetic Japanese script this authoritative English designation for the object he held. Doubtless subsequent guests were puzzled when smilingly asked by the hotel proprietor whether they would have their breakfast *rotten* "three or four minutes," or fried on both sides. After an Asiatic custom as old at least as Marco Polo's account of it, the "Hotel Nippon-China" offered not only ordinary refreshment but provided those further solaces which the Oriental traveler finds indispensable. But the enticing giggles of the gay little ladies from Japan in the adjacent room left us unconcerned as we drew the heavy wadded *futons* over us for a sound night's sleep.

The erstwhile military railway upon which we traveled still afforded terrors almost equal to those of war. The diminutive locomotive all but came to a stop as it slowly crawled up steep grades, or dashed furiously down mountain sides and around sharp curves, the while emitting billows of black smoke and cinders. As our two small make-shift coaches balanced on the rails at the very edge of the precipices, far below in the valleys we could occasionally discern the earlier wrecks of trains. The scenery through which we passed was magnificent. The hills were covered with pines, standing out green against the white snow. At Phoenix Mountain, Feng-huang-shan, the Japanese forces advancing from Korea had had a sharp engagement with the retreating Russians.

At Antung, important city at the mouth of the Yalu River which divides Korea from her northern neighbor, we were met by Lewis Palen. A Cornell graduate, Palen represented the far-flung Chinese Customs Service, in this remote spot. His official residence was a converted Chinese temple which he shared with the original occupant, the Goddess of Mercy. This celibate existence he offered us for the duration of our stay. After the cold and comfortless journey across the mountains of South Manchuria, and now under the contemplative gaze of Avokitesvara, the benign one, his hospitality was deeply appreciated. Palen was one of those gifted but volatile persons so often found in Sir Robert Hart's international service. Here we found him, a sensitive recluse on the bleak shores of the frozen Yalu, reading with intense relish Henry VanDyke's poetry. He complained that his eye-sight was impaired. Possibly it was, as he read on and on in the dull light of the winter day, or in the dimmer murk of a kerosene hanging lamp. He left soon after for Germany, for treatment of his eyes, resigning his post in the Customs.

Soon Palen was back in Manchuria to establish an extensive agricultural project in the fertile but lonely valley of the Sungari River. He colonized Russian and Chinese settlers and taught them to use modern agricultural machinery. All went well until the dreaded "Red Beard" bandits heard of this flourishing enterprise. Just as prosperity dawned, with bumper harvests and profitably marketed crops, the ferocious gangs dashed down upon the settlers and carried off their money, grain, and cattle. At length, complete tragedy overtook the project. His American manager, William Morgan Palmer of Plattsburg, New York, a Harvard graduate, proposed organized resistance to the raiders. Palmer's well armed party advanced through the fields of giant sorghum upon a marauding enemy band. But the latter, knowing too well the terrain, noiselessly crept up behind their attackers. Palmer was the first to go, shot through the head. An American of wide culture and high idealism, who was singularly devoted to China, lies forgotten under an oak on the long abandoned Manchurian ranch. Palen, balked in his ambitious venture, next turned to literature. He collaborated with Dr. Ossandowsky on that highly successful if sharply debated romance *Beasts, Men and Gods,* and retired to Switzerland to devote himself to writing.

Across the Yalu

THE BROAD YALU RIVER, boundary between Manchuria and Korea, is crossed by one of the world's great achievements in bridge engineering. To our party of three it was a picturesque venture on *pai-tzu,* sleds with iron-shod runners. These extend behind so that a fur-clad Manchurian can stand astride of them and push the sled along at high speed by means of a spiked pole, thrusting it rapidly backward between his legs against the ice. On the south bank we were in our first North Korean town. This was a different world. We had left behind the Chinese-Manchurians in their heavily wadded short jacket and trousers. Instead there were gentlemanly-looking persons strolling sedately about, pulling at long pipes, adjusting precariously balanced hats, and maintaining their voluminous white raiment in unruffled dignity. A passenger train of American pattern awaited us at New Wiju station. In a short time we were running along valleys between low rounded hills, sparsely covered with pines.

Overnight I stopped at Pyeng Yang city, important American mission and educational centre. In its river, almost a half century before, an American trading vessel, the *General Sherman,* had stranded. Korean officials, fearful of interlopers, immediately blockaded the river, burned the ship with fire-rafts, and massacred every last man of the crew. The latter, however, included only one American, a certain Captain Preston, well known on the China coast as an adventurer. The supercargo was an Englishman, and the entire crew Chinese. The ship was laden with muskets, powder, and other articles which were contraband; it had more than likely sailed on a marauding expedition. Commodore Robert Shufeldt, U.S.N., who later brought the U.S.S. *Wachusetts* to the Korea coast to investigate the case, reported that the *General Sherman* had wilfully and under constant protest ascended the Ta Tong River; that finally the Chinese crew, landing and behaving in a lawless manner, were attacked and murdered by an enraged mob. The significance of this episode was expressed by Admiral Schufeldt when he recorded how, some fifteen years later on May 22, 1882, he "signed the first treaty ever made between the Hermit Nation and any Western Power."

Now the Americans, missionaries and teachers, were beloved members of the Pyeng Yang community. The national misfortunes of the Koreans made them the most ready of all Asiatic peoples to embrace the foreign religion. Relationship to powerful America, they felt, might lead to an amelioration of their hard lot. Thousands flocked to the Y.M.C.A., to the Salvation Army. The connotation of the latter words, particularly, suggested in some way liberation. It was yet early in Korea. Annexation was a year away. The subsequent gradual reduction of the people to outward acquiescence in the alien yoke meant bitter years ahead. The sympathy and spiritual succor which the American missionary extended to this gentle and sensitive people in its national despair can never be estimated. Doubtless the advice of certain missionaries led the Koreans even deeper into the abyss. On the other hand, the counsel of wise men like James Gale and Horace Underwood, counsels of prudence and adjustment to what could only be regarded for the time being as the inevitable, saved many from futile suffering.

*   *   *

Uncle Jim was there to greet me at the Seoul Station. When one's uncle has been present to pronounce his nephew plump and bonny a few hours after the youngster has first seen the light of day; when at the age of four, hours of precious time are devoted to his entertainment; when again he listens open-mouthed to stories of far lands on sabbatical years of furlough; when one's uncle is the lodestone which brings one to the Far East and at last to this city of Seoul itself, there must be deep affection.

This uncle of mine I perceived as tall, commanding, distinguished, and wearing withal a smile of kindly humility. A greeting ensued, appropriate to the joining of uncle and nephew long separated by thousands of miles.

Gale's early years in Korea were of such a nature as to lay a remarkable foundation for a knowledge of the country, its people, and its language. For long periods he lived in Korean homes with his Korean and Japanese teachers constantly beside him. He subsisted on native food for months on end to the ultimate detriment of a naturally robust digestion. Early in the year 1891, he and that other missionary pioneer, Samuel Moffett, as traveling companion, sallied forth on a perilous exploratory journey through North Korea. During this adventurous trip, which lasted three months and took them into Manchuria as far as Mukden, they made a study of the country and its people, acquiring special familiarity with the difficult and practically unknown language. Traveling without escort, through mountains and forests infested with Siberian tigers and ferocious black bears, but by even fiercer bandits, their only casualty was "Nip," Gale's ubiquitous fox terrier. This lively quadruped was reduced for food

55

to eating sorghum candy, which served to extract most of his teeth. As a rest from this arduous life, Gale settled with his wife (the widow of John W. Heron, M.D., first Presbyterian missionary to be appointed to Korea and subsequently court physician) and her two small daughters, Annie and Jessie, in the port of Wonsan on the east coast. This post gave him opportunity to perfect his linguistic knowledge and to embark upon his *magnum opus,* the Korean-Chinese-English dictionary.

During those critical years when Korea occupied world attention as the centre of the intrigues of Japan, China, and Russia, Gale was the brilliant Seoul correspondent of the *North China Herald* at Shanghai, the principal English newspaper of the China Coast. For this and for other purposes when a degree of anonymity was desirable, he employed as *nom de plume* two family surnames combined—"Esson Third." He ceased his political contributions before the annexation of Korea by Japan in 1910. Years later, in 1923, he visited me in Manchuria. I persuaded him to make another contribution in his old vein to the *North China Herald*. His two articles under the caption "Manchuria Revisited" contrasted the new Manchuria, with its railways and modern cities, coal-mines, and agricultural experiment stations, with the complete wilderness which he had found some thirty-two years before. Old-time readers of the *North China Herald* were electrified to note the reappearance, for a moment, of the once-familiar pen-name, with its accustomed clarity and humor.

Like his great missionary compeers in China, James Gale was called upon frequently to participate in political affairs. Yuan Shih-k'ai was his personal friend, up to Yuan's departure from Seoul in 1894. Sir John Jordan, later Britain's envoy to Peking, while at Seoul as Minister Resident, often engaged his services as official interpreter and negotiator. When the King of Korea was in great distress, after the murder of his Queen by Japanese *ronin,* His Majesty begged Gale to remain beside him in the Palace. Gale's was the largest church auditorium in Seoul, built with funds raised by the Koreans themselves. Here he addressed congregations of hundreds in faultless Korean vernacular, never tiring his listeners by long discourses, for he believed in moderation in all things.

With all the honors and distinctions that he received both within and outside the Orient, James Gale remained an humble man. His religion was far from dogmatic. He was sharply impatient of injustice and hypocrisy, and of great resolution in the things that he considered as of account. When the days of bitter national humiliation came upon the Korean people, it was to *Kil Moksa* that they went for counsel and aid.

He was friends with successive Governors General, Araki, Saito, Ugaki, as well as with lesser officials of the Japanese Residency General. Avoiding the appearance of interventionist in political affairs, a sin with which missionaries have often been charged, he was often able by his nonpartisan character to lighten the load of the people he had adopted as his own.

At length, after thirty-nine years in *partibus infidelium,* as the old *mis-*

sionnaires designated the heathen lands in which they labored, he retired into an atmosphere redolent of England's greatest literary men. At Bath he occupied the house in St. James's Square in which Charles Dickens and Walter Savage Landor lived and wrote. He frequently spoke in the famous Pump Room before the Dickens Fellowship which he served as chairman. His acquaintance with the great literature of the Orient was fully matched by a knowledge and appreciation of his own. If ever missionary effort was justified—as it generally has been—it was in the life and works of James Gale. "Salt of the earth, your uncle is," boomed old Dr. Timothy Richard, Nestor of Protestant missionaries, to me one day in his Quinsan Gardens home at Shanghai.

*   *   *

The Gale residence, to which I was taken, was at Yun-Mot-Kol, the end of a low ridge, the Dragon's Head, projecting into the unique city that was Seoul. It commanded a view of a sea of thatched roofs. Here and there the monotony was broken by higher buildings, or by the Drum Tower, and in the distance the Palace buildings and the picturesque city gates. Unlike vast Peking with its vermilion palace walls, its yellow tiled roofs, and its azure skies, Seoul presented a uniform drabness, enlivened alone by the glisteningly white-robed throngs of the streets. But the children appeared in bright yellows, pinks, and greens.

The Peking Legation Quarter was virtually bereft of young femininity in those days. The arrival of two attractive young women the April of 1909 proved an event of stellar magnitude. Immediately the Students' Mess, which through the "step-cousin" enjoyed a priority, set its social machinery in operation. Luncheons, teas, dinners followed one upon the other. The Chinese mess-boys and the cooks exerted themselves to make these entertainments notable in a world devoted largely to social events. The excitement and activity extended in ever widening circles—to the Minister's, to the Colonel Barnetts', to the junior mess of the Marine officers. Picnics penetrated into hitherto unvisited precincts of the Winter Palace, arranged for, via some mysterious diplomacy, by Earl Hobart—to become in later years Alice Tisdale Hobart's hero in a magnificent trilogy of novels on the life of the foreign businessman in China. The epic excursion to Nankow, the Great Wall, and the tombs of the Ming Emperors ensued. There were romantic walks on the Peking wall, when the distant western hills shone purple and gold in the haze of gorgeous sunsets.

How could a short month exhaust Peking's infinite possibilities? The cabled reply to a request for extension of the visit came back from Seoul, "Yes, certainly." Dear Uncle Jim; hadn't he for years revered great China's capital as the *fons et origo* of all East Asia's culture, and particularly of his own Korea's, in which, like the learned Jesuit missionaries of preceding centuries, he had so deeply immersed himself?

The summer's heat then being upon us, the annual *hegira* to the temple in the western hills took place. With mountains of baggage, the ladies rode the narrow-gauge railway to the station at the foot of the Hills. Here they changed to sedan chairs which sure-footed porters would swing along up the stony mountain path, past the Eight Great Shrines, to the gates of the Convent of the Three Mountains. All was found swept and garnished by the servants, who had preceded their mistress. Cots were arranged in the various rooms, well protected by nets from mosquitoes and the even more virulent sand-midgets. Tables were set out on the terrace overlooking the plain, with Peking faintly visible in a haze of dust and heat fourteen miles distant. We men came along on horseback "By the Eight-mile Village pagoda, looking eastward to the sea...," we sang parodying Kipling.

III

SHANGHAI, 1911–1914

*Plague Special — China's Old Man River — Shanghai, City
Towards the Sea — Consuls, Courts and Compradores —
Dispensing with Justice — Liberté, Egalité, Etcetera — A
Publican in the Provinces — Salt, Pillar of China's Finance
— A Tale of Three Cities — Yoked to an Unbeliever —
Mandarins and Merchant Guilds*

Plague Special

A GHASTLY SPECTRE now appeared in the North. It was one long-familiar to China, but dressed in a new garb. Reports came through of number-less deaths in the bitter cold of the Mongolian-Manchurian border, deaths sudden and horrible. The Chinese government despatched to the affected region, in this winter of 1910 and 1911, its most capable Cambridge-trained physician, Dr. Wu Lien-teh. Heroic efforts were made to stem the advance southward of the "pneumonic plague." With armies of North China laborers returning by every land road and sea route, from the soya-bean cultivation of Manchuria, how could this be effected? The Mongolian marmot, whose fur was universally worn in China proper, was iden-tified as the "carrier" of the dreaded infection.

I myself was at the moment under instructions for my anticipated trans-fer to the Consulate General at Shanghai. I had completed two years' in-tensive study, and a half year of service in the Chinese Secretariat of the Legation. My special board of examiners, a formidable trio of "sino-logues," Drs. Tenney, Gattrel, and Princeton's Robert Gayley of the Peking Y.M.C.A., expressed their satisfaction at what they were pleased to regard as my phenomenal accomplishments with the recalcitrant lan-guage. Inwardly I realized how little I really knew of it, despite the four thousand characters, on which I had prepared myself for the final written examination, which successfully passed had entitled me to my promotion.

When the long train pulled out for the seven hundred mile run, straight south through the middle of China to Hankow on the Yangtze River, it was dubbed the "Plague Special." This was only the first of those innumer-able "flights from reality," from war, from flood, or from other human or natural calamity, which continued to feature our life in China. A couple

59

on honeymoon, we then recked little of these external cataclysms. To us the journey promised to be a merry episode. The lugubrious face of the Italian Minister, still anguished with fears of the pursuing plague, failed to darken our mood. New adventures were before us. Yet for a moment at least there was a pang at leaving that enchanting world of Peking.

"One arrives in Peking weeping; but leaves in tears," we reminded ourselves.

The "Kin-Han" railway was at the time the longest trunkline in China. Completed by Belgian engineers after 1897 with "Belgian" capital, though with more than a suspicion of concealed Russian interest, it had been redeemed through a loan obtained from British banking interests. This for the first time placed a railway in China under purely Chinese control. The railway could be regarded as an extension of the older British built line from Peking *via* Tientsin to Mukden, Manchuria. There the South Manchurian Railway (Japanese) made connections to Changchun (now Hsinking), whence the Russian controlled Chinese Eastern Railway led to Harbin and in due course either eastward to the port of Vladivostok on the Pacific, or westward to Europe over the Trans-Siberian Railway. Thus direct rail connections were provided from Hankow on the middle Yangtze River to Berlin, Paris and beyond. As far back as 1898 the American-China Development Company syndicate had obtained a concession to build a railway from Hankow to Canton. The route had been surveyed in 1899, but the concession had been transferred by the Americans to Belgian interests. It was many years before this important trunkline was completed and this only in 1936 by Chinese engineers in the face of possible war-needs.

The "Plague Special" traversed the wide plains of central China: Chihli, the metropolitan province of "Direct Rule" (now Hopei, "North of the River"), Honan ("South of the River"), Hupeh ("North of the Poyang and Tungt'ing Lakes")—three of the most thickly populated of China's provinces. The two former are subject to great periodical famines due to drought or flood. This is the "Dust Bowl" of China, although varied by alternate periods of devastating flood waters.

Hupeh is south of the Tsingling range, which constitutes the dividing line between the northern wheat and millet eating population, and the southern rice consumers. The Yellow River bisects this region with its wide sluggish stream, obstructed by sandbars and confined by elaborate dykes. It is the breaking of these dykes in the rainy season which causes the flood disasters. Centuries of deforestation have allowed the rains to wash down vast quantities of detritus from the hills, choking the river bed. Where we crossed it by the long iron bridge, we were afforded a view of the swirling, muddy waters beneath.

In China's war with Great Britain and France in 1858–60, a French Admiral proposed that his fleet be stationed where the Grand Canal crosses the Yellow River. The purpose was to block supplies of tribute rice from the south and thus "starve" the Manchu court at Peking into submission. This strategy had been employed by the British in their war with China in 1842, when the Grand Canal at Chinkiang on the Yangtze River had been blockaded. The French naval chief was not aware that the Yellow River, which changes its course from time to time, is unnavigable throughout its entire length save for small flatbottomed craft in the lower reaches.

Along the Peking-Hankow railway are several of the largest inland cities of China. With bastioned walls and picturesque gateways, these cities are to be seen dotted along the old Imperial highway, which for centuries joined the Capital with the Yangtze cities and below. As our train approached the Hupeh border, it began the gentle ascent to the Pass over the Tsingling mountains, finally entering a tunnel at the top of the divide. Nearby is the summer resort of Cock's-Comb-Hill (Chi-kung Shan) where the foreign population of Hankow, and many of the missionaries stationed in north central China had comfortable villas, located high above the summer heat of the plains.

Armies had marched back and forth across these mountains in the Warring States era of the fifth century B.C. Like modern Europe, China was then divided into often mutually hostile realms, armed to the teeth and constantly preying upon one another. The foundations of Chinese civilization were laid in this central China area through which we were passing, on the plains of Honan province in the valley of the Yellow River. The cradle of the Chinese race is disclosed in the buried cities of the Shang dynasty which flourished (contemporary with Babylonian civilization, Rameses II of Egypt, Moses, and the Phoenicians) as early as the eighteenth century B.C. Here the Chou dynasty continued to rule, in name at least, for almost a thousand years (1122–256 B.C.). China's feudal era was of this time, with some twenty-one minor principalities or kingdoms, thus antedating Europe's by almost two millenniums. A short-lived "league of nations" was organized to put an end to the anarchy. It was in the Chou period that China paralleled the cultural greatness of Greece on the other side of the Eurasian continent. It was China's age too of great philosophers—Lao-tzu, K'ung-tzu (Confucius), Mencius, and others. But it was not until the advent of the Chin dynasty from the Far West that China was unified as an Empire at the end of the third century before the Christian era.

All doubts as to the early origins of a high type of Chinese culture have been resolved by the remarkable discoveries along this region of the Yellow River. These finds consist of magnificent bronze ritual vessels, and quantities of oracle bones and tortoise shells. The inscriptions on these objects are being slowly deciphered, corroborating the relative accuracy of Chinese traditional history, and throwing new light on the origins of that remarkable literary medium, the Chinese ideograph.

*   *   *

61

In deference to His Honor, the Judge of the United States Court for China, who headed our party, we were met at the Hankow station by the American Consul General, a Mr. Mosher. During the few intervening hours before the departure of the Yangtze River steamer which was to take us to Shanghai, we visited Hankow's chief recreation centre, the Race Club. True to form, the British community had provided their invariable Temple of Sports in this remote corner of the world, six hundred miles in the interior of China. The entire foreign community gathered here daily for afternoon tea, followed by tennis or golf on the two nine-hole courses. In the early morning, racing enthusiasts watched the China ponies under training being galloped around the splendid turfed race track. A fine swimming pool, and spacious tea room, game rooms, locker rooms, and one of those traditionally long bars of Far Eastern clubs were housed in the Club House with its long breeze-swept varandahs. Tennis courts, an 18-hole golf course, and fields for other sports completed the grounds.

The club was exclusively for the Occidental population, the resident Chinese being admitted only during the races, spring and autumn, with occasional *gymkhanas* or "off-meets" interspersed. Considerable sums of money changed hands at these races. All the forms of race-track betting were permitted, "parimutuals," "cash-sweeps," etc. This was "East of Suez," they would have you know, "where there ain't no Ten Commandments" and all prohibitions are off. The club enjoyed a handsome income from the race meets. As elsewhere in China only "gentlemen jockeys"—no professionals—rode the fleet China ponies.

Hankow, like Tientsin, we found divided up into foreign "concessions," each under its own independent government. In succession of establishment, they were the British, French, Russian, German, and Japanese. These veritable European cities were stretched along the upper side of the Yangtze for several miles. The "Bund" was a fine boulevard, with shade-trees and grass-plots between the paved roadway and sidewalks. The river bank was reinforced against erosion from the powerful current by concrete and masonry bunding. At this mid-winter season of 1911, the Yangtze was some thirty feet below mid-summer high water, leaving great stretches of bare river-bed exposed. The Chinese populace, excluded from the Bund itself, took advantage of the temporary foreshore and in large numbers took squatters' right by putting up mat-shed dwellings and shops.

Beyond, in the deep channel, were the pontoons and hulks to which the large British, French, German, and Japanese steamers tied. The shrill falsetto chant of coolies working cargo came back to us over the foreshore. The streets of the British Concession were policed by tall East Indians, Sikhs, wearing picturesque multi-colored turbans and rolling their long black beards tightly under their chins. In the French Concession, Annamite police from Indo-China were on duty. They were squat, swarthy little fellows, their teeth turned black from chewing beetle-nut and lime.

Hankow, we learned, is only one of three large cities, which with Hanyang and Wuchang, forms "the Wu-Han cities." They are separated from each other by the confluence of the Han River with the Yangtze, which is here a mile or more broad. The name Hankow means "mouth of the Han." It is China's most important inland city, at the centre of rail and water transportation—"the Chicago of China." The mouth of the Han River is usually crowded with the junks engaged in the transport of cargo to and from this centre. Native shipping seeks shelter within the narrow stream from the heavy storms and high seas which frequently prevail here on the long open "reach" of the Yangtze. In shunning Scylla, they often fell into Charybdis, for heavy freshets come unheralded down the Han River valley to sweep the congested mass of junks and sampans out into the Yangtze. With the advent of the telegraph, these disasters became avoidable as warnings were flashed down in time for native craft to seek safety elsewhere before the onrushing wall of water arrived.

On either side of the mouth of the Han, convenient for junk traffic, I had my first glimpse of the famed storehouses which supply much of Central China with its salt. They are great wooden or stuccoed structures with grey tiled roofs, owned by the rich merchants who transport the salt; but they are subject to strictest government supervision. For centuries, this necessary commodity has been brought up the river from the sea-coast in huge, unwieldy sailing junks. They often carry as much as from four to six thousand bags of salt, 250 to 300 tons. The salt, coarse and grey as it comes from the earth evaporating-pans on the sea-shore, was then packed in woven rush bags of one "picul," more than a hundred and forty pounds each. Stored in these warehouses "in bond," the salt pays the balance of tax due when purchased by local distributors. Salt in China plays the part of gasoline and liquor in America, "necessities" which produce a handsome revenue. Similarly, the tax officials "lay on" all the traffic will bear. The ease with which the tax may be "upped" by an impecunious government, or in time of national emergency, is both the blessing and the bane of these taxes.

One resourceful Minister of Finance blandly announced upon his assumption of office that he would not add to the people's burdens by an increase in the rates of duty on salt. Shortly thereafter he issued orders assertedly in pursuit of the policy of "modernizing China." The metric weight system would be introduced into the salt trade. The unit of taxation had been the *ssu-ma picul,* a weight of 140 lbs., upon which the salt tax was approximately twelve Chinese dollars. The new "metric picul" introduced under the "modern regime" would weigh 110 lbs. but the rate of duty would remain unchanged, an actual increase of about 22 per cent in the salt tax!

Across the Han to the west we visited Hanyang, location of the first modern Chinese iron works. As inland Hankow, the centre of actual and proposed railway trunk lines and head of deep water navigation, came to be likened to Chicago, so Hanyang assumed the character of a Pittsburgh.

The Hanyang Iron and Steel Works was originally established by a forward looking Viceroy, Chang Chih-tung. Iron ore, he knew, could be obtained from the Ta-yeh mines a short distance down river; coal in abundance from the P'ing-hsiang collieries in Hunan up river. The raw materials could thus be economically transported by water and assembled for processing at Hanyang. Thus arose the Han-Yeh-P'ing Corporation, whose potentialities were great, but whose accomplishments, owing to mismanagement and financial difficulties, were insignificant. Japanese interests, always on the lookout for sources of materials basic to modern industry, made every effort to secure control of these valuable properties.

Wuchang across the river from Hankow, Hupeh's provincial capital, is a venerable walled city. The Yellow Crane Tower perched on a jutting rock above the city has formed the theme of many Chinese poems. The city is famed in story and legend. It existed as a castellated town while Hanyang and Hankow were mere settlements of boatmen and fishers.

China's Old Man River

THE PEKING refugees from the "Plague Special" separated to travel on two river-steamers, the *Kutwo* and the *Tatung,* both flying the British flag, although belonging to two different firms. These friendly rivals were the "muckle hoose" of Jardine, Matheson & Co., known under the Chinese *hong name* of *E-wo,* "Righteousness and Harmony," and Butterfield & Swire, *T'ai-ku,* "Exalted and Ancient." The former was founded by a Scotch doctor, William Jardine, in the early part of the nineteenth century. The revocation of the East India Company's charter terminated "John Company's" commercial monopoly in China in 1838; private British firms now were free to embark upon the lucrative Canton trade. The later competitor of Jardine's in shipping and various trading interests, such as sugar and piece-goods, was the vigorous young British firm of Butterfield's.

Opium, and outright smuggling of other commodities, played a part in the profitable beginnings of some of the early China coast firms. The disappearance of all Chinese authority at the treaty ports during the T'ai-p'ing rebellion in the 1850's, made it possible to discharge or load cargo without Customs formalities and gave opportunity for connivance with dishonest Chinese officialdom to escape payment of import duties. The Chinese Maritime Customs was established in 1854 at first under a joint American, British, and French board of inspectors. This arrangement introduced an element of probity and vigilance into the administration of the Chinese Maritime Customs by means of supervision by foreigners, nominated by the consuls, but in the service of the Chinese, paid by them, and working under the authority of the Chinese executive. The collection of Customs duties was regularized thenceforth.

The Yangtze was thrown open to foreign-owned steamers by the terms of the second series of Sino-British Treaties signed at Tientsin in 1858–1860. Eleven new "treaty-ports" were opened, including the principal trading cities on the Yangtze as far as Hankow. It was not until sixteen years later, in the Chefoo Convention (not ratified until 1885) negotiated by Li Hung-chang and the hasty and high tempered British representative Sir Thomas Wade, that further ports on the upper Yangtze were opened to trade and the river to navigation as far as Chungking. This last city is about 1200 miles from the river's mouth and was not actually opened to foreign trade until 1890.

When foreign steamers, under European officers, began to ply the powerful yellow current, the "Long River" took its place, in the estimation of Westerners, equally with the Mississippi in romance and story. Only the Nile and the Danube can compare with the Yangtze as highways of humanity over the ages.

The early steamers were side-wheelers, with two smoke-stacks side by side and a great walking-beam. They thus followed the Mississippi model and many were designed and built in America. The China Merchants Steam Navigation Company took over the old American river steamers of Russell & Co. Some of these continued to ply the river down to my time. I recall particularly the old *Kiang Kwan,* which waddled up and down the river on her big side-wheels. She, as all the C.M.S.N. Co. fleet, was painted a canary-yellow with a large staring eye on the wheel boxes. "Suppose ship no gottee eye," sententiously observed the Chinese boatswain in the pidgin-English lingo of the River, "no can see." "No can see, suppose how can walkee?"

Others of the steamers, such as the *Tatung* upon which Judge Thayer and our party traveled, were built in Scotland. They had one tall smoke-stack and twin propellers. Enormous space was provided in the holds or between decks for the bulky cargo they carried—chests of tea, bales of cotton and cotton-yarn, ramie-fibre, packages of porcelain taken on at Kiukiang, tubs of indigo, and the like. Their several decks accommodated hundreds of native passengers.

Steam shipping on the Yangtze, reaching until recent years as far as Chungking in Szechuan, and even beyond, was long largely in the hands of foreign interests. Aside from the British companies already mentioned, the American firm of Russell & Co. operated coast-wise and riverine fleets until it sold out to semi-official Chinese capitalists in the late 1870's. This action, however necessitated or excused by the concentration of American attention upon development of our own resources at home, was a blow to American commercial prestige in China. The fleet sold to the Chinese became the China Merchants Steam Navigation Co. It continued to be operated largely by foreign employees, both as to officers on the ships and as to marine superintendents ashore. The Chinese showed for many years little interest in developing a native mercantile marine personnel.

The ostensibly state-owned C.M.S.N. Co. produced enormous profits. It was thus the prey of successive political groups, especially after the Revolution. Whenever China was engaged in war, the fleet and wharfage

65

properties were promptly transferred to the protection of a foreign flag, usually the American. This was done through some foreign national as purchaser, though actually as trustee owner.

Following the example of British and American enterprise, the Japanese operated for many years a well-equipped fleet on the Yangtze, the Japan-China Steamship Company. This venture was successful, especially in serving to promote Japanese trade, but frequent boycotts upon Japanese business continued to grow out of perennial political friction between Japan and China. Both the Germans and the French operated a few steamers on the Yangtze prior to 1914, but they finally withdrew, selling their vessels to the well-entrenched British companies, or to Chinese operators who were desirous of entering this profitable field.

Shipping on the Yangtze is prodigious, as we observed on our way down river. Save for a rocky defile near Wuhsueh and the turn in the river at Ma-t'ang Bluff, the great yellow stream cuts its way through silt banks, eternally crumbling into the current. A farm today on the left bank may become a sandbar on the right bank tomorrow. The restless river is eternally changing its course. In its day of operation, the largely foreign-officered lighthouse and buoy service of the Chinese Maritime Customs was kept busy re-marking the changing channel. This channel may be incredibly deep, as off Wuchang where some 90 feet is recorded; or again so shallow that passengers are reminded by communicative ship's officers that all Yangtze steamers' bottoms are equipped with rollers so as to cross over the shallows! The *Yangtze Pilot* was the annual handbook which kept the shipping world informed of conditions on the world's greatest riverway, which takes its beginning in the eternal snows of Central Asia.

A special race of foreign river navigators developed. New England skippers and Scotch engineers predominated. Tradition held that if you wanted the "chief," you just called "Mac" down the engine-hatch and he appeared. A well-known "Down East" captain, a very stout man, came to a tragic end. After sailing the river for half a century, late one night he slipped off the long elevated plank-way, which led from the Hankow Bund onto the pontoon to which his ship was tied. The current was deep and swift and carried the refuse of a thousand miles of unsanitary China. The rotund captain easily managed to float and cling to the planking. But in the time taken to hoist his heavy form up onto the gang-plank, he swallowed some of the polluted waters. He was dead of cholera by the next morning.

The C.M.S.N. Co. steamers, too, were particularly popular with the native traveling public for their elaborate Chinese menus. As the fleet was a Chinese semi-governmental enterprise, high Chinese officialdom traveled free. But, in the lavish custom of China, such privileged passengers made up for this economy by distributing handsome "cumshas," i.e. tips, to the Chinese stewards. The latter accordingly saw that their guests were equally lavishly entertained—at the Company's expense.

66

Among the most picturesque characters on the River was a Captain known as "Holy Joe." This sobriquet was derived from his having been deeply devoted to religion in his youth. In later years this piety soured from the exacting nature of his navigational duties on the River, and was replaced by a degree of genial cynicism.

Shortly after the war broke out in 1914 "Holy Joe's" steamer was tied up one day at the small river-port of Kiukiang, loading chinaware from the nearby kilns. A venerable local American missionary of Teutonic origin and name was under suspicion of being active in disseminating pro-German sentiment among the lower-class Chinese. As usual, vast confusion reigned below-decks as native passengers, baggage and cargo crowded on and off the steamer through the narrow gangways. The captain was on the watch for the enemy. Slipping down to the main deck, his worst fears were realized. There to be sure stood a white man vociferously haranguing an attentive and appreciative audience of coolies in perfect Chinese colloquial. The captain himself, despite his many years in China, was like most shipping men disdainfully ignorant of the "native lingo." "Ah, I'll teach you to belay that stuff, you son of a Hun," he shouted as he sprang upon his victim and proceeded to choke him speechless. A Chinese person in long blue gown struggled desperately to release the clutching hands.

"Stop, stop," he pleaded. "This my master. He belong American missionary from Hankow-side. Thief-man have steal he trunk, and my master only askee these coolies what-side have take."

The vigorous spy-hunter relaxed his hold only as the features of his victim of mistaken identity were turning a deep purple.

Shanghai, City Towards the Sea

THIS WAS not my first visit to the fifth port of the world. Its designation is both poetic and geographic. It lies in fact some forty miles or more from the Eastern Sea up the Yangtze and on the latter's deep tidal affluent, the Whangpoo. A few months earlier, I had been deputed by the American Minister at Peking, the Hon. William J. Calhoun, to carry a copy of the new State Department diplomatic codebook to the Embassy at Tokyo. The mission was one of considerable responsibility. I had taken a small German steamer from Tientsin to Shanghai, thence another, the *Princess Alice,* to Yokohama.

"If you fail to deliver the code safely into the hands of Mr. Jay at the Tokyo Embassy, you needn't bother to return," was the caustic admonition of First Secretary Lewis Einstein as I left Peking.

Consequently I kept the formidably-sealed packet close to my person throughout the entire journey. The U. S. diplomatic code apparently occasionally fell into improper hands. Einstein told me that when at the St. Petersburg Embassy, he had been offered photographic plates of the entire United States secret cipher. The price demanded was exorbitant.

"What do I want with the plates, when I have the book itself locked up in the Embassy safe," he advised the would-be vendor.

This disclosure led to the issue of a new and more intricate telegraphic cipher by the experts of the Department of State.

Shanghai, as I now viewed it again as a member of the staff of the American Consulate General, still preserved much of the old-time treaty-port character. The life of the foreign community proceeded at a leisurely pace. Transportation was by the "victoria," a four-wheeled open carriage drawn by a pair of diminutive "China ponies." These latter were of a recalcitrant breed. In addition to the driver, or *No. 1 mafoo,* on the box, there was a *No. 2 mafoo.* It was the function of the latter to leap down whenever the carriage was to stop or turn a corner, run forward, seize the ponies' bridles, drag them to a halt, or forcibly turn them in the required direction; then to run back and awkwardly remount the box beside the driver, for the *mafoos* wore long-skirted gowns, and winter felt or summer straw official hats with red silk tassels. The *mafoos* of the wealthy *taipans,* as the managers of the big foreign firms were called, were elaborately uniformed in silks and satins. Such flowing draperies were often a great inconvenience to the *No. 2 mafoo* in his acrobatic stunts with the ponies; and he frequently lost his footing to be ignominiously dragged along by the spirited steeds, who seemed themselves to take special joy in the discomfiture of their constant tormentor.

The China pony is "tamed" not domesticated; he is always bred in Mongolia where the mares are kept. These animals never lose a certain wildness of their earlier free life on the Mongol steppes, despite the harness that civilized man imposes upon them.

Prominent citizens and their ladies drove in the late afternoon up and down Bubbling Well Road. Along this famous winding boulevard were the spacious estates of the local *taipans.* Their villas had deep verandahs, for coolness during the long hot summers, supplemented by bamboo-matting screens. In this, the latitude of New Orleans, both temperate and tropical shrubs, trees and flowers grew luxuriantly in the grounds. Tennis courts were provided for the afternoon tea parties in the English manner.

An abundance of efficient servants enabled the mistresses of these homes to entertain on a lavish scale. Folks either invited their friends to dinner or dined out, with unvarying regularity. The dinners were preceded by elaborate *hors d'oeuvres,* accompanied by sherry, gin-and-bitters, and other *apéritifs.* Cocktails were not yet popular in British dominated Shanghai of 1911. Numerous courses followed: soup, fish, game *entrée,* joint (roast), savory (usually a welsh-rarebit confection), dessert, and cheese. The ladies then withdrew, the gentlemen remaining over their coffee, port, liqueurs, and cigars. The Chinese cooks displayed characteristic taste and talent under the supervision of their foreign mistresses. A special feature of these Lucullan feasts was the game course. Teal, woodcock, pheasant, snipe, venison, wild goose, were regularly available in the local markets, as well as ordinary meat cuts and farmyard poultry. All were incredibly cheap. Excellent wines accompanied appropriately each course.

Devotion to sports throughout the day, riding and tennis especially, enabled the gourmets and the bibulous to withstand the menaces of "liver" and gout until a sufficiently old age. By such time most of them had amassed enough income to retire to the relative simplicity of living in their homelands. There were no movies, cabarets, or theatres to occupy the evenings, unlike the plenitude of these amusements in later Shanghai life. The bridge table, accompanied for the men by successive Scotch-and-sodas, accounted mostly for the hours after dinner.

This invariable pastime was broken into by occasional functions, which all social Shanghai attended. These were the productions of the "A.D.C.," Shanghai's Amateur Dramatic Club. Since the founding of the community in the 1860's, performances had been given several times a winter with such artistic and financial success that the club came to build its own "Lyceum Theatre." Much histrionic talent was in evidence. While the whole range of lighter drama was represented, no season in my days at Shanghai failed to produce the ever vernal Gilbert & Sullivan musical comedy.

Shanghai possessed, even then, a municipal orchestra, whose performances, before 1914 under a German conductor, since World War I under an Italian *maestro,* have always been of high merit. Occasionally, it must be added, a bedraggled group of Thespians would favor Shanghai with a week of feeble imitation of the London music halls. Before reaching Shanghai, these companies would have toured India and played at Singapore and Hongkong. They usually showed the wear and tear of the heated tropics on performance and costume. On the other hand, the most noted artists, on their frequent world tours, never failed to include the Far Eastern metropolis.

A succession of national folk-days were enthusiastically observed by the respective communities. The cycle began with St. Andrew's Eve, when the Scotch made merry with highland flings and haggis. St. Patrick, St. George, His Britannic Majesty's Birthday, the Glorious Fourth and Bastille Day all furnished occasions for official receptions, when guests of other nations joined at high noon in hearty toasts to President or King. Then followed the formal balls in the evening. The American community usually excelled all others in their elaborate celebration of Washington's Birthday.

Week-ends were spent on luxurious houseboats. Shortly after our arrival at Shanghai a party of us secured the *Nirvana* and the *Frances,* owned respectively by Mr. J. A. Thomas, the pioneer chief of the great British-American cigarette company, and by Mr. T. R. Jernigan, the prominent American sportsman and lawyer, who wrote delightful books on China in law and commerce and on shooting in the Yangtze delta. Our forty-foot, shallow-draft craft were each fitted with a long cabin containing bunks and well-equipped kitchen galleys. The crew's quarters were

69

well aft. All was in command of an ancient mariner known as the *Laodah,* "Old and Great." During the unoccupied week, Shanghai's fleet of house-boats was moored in the shelter of Soochow creek. Only "skeleton crews" ostensibly remained aboard, but in fact the boats more often housed during such undisturbed time the wives and numerous progeny of the crew.

By Thursday night or early Friday morning all native feminine and infantile humanity disappeared, as vigorous scrubbing of decks and other preparations for the week-end got under way. Soon the owner's cook and "boys" appeared with great hampers of provisions. The pleasure-craft took on a purposeful appearance. Last of all came the house-boat party of ladies and gentlemen. The vessel cast off with much shouting of stentorian commands by the *Laodah.* Wending its way through Soochow creek's intricate traffic, either by poling, or by grappling the surrounding sampans and junks with boat-hooks, the house-boat emerged into open water. All the waterways in the Yangtze delta are subject to the tide. The crew neatly timed their movements to secure the aid of this incoming or outgoing current. Their labors at the heavy stern scull or *yu-loh,* by which the boat is propelled, were thus materially lightened. If the wind proved fair, the stout mast was stepped and a great sail hoisted. The sweating "galley slaves" at the ponderous *yu-loh* momentarily rested from their labors.

On the houseboat voyage on which our party embarked, the ancient walled city of Soochow, some sixty to seventy miles from Shanghai, was the objective. As the initial distance was too great for manual propulsion or even for sailing, we attached ourselves to the end of a long "boat-train." This consisted of a string of several native house-boats, towed by a steam-launch. All through the night, the train dragged its length at high speed up the deep and winding creek and through innumerable canals. Stops were made at intermediate towns, where Chinese passengers embarked or disembarked with mountains of luggage. The gurgle of the water against the boat's sides, the occasional muffled blast of the launch's whistle as it neared a station wharf, and the distant murmur of voices on the train ahead of us, lulled us to comfortable sleep. Long before turning in, the cooks had prepared for us a sumptuous dinner. Here was the ideal voyage, with no sea sickness to steal our appetites or disturb our rest on these placid inland waters.

Up betimes, we found ourselves on a wide stretch of water. In the distance the famous fifty-eight, ... no fifty-seven ... no fifty-eight, arch marble bridge glistened in the early morning sun. No one, they say, ever can count the graceful shining white arches twice the same. We were on the Grand Canal, as it passed the crenellated walls of Soochow, famed in legend, ancient capital of the kingdom of Wu. From this city came martial heroes, and many noted men of letters and painters. "Lady Soo," as the city is poetically named, resembles her distant sister, the Queen of the Adriatic. The streets we found were canals, crossed by innumerable half-

70

moon bridges. As in Venice, the houses rise up from the water's edge. Thus, the early morning domestic activities of the populace were entirely visible, as well as being somewhat hazardous to us. Our house-boats were now slowly sculled along these watery streets beneath open windows through which household refuse was being thrown. We had earlier cast off from the boat-train.

The city contained innumerable gardens and many historic spots. Its distinctive beauty is represented by the saying,

> *above are* "Beneath Heaven's skies of blue,
> *Beneath* Only equal are Hang and Soo."

Hangchow is the lovely city by the West Lake, the glorious twelfth and thirteenth centuries capital of the southern Sung Emperors, described with boundless admiration by Messer Marco Polo. Our principal excursion ashore led us to the famous pair, the "Pen and Ink" pagodas, which doubtless have accounted, since their erection in the sixth century, for the literary eminence of Soochow's scholars.

*   *   *

As at the old capital, Peking, social intercourse between the foreign community at Shanghai and the Chinese was still limited to the demands of official relations and business transactions. The highest Chinese functionary at Shanghai was the *Taotai,* or "Superintendent of the Circuit." His jurisdiction exceeded that of an American city mayor but was less than that of the governor of a state. Yet the Shanghai *Taotai's* post involved functions which gave it exceptional importance. He was the point of the Chinese official phalanx projected against the ever aggressive foreign front which sought to extend and increase its privileges under the vaguely phrased treaties with China. He dealt directly with the Shanghai consuls, collectively or individually, in their manifold interests and demands.

After 1900, the Shanghai *Taotai* was the custodian of the immense Customs collections. These were earmarked for periodical payment for account of the huge punitive indemnities owed to the foreign powers under the terms of the 1901 Boxer Protocol. Possession of inactive cash balances, awaiting the due dates of payment of indemnity installments, offered immense possibilities. Utilization for personal profit of idle public funds has not been unknown even in our own system of local or state government and such had always been the recognized perquisite of officials in China.

The post of the Shanghai *Taotai,* with its innumerable sources of revenue, regular and irregular, was so opulent that it was reported to be "syndicated." A group of Chinese capitalists raised the amount which would satisfy the Court at Peking. In return, they obtained the right to appoint their own representative to the "Taotaiship." The financial possibilities were then fully exploited, all collections over the amount guaranteed to the Peking government being retained to the profit of the syn-

71

dicate. In 1911 the Shanghai *Taotai* was a ponderous mandarin. His chief *factotum* and active business manager was an able Eurasian gentleman, whose complete mastery of English was a rare talent in Chinese officialdom at that time. As my consular duties led me frequently to the Taotai's *Yamen,* we came in the protracted years of our acquaintance to speak of our friendship in the classic phrase as "friends of three dynasties"—the monarchy, the era of the warlords, and the Republic.

An American citizen who had early demonstrated his marked abilities in educational circles, was for some years foreign adviser to the *Taotai's* office. The hand of this astute *deus ex machina* was to be discerned in most of the negotiations between the mandarins on the one hand and the Consuls and the Municipal Council on the other. It was generally held that in the Chinese-American treaty of 1903, the copyright provisions were devised by this able adviser to the advantage of his employers, the Chinese. It was thereby stipulated that books, such as for example American text books in great demand, must indicate on the title page or elsewhere that they had been printed especially for the China trade. Otherwise they could not enjoy copyright protection in that country.

The progenitor of all American "advisers" to the Chinese government was the first American Minister to take up residence at Peking, Anson Burlingame, a man of singular courage and spirit. When Charles Sumner was brutally attacked and beaten in the Senate Chamber by Preston S. Brooks of South Carolina, Burlingame had vigorously denounced the cowardly act. Although of Massachusetts origin, Burlingame had spent some time at my own University of Michigan. While thus in the "backwoods," he had learned to handle a rifle expertly. As the one challenged, Burlingame was entitled to choose the weapons and the place. He chose rifles and the brink of Niagara Falls. The duel never took place. Burlingame's distinctly American temperament and outlook led him to advocate, from 1863 to 1865, a "cooperative policy" of the Powers with China. Up to then, all approaches of Europe toward China had been by way of *force majeure.* The succession of Sino-foreign treaties from 1842 onward had been imposed by fleets and armies.

Burlingame and the enlightened Manchu premier, Prince Kung, had become fast friends. Upon Burlingame's retirement as American envoy, he was invited by the Chinese government to head a mission to the capitals of the Powers. This was designed to explain China's position in international affairs. She was indeed anxious to adopt modern methods—railroads, telegraphs, etc. But conservative China must not advance too fast. *Festina lente,* hasten slowly, should be the guiding principle. On the other hand, the growing foreign communities in the treaty ports, at Canton, Shanghai and elsewhere, were impatiently demanding extension of their privileges. Burlingame apparently converted his British, French, and Russian colleagues to his notion of getting things done by friendly consultation and orderly processes. There is evidence for believing that Sir Robert

Hart had a hand in quietly promoting these ideas. Burlingame was to persuade the Powers to delay further treaty revision. The mission first arrived at San Francisco, where under Burlingame's inspired rhetoric, it was received with great enthusiasm. Secretary of State Seward moved cautiously, although he lent his approval to the Treaty of 1868 signed by Burlingame on behalf of China. Its extreme liberality later became a point of embarrassment in Chinese-American relations. This was just before the agitation in California against immigration of Chinese labor in the 1870's.

The initial promise of the mission waned as it proceeded to European capitals. Lord Clarendon was induced to make a favorable declaration of British policy towards China. Little was accomplished at Paris and Berlin. The sanguine envoy succumbed to illness at St. Petersburg and the remaining members of the mission hastened home. Its prospects had depended largely on the personality of the principal envoy himself. Those familiar with China at the time declared Burlingame's statements misleading, as creating a false and disappointing optimism. It was in fact many decades before China was sincerely prepared to modernize herself. This was not to be until the reactionary Manchu Empire was swept away and the painful era of civil war and internecine strife had purged the land of some of its ancient predilections. Nevertheless the optimistic and cooperative spirit of Burlingame has predominated in the American attitude towards China from that day to this.

Consuls, Courts and Compradores

WHEN I REACHED SHANGHAI in February, 1911, I was at once impressed by the special dignity enjoyed by the "Consular Body." These officials, representing the Powers, possessed a character elevated far above their colleagues in most lands, where they are restricted to certain routine functions relating to commerce. In Shanghai they enjoyed a semi-diplomatic status, derived from their representative character *vis-à-vis* the powerful semi-independent provincial viceroys with whom they were in official relations. Moreover, they were the titular rulers of the International Settlement and the French Concession, which comprised the foreign controlled *enclave* of Shanghai. They were superimposed above the hardworking Municipal Council elected from and by the foreign "rate-payers." In virtue of the authority conferred by the so-called "Land Regulations" and by successive agreements with the Chinese officials, the Council itself was charged with the actual administration of the city.

Finally, the Consuls possessed judicial authority over their nationals, in association with the special courts that were provided. They were subordinate only to the august Ministers of the Powers resident at Peking. From them they received instructions in certain matters of high policy, as ultimately determined by the Foreign Offices in the various capitals of the world when matters assumed such importance as to require decisions. But ordinarily the Consuls were left to their own devices, and they in turn permitted the Municipal Council to "gang its ain gait."

As a minor satellite in the Consular galaxy, my title was that of "United States Deputy Consul General and Interpreter." In this capacity I was permitted to share in some of the refulgence of my exalted superiors. My immediate chief was Consul General Amos P. Wilder, who possessed the highest reputation as a public speaker. Dr. Wilder had abandoned journalism in Wisconsin, where he had edited a paper, to assume the post of Consul General at the British crown colony of Hongkong. This assignment had been followed by the even more responsible post at Shanghai. He was said to have been on terms of personal friendship with President William Howard Taft; both were Yale alumni, Taft '78, Wilder '84.

There was, however, the inevitable fly in the ointment. This was the moot-point of whether the Judge of the United States Court for China or the Consul General held top rank in the local official American hierarchy. The question had previously become so acrimonious that it had even precluded the two highest American officials, the Judge and the Consul General, from attending the same public, or even private, functions. Dr. Wilder's ready wit solved the knotty problem for the moment. At a large community dinner at the Shanghai Club, he ostentatiously signaled his jurist colleague to precede him into the dining room. In his subsequent speech as toastmaster, the Consul General hastened to explain that Judge Rufus Thayer's prior entrance into the dining room was not due to official precedence but to an over impatient appetite. In later years the State Department was called upon to fix procedure formally. In a gathering of American citizens only, the Judge of the United States Court for China took first place; in an international assemblage, when citizens of other nations were present, the Consul General was *primus inter pares* and outranked all.

Dr. Wilder's gifts made him in great demand. He had a sonorous voice and a histrionic manner, and heartily enjoyed public speaking. At that time he was one of the few total abstainers in the Shanghai official community. This was a rare quality in American consular officers, for whatever their personal predilections, the international character of their social relations involved serving wine at their tables. Dr. Wilder's unusual principles at any rate had an advantage on grounds of economy, for there was no official entertainment allowance in those days of a frugal government. Moreover, his abstinence especially commended the Consul General to the more "fundamentalist" members of the large missionary community. The question whether or not the punch to be served at the official Fourth of July reception at the consulate should contain a "stick" frequently split the American community asunder.

Consul General Thomas Sammons, Dr. Wilder's successor, was almost equally abstemious; but as he served the customary wines at his official dinners, and unfortunately possessed a naturally florid complexion, he did not enjoy an esteem equal to that of his predecessor with his compatriots from the "bible belt." Dr. Wilder reinforced his sentiments toward wine with an unusually militant zeal, expressed in frequent "prohibition" addresses. The more cynical assigned this to two motives, the one as providing a vehicle for continuing his forensic practice, the other a natural parsimony in social entertainment. In Consul General Wilder's talented family, son Thornton, then aged thirteen and later to become "playwright" Thornton, was already disclosing literary talents. His favorite juvenile at this time was *The World Almanac*. From this he propounded upon his elders, including my un-encyclopaedic wife, statistical questions, which would stump our current "Information Please" wiseacres.

Dr. Wilder established a weekly gathering of American citizens and their friends of other nationalities known as the Saturday Tiffin Club. This clashed with a similar organization conducted by a prominent missionary and educationalist, and director of a cultural and religious organization. As is so often the case, Dr. Wilder's newer organ grew in popularity at the expense of the older, and the two leading American speakers of the port developed a keen rivalry in their otherwise amicable relations. Ultimately, however, his rival scored heavily against the Consul General when at two successive lawn-parties he had as guests of honor Dr. Charles Norton Elliot, President Emeritus of Harvard, and the Hon. George Woodward Wickersham, Attorney General of the United States in President Taft's Cabinet. These two distinguished visitors at Shanghai quite "stole the show" for the more resourceful *impressario*.

The old-time American consul obtained his post usually for services to the political party to which he adhered. Failing of reelection, a member of Congress frequently was consoled with a foreign post. As a former politician, he was usually a practiced orator, with however little or no knowledge of consular business. One such consul, who spent many years in the smaller ports of China, had been a member of the Massachusetts State Legislature. By profession a clergyman, he had been instrumental in securing the passage of certain "blue laws" in his State. Not all consuls had such impeccable origins.

Frequently the American Consul in China had only one opportunity in the year to come prominently before the international public. This was by way of the patriotic oration delivered on the Glorious Fourth, usually a pyrotechnical display of oratory. The more prosaic affairs of his office were attended to by a seasoned, if poorly compensated Vice Consul. Hence tradition arose that a good public speaker was usually an inept consular officer.

The intervening establishment of a career service has happily made these features of the consular personnel a thing of the past. No service today can claim a more efficient and thoroughly trained body of consular officers than the American.

There was extenuation for the financial peccadillos of some at least of

75

the early consuls. This could be based on the small compensation allowed them. Meager salaries were thus supplemented by "unofficial fees." Sometimes the irregular issue of passports to Chinese desiring to enter the United States, was carried on through the connivance of a locally hired Vice Consul or interpreter, most frequently not an American citizen, who "split" the proceeds with his Chief.

Such practices were usually confined to the South China ports, particularly Canton, for almost all the Chinese laborers emigrating to the United States came from this urban region. The laundrymen and restaurant-keepers in America are entirely Cantonese, speaking a dialect not understood by their fellow countrymen of the North. Early in my consular career at Shanghai I was made officer-in-charge of the issue of "Section VI Certificates." By means of this document, Chinese officials, merchants, travelers and students were permitted under the immigration laws to enter the United States. Laborers are excluded under any circumstances from entry as a result of the anti-Chinese labor agitations of the 1870's and the 1880's with the resultant treaties.

One day I was visited by a suave Chinese gentleman who introduced himself as long a practicing physician at St. Louis, Missouri. Having returned at length to his ancestral land of China for a brief visit, he found he had become so "Americanized," so he rather ruefully informed us, that he felt quite out of place and craved American company. Would I favor him, together with the administrative Vice Consul, by accepting an invitation to a dinner which he was arranging.

I vaguely sensed something suspicious in the debonair little man, dressed immaculately in American-style clothes and—what was unusual for a Chinese—with a slight baldness that befitted his announced profession. I referred the invitation to my senior colleague who similarly "smelled a rat" and we both declined on grounds of other engagements. With all the appearance of deep personal disappointment, the "Doctor," when about to take his leave murmured something about proposing to take his dear nephew back to St. Louis with him for further education.

Next day in fact he escorted the "nephew" into my office—a heavy fellow, rolling his eyes uneasily, we could see, in such unaccustomed surroundings. One glance at the "student" and I ordered him to take off his shoes and socks, and to spread his open palms upward before me. Calloused feet and hands identified the man as a common laborer. The "Doctor" and his "nephew" passed out of the door precipitately. I reported to the Department of State this obvious attempt to introduce into the States one of the prohibited classes of Chinese. In doing so I furnished copies of my letter to the Consulates General at Hongkong and Canton. Replies were soon received that the "Doctor" had become well-known for such practices in the South before trying it on at Shanghai. A copy of my letter also sent to the Consulate General at Tientsin reached there in time to frustrate the same design. There the "Doctor," so I was later told unofficially, had had the effrontery to declare that of course he could obtain a certificate from the Vice Consul at Shanghai for "the usual gratuity of five hundred dollars; but that he would be glad to provide instead the appropriate official in the consulate at Tientsin with an identical amount for the service." The same man conveniently "forgot" to take away with him a small box containing a diamond ring which he carelessly placed on the Vice Consul's desk at Canton. He was called back and the ring restored to him. The profits of this coolie-running into the United States were enormous. I had put a period to at least one career which had been responsible for a protracted era of successful evasion of the immigration laws.

*　　*　　*

Prior to the establishment in 1906 of the United States Court for China, American citizens were amenable to consuls, officiating in limited judicial capacity and frequently inexperienced in the law. Many ineptitudes and irregularities ensued in both criminal and civil cases. The British government early established His Majesty's Supreme Court in China, which assumed jurisdiction over all British subjects save in minor cases which were still handled by consular officers. A Judge of the United States Court for China set up his headquarters at Shanghai in 1906, assisted by a District Attorney, a Marshal, and a Clerk of the Court. All cases between Americans or cases in which action is brought against American citizens by other nationals, were dealt with by the Court, including probate matters until 1943 when extraterritorial jurisdiction was abolished.

These latter cases appear to have resulted in irregularities prior to the establishment of the U. S. Court for China. Stories were current in Shanghai of how the estates of deceased Americans, in cases where relatives were not present, had been liberally mulcted by consular officers, either through the exaction of exorbitant fees which they pocketed, or by deliberate suppression and conversion of assets. These practices at once ceased with the introduction of the new judicial regime.

Even under the strictest adherence to recognized procedure, criticism arose against the Court. Western jurisprudence frequently violated what the Chinese regarded as "justice." One conspicuous example occurred during my residence at Hankow. A United States man-of-war lay at anchor in the mile-wide "reach" of the Yangtze. A Chinese shoe-maker boarded the ship to ply his craft among the crew. Some of the latter were in an hilarious mood, and were annoying a shipmate who apparently was just recovering from a spree ashore. Finally in their horseplay, they dared their victim to throw the unlucky cobbler overboard. To their consternation, he immediately did so. A heavy sea was running, whipped up by a strong up-river wind against a seven-knot current. The man immediately disappeared in the boiling yellow stream. Although a boat was put off, he could not be found. The sailor was tried in the United States Court for

China charged with manslaughter. He was acquitted on grounds that the *corpus delicti,* the body of the lost man, had not been produced. The Chinese government lodged a vigorous protest against this, to them, glaring miscarriage of justice. The Court's decision was, of course, entirely in accordance with the practice of Western jurisprudence in such a case. Finally a liberal *solatium* was paid by the United States naval authorities to the family of the victim and the uproar subsided.

Conflicting notions of justice between Chinese and foreigners had appeared from the beginning. As far back as 1821, an American seaman named Terranova was charged at Canton with the death of a Chinese boat-woman who was killed when the sailor happened to throw a heavy jar overboard. At the demand of the local Chinese authorities and upon threat of stoppage of trade, the American was surrendered to them and promptly strangled. This and other "miscarriages of justice" in connection with cases of "accidental homicide" led to the insertion in the first American treaty with China in 1844, of the extraterritoriality clause. Thereafter Americans resident in China were no longer amenable to Chinese law, but to their own consular authorities. Caleb Cushing of Newburyport, Massachusetts, American Treaty Commissioner, based these exemptions on traditional practice in Mohammedan countries, where Christians enjoyed their own court procedure. The establishment of the United States Court for China, in 1906, brought this unique judicial procedure to its ultimate development. The Court was governed by the Federal codes of the District of Columbia and of the Territory of Alaska.

*   *   *

The Chinese figure known best at this time in Shanghai and the lesser treaty ports was "The Compradore." This term, doubtless of early Portuguese origin, designated the person through whom the growing volume of imports and exports was effectuated. He was the shrewd, hard-headed Chinese business agent without whom the foreign merchant could not effectively come into contact with his native clients. The Compradore in recent times became almost extinct. His place was taken over by a younger generation of Chinese businessmen, who studied up-to-date commercial methods in schools of business administration, institutes of technology, and the many similar schools of professional training in the United States and elsewhere.

The old-timer, the Compradore, could have traced, if he had known any history (he usually did not), his vocational lineage back at least to Howqua, Wu Tun-Yuan, that genial "cohong" merchant who was the go-between for the early American traders at the "factories" in Canton. From powerful Jardine Matheson & Co. down to the latest struggling German firm, the Compradore occupied a pivotal position. Clad in long silk gown, with skull-cap on the back of his head, he sat in his own separate offices. Here his relatives to the most distant degree of relationship, crowded the

78

dark and narrow rooms. In the operation of his various agencies and the extension of credit to native dealers, which was one of his principal functions, nepotism was a virtue. As was general in China from highest government official down, he could rely best on his family connections in positions of trust and confidence. All Chinese employees of the firm were guaranteed and controlled by the Compradore. Group activities were limited to the family circle in China.

Doubtless the reputation for impeccable honesty which is so generally credited to the Chinese businessman stemmed from this functionary. It was to the Compradore's interest to remain honest, as his emoluments were usually gratifying. His operations might involve figures of hundreds of thousands of tael, which he owed his foreign principals, and which in turn were owed him by his native connections. Debts in large amounts were often secured only by verbal agreement, or by informal memorandum. In the larger foreign firms, the Compradore's commissions and profits often approached the fabulous. This resulted in the erection of palatial residences in the security of the foreign concessions, the spacious grounds of which were sealed from outside gaze by high brick walls or bamboo palings. Within, the wealthy Compradore gave rein to the Chinese delight in rockeries, lotus-ponds, arbors, and bamboo groves. Flowers and shrubs were cultivated in that variety which China, mother of gardens, so generously affords. His wives, concubines and many children disported themselves in these pleasure grounds. Alas, the Compradore sometimes overextended himself in indiscreet speculations, resulting in heavy losses to his principals, the foreign firms.

The numerous "ningpo-varnished" rooms of the Compradore's home were furnished in lustrous blackwood, often encrusted with rare picture marbles from Yunnan, or with semi-precious stones, cornelian, agate, and carved Wenchow soapstone. His wealth enabled him to cultivate a taste, inherent in all Chinese, for the exquisite products of the native art. His collections of archaic bronzes exhumed from the Yellow River valley, of ritual jades buried for centuries in princely tombs or their modern counterparts cunningly fashioned into jewelry, of rare porcelains from the Imperial kilns of Ching-teh-chen, often rivaled the Palace collections at Peking.

Most prized of all were his paintings, monochromes of misty mountain landscapes, or Tatar horsemen and their spirited mounts, and gay flowers and brilliantly plumaged birds. These were of an artistry achieved in fully developed form centuries before the Italian primitives. Such paintings were tightly rolled, tied by silken bands with carved jade fasteners, and lovingly pressed into polished teak-wood cases. They were brought out only occasionally for the appreciative examination of his friends, *connoisseurs* like himself. Though he was often virtually illiterate (he could obtain writers and clerks for a few taels a month) his admiration for calligraphy —the artistic execution of Chinese character writing—was boundless.

Thus on the walls of the rooms hung silken scrolls on which were written in bold black or gold ideographs sentiments from the classics or the poets.

I have visited the Compradore in his luxurious country villa, which he affected to call his "thatched hut" in the manner of the poets of old. Here like the ancient recluse he could retire to contemplate the joys of rustic life. Such villas were usually on one of the many lakes of the Yangtze delta. My friend, Compradore of an old American firm, invited a party of us to his country retreat, built upon a low promontory overlooking the broad expanse of Lake T'ai. The house was a commodious European-style edifice, completely furnished in the most approved Western fashion. We were served foreign foods and wines and slept on "beauty-rest" mattresses, or what passed for that invention in 1912. Much of the day we idled in canopied pleasure-boats on the lake's placid surface.

The T'ai-hu, the Great Lake of the Yangtze delta, has not always permitted such peaceful dalliance. Its shores have been haunted by pirates who, despite the officers of the law, despoil the rich merchants and traders whose well-laden junks cross its expanse. For centuries it was regions such as this which have supplied the Chinese novelist with material for his most romantic tales of slant-eyed Robin Hoods and Buddhist Friar Tucks. Compradore Yung could well afford to place the necessary ounces of silver in the robber chief's ready palms so as to insure that he and his guests could sleep peacefully on "the water-margins" of the lake.

Dispensing with Justice

ORIGINALLY established as a British "concession" under the provisions of the Treaty of Nanking signed in 1842, Shanghai became, in time, an unwieldy political entity. The United States had also been presented with the opportunity to secure for itself a similar exclusive area. Its location was north of the British Concession and beyond the Soochow creek, known as Hongkew. The name literally means "the Rainbow." So far as territorial control by the United States was concerned, it was as evanescent as that celestial phenomenon. The American government adhered firmly to the principle of non-acquisition of Chinese territory. In order to retain this valuable and convenient area, largely occupied in the early days by missionary establishments, the English and American residents decided on a merger of the original British Concession and the American settlement of Hongkew. Thus the "International Settlement" came into being in 1862 while the T'ai-p'ing rebels were swarming around Shanghai.

The French remained aloof by securing during the dislocations of the rebellion a further piece of ground south of the "Yangkingpang." This latter was a malodorous creek forming the southern boundary of the International Settlement. In the French Concession the right of France, represented by the Consul, ran exclusively. Beyond this was the ancient walled city of Shanghai, dating from earliest times. Its narrow streets and dark, smelly lanes continued to be of interest only to visiting globe trotters.

80

There they could have a glimpse of the celebrated Willow Tea-House which came to provide the decorative pattern of favored blue and white China-ware. Rarely did a Shanghai resident set foot in the "native city."

Within the areas assigned to exclusive foreign control, there already resided a rapidly growing Chinese population. These numbered, by as early as 1862, at least five hundred thousand. They retained title to their lands until such time as they might voluntarily sell them to foreign owners. Land coming into the hands of Europeans or Americans was registered in the Consulates of the respective nations, and the deeds were recorded and stamped by the local Chinese Land Office as well. Once such deeds were stamped, the title could not be questioned. This arrangement took the place of our western "title guarantee" agencies. Evidence of original Chinese ownership was provided usually by *fang-tan,* strips of thin Chinese paper duly describing the land and bearing the seal of the local officials. In time, lawyers and some missionaries obtained considerable income by securing as trustee owners registration in the foreign Consulates for Chinese owned land. This made transfer and sale of lands more certain and expeditious, and thus enhanced the value of real property.

We juniors had a go at almost every type of work in the American Consulate General—even occasionally that of assistant jailor of the Consular "hoosegow," where recalcitrant sailors and inveterate beach-combers were incarcerated by order of the U. S. Court or the Consular Judge. Among my duties was that of registrar of deeds. The practice of trustee ownership grew to considerable proportions owing to the liberal fees derived. As Consular "land-officer" I was a somewhat unwilling party to one of these transactions which presented some features of unusual interest. A prominent American lawyer was the "registered" owner of a certain property called "The Wheel." This site was entered from a road controlled by the Municipality, but extended into territory under Chinese jurisdiction. It thus suffered from two masters. It was known, as its name suggested, to harbour a number of roulette wheels.

In an attempt to rid the Settlement of public gambling establishments conducted under American auspices, the U. S. Court's District Attorney had given notice that any American citizen, even though only a "registered," i.e. trustee, owner of real property, would be held responsible for such activities as were carried on. The establishment in question was actually operated by a notorious gang, with suspected American direction in the background, though nominally under a Cuban citizen. In the present case, the American trustee owner decided, out of abundance of caution, to divest himself of the embarrassing property. Coming to my office in the Consulate, he requested me to transmit the deed to the Chinese Land Office for cancellation and for the issue of a new deed to a complaisant Spanish subject. A considerable delay ensued. My American lawyer client urged me almost daily to hurry the Chinese Land Office to complete the transaction. The Chinese authorities, being cognizant of the shady character of the property, were obviously holding out for extra fees.

Finally on a Saturday afternoon, when I had returned to my home in the French Concession, some four miles distant, I had a pressing telephone call from my lawyer friend.

"Will you come down to the Consulate so that I can sign off on that deed?" he begged.

I demurred on grounds that the day was an official half holiday, and that Monday would do as well.

"It will be worth seventy-five taels to you," urged the man-of-law, evidently overlooking the fact that the old days of "unofficial fees" among American consular officers were past.

"All right," I replied, "if you really want it that bad."

The reason for the urgency was disclosed when we learned that "The Wheel" began to revolve merrily that very Saturday night.

During those earlier years of slaughter and pillage when the T'ai-p'ing military operations reached the very confines of the foreign-controlled areas, great numbers of Chinese refugees added enormously to the native population of Shanghai. The wealthy particularly came to discover the protection afforded within the areas under foreign flags. In all subsequent periods of disturbance the Settlement's Chinese population was further augmented. At the beginning of the Sino-Japanese war (1937) tens of thousands of Chinese refugees added to already crowded conditions. The number of foreign residents continued to decrease markedly in ratio to the rise in the Chinese population.

Virtually withdrawn from the jurisdiction of their own authorities, the problem of policing this enormous and heterogeneous populace early became acute. Facilities for civil litigation among the Chinese engaged in business had also to be provided. It was agreed accordingly that "Mixed Courts" presided over by Chinese magistrates should be established. The "City State" of Shanghai, i.e., the Municipal authorities charged with the preservation of peace and order, was directly concerned in all criminal cases. Foreign citizens were often involved in litigation against Chinese subjects, such cases being heard in the Mixed Court. Thus to insure proper judicial procedure, "Assessors" from the principal Consulates were assigned to sit concurrently with the Chinese magistrates "to watch proceedings."

Actually no verdicts or orders of the Mixed Court Magistrates were enforceable without the concurrence of the Assessors. Ordinarily the latter interfered but little in the decisions of the Magistrates, especially in disputes between or involving Chinese where the Magistrates' knowledge of Chinese customary and statutory law was supreme. There were occasions, however, when sharp clashes occurred between the foreign and Chinese officers of the Courts. My first day on the bench as "Acting Junior American Assessor," was full of thrills. As I possessed at the time no specialized

82

knowledge of law, Occidental or Chinese, I was obliged to lean heavily on my colleague, a learned and experienced Magistrate whose surname, Teh, had the highly appropriate meaning, "Virtue."

At this session, a Chinese was charged by the Settlement police with having purloined a *sampan,* a small native boat, on the Dixwell Road Creek.

"To be sure," observed His Honor the Magistrate, "as this creek is not within the boundaries of the foreign leased areas the defendant is ordered to be handed over to the Chinese authorities beyond the Settlement for due trial."

I unwittingly concurred, for as a matter of fact I had no specific idea of the location of the creek in question. Immediately a British representative of the Municipal police intervened. He maintained that the creek *did* lie within the jurisdiction of the Settlement authorities. On this I deferred signing the order on the charge-sheet, "to hand the prisoner over to the native authorities," until I could consult a more experienced colleague in chambers. Oddly enough the Senior British Assessor advised me that he supported the Magistrate's contention, whereupon I gave my necessary concurrence to the original order. Immediately there was a great flurry in Municipal Council quarters. The American Consul General was informed that this was a grave surrender of Settlement jurisdiction. The police would not under any circumstances comply with the Court's order to turn the accused over to the Chinese authorities.

Consul General Wilder and my colleague, the Senior American Assessor, supported me. Until the police yielded, notice was given that the American assessors would refrain from attending criminal court sittings on Tuesday and Thursday mornings, the two days allotted to them each week. The courts continued to grind out daily a large number of cases in this city of several millions but the volume was too great for the British and German Assessors to handle in the absence of the Tuesday and Thursday sittings of the American assessors. The congested jails began to fill. One third of Shanghai's judicial machinery was at a standstill. The Gordian knot was finally cut by the simple expedient of dismissing the case and releasing the accused. In my inexperience, I had blundered upon one of the most contentious questions of all Shanghai's history, the Council's jurisdiction over tidal creeks. Within or without the foreign areas, the Chinese maintained that they held exclusive authority over such waters.

Difficulties incident to language often arose. A "hire-carriage" driver was charged with having contravened traffic regulations. He was an old offender, with many previous convictions. Looking at the pathetic figure which a Chinese defendant always manages to present, I suggested that in lieu of the usual cash fine, he be sentenced to three days in jail. This I considered a sufficiently severe penalty, while not impinging unduly upon the fellow's slender purse. *"Chia* three days" directed the Magistrate. *Chia* I took in one of its senses, "to add to," thus inflicting an additional three

83

days imprisonment. This would, I felt, keep the man too long, i.e. six days, from his means of livelihood and his horses. After some heated argument, magistrate Teh and I discovered how far apart our proposals were. *Chia* means "to add to," but means also the *cangue,* the wooden collar fastened around the neck of a petty criminal and upon which his crime was written in bold characters. He was then exposed for the prescribed period of his sentence at the scene of his offence. It was a humiliating punishment, and "repeaters" were subjected to it customarily. When we had straightened out our linguistic misunderstanding (which was made the more readily as both words are pronounced with the same *tone*), I reluctantly agreed to follow precedent and have the man exposed for three days. This punishment, as well as the strokes of the bamboo, were discarded under the more humane Republic.

Major cases, criminal and civil, also came before the Magistrates and Assessors. One stormy night my apartments on Bubbling Well Road were entered. Family silverware of considerable value was carried off. Later a Chinese was arrested by the police as he was transporting a large bundle of loot in a ricksha. Most of my silverware as well as many other articles were recovered through pawnshop tickets indiscreetly carried on his person. The fellow turned out to have worked a very clever and dangerous "racket." He was an experienced house-servant, speaking English. His practice was to secure a position in a foreign household long enough to familiarize himself with its valuables, make a duplicate key to a door and then contrive to get himself dismissed. On the first stormy night, when wind and rain drowned other noises, he would return and leisurely help himself to his former employer's goods. In choosing to rob the home of a Mixed Court Assessor he had been unlucky. I myself could not sit on the bench at his trial, being an interested party. A colleague, however, who did not ordinarily believe in the quality of mercy, awarded this dangerously clever burglar a sentence of several years.

Persons charged with various degrees of homicide frequently appeared before us. Husbands, too, demanded punishment for erring wives, producing as incontrovertible evidence the queue of the male seducer, which was customarily sheared from the latter's head when found *in flagrante delicto* by the injured spouse. Civil causes revolved about high sums, when suits were brought to enforce contracts involving large quantities of import and export cargo. There is much to be said for the old adage that a "Chinaman's word is as good as his bond." Yet the Oriental concept of a contract is not as legalistic as our own. An enforceable agreement, in his opinion, should in all equity be mutually advantageous. Thus if "exchange," that is, the cost of foreign moneys, such as pounds sterling or gold dollars, in Chinese currency, went against a Chinese dealer who had taken chances by not making a "forward contract" with his bank, he frequently asserted that the transaction should be held void. This on grounds that he would lose and not profit by the business. Foreign importers thus often found themselves with large quantities of cotton piece-goods, machinery or the like on their hands of which the Chinese consignee refused to take delivery. Under the mongrel law administered in the International Mixed Courts, a mild form of imprisonment for debt was still practiced. Many a debtor languished in the Mixed Court detention house for months or even years, while his creditor vainly sought to extract the money owed, either from him or his relatives. Where capital punishment was imposed for high crimes, the convicted were turned over by the Mixed Court to the outside Chinese authorities for the final rites.

"My dear Father," I wrote from Shanghai on June 5, 1912, "...One of the curious functions now performed by the Assessors, since the Revolutionary changes in Shanghai, is that of coroner. Whenever a Chinese dies under at all doubtful circumstances in the Settlement, his body is sent to the public mortuary for an inquest held by one of the Mixed Court Magistrates and the Assessor for the day. I have now attended three inquests: the first a woman of the laboring class who dropped dead while at work on the street, the second also a woman who as the result of a family *fracas,* swallowed a dose of raw opium, a favorite method of committing suicide among the Chinese. Yesterday afternoon we held an inquest on the body of a once well-to-do merchant, who had been detained in the Mixed Court for three years for debt. He had just satisfied his creditors and was brought into the Mixed Court office for final dismissal when he placed his hand to his forehead, leaned back against a rail and when given a chair he gradually lost consciousness. The attending physician stated that in his opinion the man died of apoplexy, though only an autopsy could decide the matter —death from natural causes was the verdict. This work is certainly far from any of my expectations—coroner—but the duties of a consular officer in China are varied, to say the least."

Service on the Mixed Courts had its humorous as well as its tragic aspects. A veteran Magistrate with whom I frequently shared the bench, was Mr. Sun. He was from that inland province of scholars and braves, Hunan, which he pronounced in his native dialect *Fu-lan,* with curious other consonantal transpositions also characterizing his speech. Emaciated and stooped, with long thin mustache, scarcely concealing the absence of several upper and lower front teeth, he sat usually crouched forward in an attitude betokening intense concentration and even sympathy. I have seen a culprit, disarmed by this merciful appearing judge, begin an interminable tale of wrongs, adding more pathos as he noted the apparently satisfactory effect upon the listening Magistrate. Just as the accused might be launching on an impassioned peroration, declaring himself entirely guiltless of the charges brought by base calumniators, etc. Magistrate Sun would unexpectedly assert himself. Drawing back with startling suddenness, he would bring his magistrate's ferule down on the desk with a crash. *"Ni sa huang"* ("Perjurer and liar") he would hiss into the face of the astonished culprit, as he thrust his sharp features forward. The learned judge would then summarize briefly but in masterly fashion the probable character of the female ancestors of the accused, back unto the third or fourth generation, since they had produced such an unprecedented prevaricator and swindler as the witness. Usually the fellow in his terror would forthwith blurt out the truth.

It was, however, the Assessor whose sympathies or interests were chiefly invoked. A group of foreign lawyers developed a flourishing court business in Shanghai by assiduously disseminating through their native interpreters the notion that, if a case was to appear before a certain foreign Assessor, it would be well for all concerned to employ a lawyer of similar nationality. A Chinese married couple were accused of maltreating a small slave girl. The child was brought into the court. The defendants strongly asserted their intense fondness for the child and the quite parental love they lavished upon her. At this moment an American lawyer bustled in, begging Their Honors' pardon for appearing late, but he had only just now received his clients' instructions. Whatever slight bruises might be visible on the child had been the result of some tiles most unexpectedly dropping on her from the roof-eaves as she happily played in the garden. Noting that the child was unusually heavily clothed for the prevalent warm weather, Magistrate Sun ordered a court attendant to strip the child of her upper garments. There on her back and especially below we beheld the livid welts, where the alleged falling tiles could scarcely have reached. One glance and the disconcerted American attorney hastily gathered up his papers and left the court amid loud guffaws from the onlookers. Magistrate Sun solemnly rapped for order.

A laundry-man appeared before us one day charged with contravening the Municipal sanitary regulations which prohibited the practice of spurting water from the mouth upon clothes to dampen them before ironing. "I would never do such a thing and besides it was my brother who was ironing the clothes," expostulated the accused, as he smirked knowingly at me with his one good eye. Something about the fellow seemed familiar to me and prompted by the feeling that the man was honest enough in his claims, I suggested that his explanation be accepted and the charge against him dismissed. When I reached home that afternoon my wife informed me that a number of presents had come in for me from our laundry-man. There were some linen handkerchiefs, a box of Manila cigars and two bottles of native *samshu* on the table. A few moments later the now familiar features of the one-eyed defendant of the morning's court session emerged from the kitchen quarters.

"I hope Master much likee cigars; thank Master velly muchee," he grinned.

"A judge suborned," I admitted.

Detective-Sergeant Cruikshank, ponderous and bemustached, was the veritable Javert of the Shanghai municipal police force. One day he dragged in a diminutive Chinese coolie, who clutched a cage containing a

86

fine Hartzwald canary. This dangerous criminal had unquestionably come into possession of the bird improperly; but as he doubtless had numerous other high crimes and misdemeanors chalked up against him in the police records, the case was remanded for a week in which to make appropriate investigations. Detective-Sergeant Cruikshank was personally entrusted with the custody of the canary. A week later the Sergeant appeared in court himself carrying the identical cage, but within it a fluffy, brownish fledgeling not even remotely resembling the handsome songster of the early session. What, demanded the court, had happened to so transform the original cause of the proceedings.

"Ah weel, Your Honors," explained the crestfallen police officer. "I thought it would hae been safe to turn the bir-r-die over to my cook to look after. But I can no tell what has transpired in the meantime."

Case dismissed!

My American colleague in the Mixed Court one day dealt with the alleged theft of a pair of fine grey geese, which were produced in court as evidence against the accused. The story of how he had obtained full legal title to the creatures was so circumstantially and convincingly related by the prisoner at the bar that he was not only liberated by the Magistrate, in which decision the Assessor readily concurred, but possession of the birds was restored to him. It was noticed that he left court with all speed, with the geese in his covered basket.

That night the Assessor returned to his villa known as "The Back of Beyond," well outside the city. The first thing that he noted was that a brace of his prized grey geese was missing from the lagoon.

Distinguished visitors from afar frequently joined the Magistrates and Assessors, sitting on the bench as guests. One of these, Professor Harry Thurston Peck of Columbia University, noted for his ready wit, observed dryly after watching a busy court session, "I certainly do admire how justice is dispensed—*with*."

By way of introducing the Spring Session of 1912, the Mixed Court Magistrates invited their colleagues, the Assessors, to attend a feast in the famed "Hardoon Gardens" of Shanghai. The five upright and learned Judges doffed for the nonce their judicial severity. Kuan, the Senior Magistrate, was of Falstaffian proportions. There were four Associate Magistrates. Pao and Teh were "Bannermen," as the Manchus called themselves from their ancient clan organizations indicated by variously designed or colored banners. Sun maintained a Confucian austerity. Nieh was a jovial and somewhat cosmopolitan soul whose duties were largely in the Mixed Court of the French Concession. The professional asperity of manner normally affected by the Magistrates towards the Assessors, likewise was dropped for this occasion. The guests represented the principal Powers, three British, three American, two German, a Japanese and a Belgian, the latter young enough, but tall and luxuriantly bearded after the manner of His Majesty King Leopold II himself.

The feast was set in a pavilion of the gardens, laid out in all the elaboration which the limitless wealth of the owner, a Bagdad opium merchant, could provide. Rockeries, arbors, pebbled walks, and lagoons, flowering shrubs and shady trees extended over many acres in the heart of Shanghai. Here and there were charming pavilions set back among the trees. Servants hurried back and forth as they brought on the innumerable courses, from the original "cold whets" of uncooked cockles, ancient eggs coagulated long before in quick lime, dried melon seeds, sliced Yunnan ham, cold roast duck and chicken, to the final quartered Chefoo pears, honeyoranges and jasmine-flavored tea served in delicate porcelain bowls. Not even in ancient Rome, drawing on the world for its luxuries, could Caesar himself have provided a feast greater in variety. Strange and exotic viands appeared in steaming pewter dishes. A soup to begin with, served in a huge melon; as one dug into the rich pulp, care must be taken not to pierce the frail receptacle. Dried bear-paws and "fruit-eating wild-cat" from Manchuria, "silver-ears" (tree fungus) from Szechuan, shark's-fins from the Formosa Channel, and bird's-nests from the cliffs of Malaya, seacucumber from Macao, salamander from Kwangsi—all these rare foods titillated the palate as the feast wore on.

Suddenly staccato voices arose at the end of the table. The Belgian Assessor and the French Mixed Court Magistrate were engaged in a furious game of *mora*. The antagonists thrust forward their hands with one or more fingers extended, the meanwhile each shouting the expected sum of exposed fingers in the two hands. *"Four* seasons bringing wealth," "five," "six"—each number bellowed was followed by the customary auspicious adage. He who guessed the correct aggregate of fingers in this game of quick eye and ready tongue, imposed a penalty of a draught of ricewine upon the loser. The Belgian trailed badly, drinking his losses in cup after cup. Hopelessly beaten, he challenged the victorious Magistrate to an even more exacting ordeal. Let the mild rice-wine penalty be exchanged for champagne! To begin with, a salute to each other with two brimming glasses. The potency of the unaccustomed grape soon dulled the Chinese Magistrate's keen eye. Again and again the elated Belgian pushed his advantage, calling right number against the Magistrate's wrong. With successive potations following quickly one after the other the loser's eyelids soon drooped, the game lagged. At last the vanquished player lay back in his chair and the deep slumber imposed by the vine-decked god of the Mediterranean overcame him. The feast had come to an end.

"One intoxication dispels a thousand sorrows," said an ancient poet.

Liberté, Egalité, Etcetera

THE ANNUAL autumn flower show was soon to be held in the spacious parimutual rooms beneath the grandstand of the Shanghai Race Club. Our gardener was arranging for the hundredth time the myriad blooms of his many chrysanthemum pots. China produces this noble flower in a glory of colors, forms, and sizes; with time, skill, and infinite patience being furnished by our gardeners, the glorious *chiu-hua* is trained in a multitude of shapes. Entries of their prized plants for Shanghai's bi-annual competition were made by the foreign "master" or "missie." It was your Chinese gardener, however, who assumed the glory among his compeers when the "Judge Peter Grain Silver Cup" was awarded for the finest display.

The North China Daily News and Supreme Court Gazette, venerable British organ whose motto read "Impartial not Neutral," carried epochal news to all Shanghai's breakfast tables that bright October morning of 1911. The aged Manchu Viceroy at Wuchang had been forced to flee from his post; his colleague in distant Szechuan, Tuan Fang, had been executed by his own troops. An obscure army officer, Li Yuan-hung, had reluctantly assumed the headship of the long planned anti-dynastic revolution. The court in Peking was in a panic. Attempts would be made that very day to seize the Shanghai Arsenal.

Accustomed to the *opéra bouffe* armies of the Imperial regime, the whole affair failed to impress us seriously. Chinese troops were still clothed in baggy blue uniforms, with cloth shoes on their feet and turbans wrapped about their heads. On their chests they carried the large ideograph *Yung,* "brave." Fluttering triangular banners terrified the enemy with their fiercely drawn spotted leopards and fire-spouting unicorns. Rifles were of all dates and makes, an assemblage of weapons bought from Krupp, Creussot, Skoda, and Vickers-Armstrong ever since the T'ai-p'ing Rebellion, and some dating from before. The artillery was from an even greater variety of sources. In the China of those days military weapons were for appearance's sake, to overawe the enemy, but not for lethal use. Drill consisted in calisthenics, resembling the actors' acrobatics on the Chinese stage.

"Now arms, however beautiful, are instruments of evil omen, hateful to all creatures . . . and not the instruments of the Superior Man; he uses them only on the compulsion of necessity," we had read in the writings of the Old Philosopher. "When hostilities begin, weigh the strength of the enemy; if your organization is not equal to his, do not engage him in battle; if your provisions are not equal to his, do not protract the war; if the enemy is numerically strong, do not invade his territory; (but) if the enemy is in every way your inferior, *attack him without hesitation."* These and similar prudent precepts of the Six Military Classics governed the theory and practice of war in China for two millenniums and more.

China had been at peace for a decade. Soldiers had been scarcely visible and the cross-country riding parties, the picnics to the Shanghai Hills, the house-boat excursions up the innumerable creeks and canals, had never been disturbed by martial evidences.

Thus on that fine autumn day we summoned a victoria and proceeded to the vicinity of the Arsenal. Its location was at the Lunghua Pagoda, south of Shanghai near the Huangpoo river. As we drove along we ob-

89

served numbers of the city's coolies and the country-side peasants, with unaccustomed awkwardness, carrying in their hands obviously hitherto unused rifles and revolvers. They wore brand-new leather bandoleers over their shoulders. They displayed the utmost indifference as to the direction in which the muzzles of the pieces were pointed. It was a gay occasion for them all.

"Who can do away with the instruments of war? By them the lawless are kept in awe, and accomplished virtue is displayed."

The small garrison at the Arsenal had discreetly decamped, probably hastily exchanging their uniforms for civilian *mufti* in the usual manner of dispersing Chinese soldiery. Such was the innocent beginning of the succession of revolution and counter-revolution which was to keep the country in a turmoil for so long. Soon enough, a portion of the population adopted war as a profession. Henceforth the revenues of the country were to be wasted and the energies of an industrious people dissipated in civil wars which threw the country back into the confusion of the traditional Warring States.

China used to be described with scorn as the perfect type of pacifist nation. This in modern times has been applied more accurately to a China unable to defend itself from outside aggression. Certain ideas of a highly sedentary and pacifist civilization in China were disseminated first by the European travelers of the Mongol domination of Cathay (1279–1368). In the seventeenth and eighteenth centuries the letters of the Jesuit missionaries lauded the peaceful disposition of the Chinese.

It happened that China was then enjoying unusual periods of quietude, which have regularly alternated with eras of warfare and confusion. These concepts of China persisted, to mingle with the more realistic knowledge of recent days. Defeated in every engagement with a foreign power from 1842 to 1900—Great Britain and France in the 1840's and 1860's, France in 1884, Japan in 1894, the Powers acting in concert in 1900—it remained for the war of no quarter with Japan to remind the world that China has a history of military heroism and glory unsurpassed by any other race.

The innate combative, ambitious, predatory, domineering qualities of human nature which have inspired wars all over the globe and in all time, have been equally effective among the Chinese. On the other hand, the misery, destruction, lawlessness, and inconclusiveness inherent in war have been apparent to the Chinese, perhaps even more than to other nations. Their political history, therefore, abounds in as great a variety of wars as does that of any other country. Their literature is equally rich in treatises on the art and conduct of war, and philosophical injunctions against its employment.

During the uprising I then witnessed, the vestigial Manchu garrison, which had held China for two and a half centuries, disappeared overnight. Many were massacred. The entire effete hierarchy of Manchu officials from

Viceroy and Tatar General down to the humble pensioned "bow-man," either took anonymous refuge within the protected foreign areas, or merged in the Chinese population, thus giving some ground for the prevalent notion that China always "absorbs" her conquerors.

The Shanghai *Taotai* was of course the first to disappear, to the great confusion of his financial records—a type of public disaster which often contributed to the augmentation of a Chinese official's private bank account. As happened in the disorganization of Chinese public administration in the T'ai-p'ing rebellion sixty years earlier, the foreign officered Customs now added further to its scope and authority. It proceeded to deposit its entire collections of duty in the Hongkong & Shanghai Banking Corporation. This British financial organ thereafter until the Nationalist Revolution of 1927 acted as chief paymaster for all of China's foreign indebtedness. This, and the depository semi-official banks of the other Powers, continued to keep on deposit the large balances of Chinese government funds as the *Taotai* had done previously to his syndicate's great profit. Chinese consequently charged that the foreign banks operated largely with these Chinese government balances as working capital. Thus was China's fiscal regime taken further out of her own hands.

The Mixed Courts similarly underwent a metamorphosis. Hitherto, the Chinese magistrates enjoyed full judicial authority. They were appointed by, and as the representatives of, the Chinese government. The Assessors of the foreign Powers, in theory at least, acted only in an advisory capacity with power to report to the Consuls in case of obvious miscarriage of justice. Now the Assessors assumed the predominant role; the new Chinese magistrates were appointed by the foreign Municipal authorities who also paid their salaries. The Court's business was at once expedited, but a new cause for friction developed between the Chinese and Municipal authorities. This was only solved in 1926 by the "rendition" of the Mixed Courts and their magistrates to Chinese control. In other respects advantage was taken of the extreme weakness of China at this moment of political transition. Roads were extended outside the conceded foreign areas, a subject of heated, and occasionally bloody, dispute. A new group of officials emerged, displacing for the time being the old professional mandarinate. These newcomers usually were the most enlightened for that time, many of them having some knowledge of English or other foreign languages.

The system of two thousand years could not be swept away in a day. True, the alien Manchu monarchy disappeared never to return, save for a reluctant brief moment when a reactionary "pig-tailed" warrior, General Chang Hsun, made an abortive attempt to restore the abdicated Emperor to his throne in 1917. My infant acquaintance of the Imperial audience of 1908, and now almost grown-up, Emperor Hsuan T'ung (to use his reign name), was permitted to remain with his family in the twilight of the Forbidden City of his ancestors under the favorable treatment clause of the abdication agreement. Finally, in 1924, he became the victim of the swash-

91

buckling "Christian" General Feng Yü-hsiang, who drove him out. The deposed Emperor, now plain Mr. Henry P'u Yi, a commoner, sought refuge in the Japanese Legation, under the protection of the overseas island folk whom his forefathers had looked upon with contempt. From the foreign concessions at Tientsin he was ultimately spirited away to Manchuria, land of his ancestors. At a "New Capital," the former Changchun renamed Hsing-king, he reigned in majesty, but did not rule in fact, after the manner of the ancient Emperors of Japan.

In the meantime, the old Confucian mandarinate of China sought to recover the ground suddenly wrested from them by the hot-blooded southern revolutionaries, indoctrinated with fantastic political notions from abroad. They had as their natural chieftain one of the most adroit and experienced of all Chinese officials, Yuan Shih-k'ai. He had been Li Hung-chang's high commissioner to Korea in the old days before the disastrous war of 1894. In 1898, by disclosing the Emperor Kuang Hsü's plot to reform the Empire, he had won the favor of the Empress Dowager Tz'u Hsi. The Old Buddha had made him Grand Councillor and Junior Guardian of the Heir Apparent. In 1900 during the Boxer rebellion, Yuan had played an extremely astute game while governor of Shantung province. When the fanatical Boxers claimed supernatural powers to resist bullets, he said "let's try and see." So he set them up against the wall and had them shot down. He had trained China's modern model army and established a Chinese West Point at Pao-t'ing-fu. Through him, the mandarinate looked for the conservation of their age-old vested rights to exploit the supine and inarticulate cotton-clothed populace of China.

Chess is a game played in China from remotest antiquity. Because a man is a good chess-player is no reason why he should be regarded as good for anything else, observed Master K'ung to one of his disciples. However, chess, as any game played for the game's sake, is the abstract form of struggle. In concrete form we watched the chess-game proceed at Peking, Nanking, and Shanghai. That earliest of overseas trained statesmen, T'ang Shao-yi, persuaded Dr. Sun Yat-sen to yield the provisional Presidency to Yuan Shih-k'ai. An undertaking was given that Nanking would be the new capital of the Republic. The revolutionaries maintained that Peking was permeated with the corruptive atmosphere of an effete court. Yuan acquiesced—with mental reservations. In the midst of busy preparations for removal, a sudden mutiny broke out within the ancient walls. It was promptly suppressed of course, but the transfer to Nanking was postponed *sine die*. President Yuan's continued presence at Peking was found necessary to insure peace and order and *the safety of the Legations.*

This was the first symptom of non-compliance with the revolutionary program. *Le plus ça change, le plus le même,* could well have been adopted as Yuan's motto—"forever the same." The disgruntled revolutionaries gathered at Shanghai. Less than two years after the first revolu-

92

tion in 1911, in the heat of August, 1913, period of "excited crickets" of the Chinese calendar, machine-gun and artillery fire was again heard in the neighborhood of the Arsenal. General Ch'en Ch'i-mei's troops were attacking the counter-revolutionary garrison installed by Yuan's officers at Lunghua. The units of the Shanghai Volunteer Corps were called out to keep stragglers or larger armed bodies from entering the Settlement. A Brigadier General, seconded from His British Majesty's regular army, was in command of the Shanghai volunteer defense force, "A" Company, "B" Company, the Customs Company, the American, and the Portuguese, all fully uniformed and equipped. There was too a mounted "Light Horse" and a "Maxim gun" Company. We were the direct descendants of the volunteers who on that distant day of April 4, 1854, helped the British and French regulars to throw back the "Long Haired" rebels, the T'ai-p'ings, in the sanguinary battle of Muddy Flat, now the area occupied by the Race Course. After half a century and more, naval contingents from the war-ships in the harbor were again landed for shore duty.

A full moon rose over the scene. Quiet during the heat of the day, the moment the sun set thunderous gun-fire made sleep impossible even for those residents not on military duty. The foreign volunteer contingents were distributed along the confines of the International Settlement; colonial troops up from Indo-China put out *cheveux de frise* barriers at street terminals in the French Concession. Our American Company was quartered in the sheds of the electric street-car company. Despite the heat we tried to sleep when off duty on the hard seats of the cars. No use; enormous black mosquitoes feasted on us. When on sentry duty, we were almost as upset. The good ladies of the Settlement, making the round of our posts in carriages, continuously pressed upon their valiant defenders bottles of warm beer and sandwiches, which we continued to drink and eat in all appearance of thankfulness.

It was merely play, however, until the Commander of the American Company ordered us to fall in, route-march order. The grim dawn had come after a sleepless night. Across the Settlement we tramped northward as far as Markham Road Bridge where it crosses the Soochow Creek into Chinese territory, the much fought-over district of Chapei of later notoriety. Through the semi-tropic heat and humidity, we carried our heavy service rifles and a full complement of ammunition, water bottles, *et cetera*. We were joined by the Maxim and Portuguese Companies, a total of perhaps 200 men.

"You are to cross the bridge, and in skirmish order advance upon the Chapei Police Station, which is believed to be strongly held. The field hospital will be in the high building to the right of the bridgehead."

Here was a forlorn hope, a cause lost before begun; 200 men to invade China! Actually we accomplished it with the firing of only one shot. One of the Americans let off his rifle by accident after we had got into the Police headquarters compound! At once heavily armed Chinese police

93

and soldiers, hitherto invisible, swarmed out from every quarter with rifle-bolts thrown in for action.

I was appointed official interpreter on the spot. The Chinese were so amazed at our appearance that they had never imagined we were a conquering host. As fellow soldiers we all soon fell to drinking tea together very sociably. I flatter myself that I never again did such a suave bit of interpreting. We Americans, none too comfortable as trespassers on Chinese soil, sent word of our predicament to the American Consul General. I was the messenger. I dropped around to my house and had a much needed bath on the way. Consul General Amos P. Wilder was considerably perturbed when he learned that the traditional American policy of non-intervention had thus been violated by armed invasion of Chinese sovereign territory by a group of normally peaceful American citizens, upon the orders of a British commander.

As for myself, I yearned for a good night's rest at home. I suggested to the American representative that perhaps the scheming nabobs of the Shanghai Land Investment Company, Ltd., a Hongkong British registered company, had engineered this latest rape of Chinese territory. Chapei, incorporated into the Settlement, would make a profitable new subdivision. The Consul General ordered the American Company forthwith withdrawn. Our military prowess had been fully vindicated, however. With the expenditure of a single cartridge, and without recourse to "the field hospital in the high building to the right of the bridge-head," we had captured an area which it took the combined land and naval forces of Japan many weeks to occupy, with enormous destruction of property, on two later historic occasions, in 1931 and again in 1943. We adopted informally as the regimental motto of the American Company, S.V.C., *Suaviter in modo, fortiter in re—gentle in manners, but resolute in deed*.

One day in early August, 1914, I stood at the Shanghai Customs jetty watching the first British and French contingents of civilian volunteers as they embarked for Europe. My friend the Imperial German Vice Consul, Herr von Tippelskirch, remarked to me with a meaning smile, that it would soon be all over: those fellows would not reach Europe in time for active service. The night before, the dinner-dance at the Kalee Hotel had been cancelled. Occasion was always availed of when a German man-of-war was in port, to secure its excellent band for dancing. But the *Emden* had slipped down the Huangpoo river in the afternoon on a swift ebb-tide, crashing into a cluster of sampans and junks as she negotiated at excess speed the difficult bend in the river in front of the American Consulate. I had watched planks, masts and perhaps a few luckless boatmen, thrown into the air as the sharp bow of the cruiser crunched into the mass of native craft. Neither the *Emden* nor many of those early volunteers were ever seen in Shanghai again. The repercussions of the European Armageddon were to be felt in China, with profound and permanent effects upon the status of its European communities.

With the entry of China into the World War of 1917, largely prompted by the United States, German nationals and their allies were evicted from all official Chinese posts in Customs, Postal or Salt Revenue Services. Their public and private property was seized by the Chinese government. They found themselves henceforth excluded from all international group activities, social or commercial, in China. After the signing of the Armistice on November 11, 1918, all their men and women and children were expatriated from China and Japan and returned to their native land. The white marble expiatory monument, erected on Hatamen Street at Peking in memory of the German envoy, Baron von Kettler, murdered in the 1900 Boxer uprising, was taken down and re-erected in Chung Shan park as a "Victory Monument."

That familiar *daemon* of mine, "the Duke," passed through Shanghai as the word of the World War's outbreak came to us. He left again on the crack Suez liner *Gneisenau* for his consular post in rain-deluged north Formosa. As we parted once more, we pledged ourselves for old-times' sake in the last Münchner Hofbrau brought to the China coast for many a year.

A Publican in the Provinces

MY ASSOCIATION with Sir Richard Dane in the salt revenue administration began at Peking in late 1914. Roy Talbot, in the Chinese Customs service, who had come out to China with me in 1908, spent a few days with me in Shanghai that mid-summer of 1914. Roy informed me that Sir Richard Dane had written him of his desire to have an American to supervise the salt revenue in Central China.

"Why not you?" urged my old friend. "You know the Chinese and their language and that's what they want chiefly." As an *attaché* in the Legation at Peking during the protracted negotiations over the abortive "Currency Reform Loan," it had occurred to me that active participation in Chinese fiscal administration would prove interesting. But this notion I had given up when the American banking representatives had withdrawn from the international financial consortium under President Wilson's disfavor in March 1913.

It now appeared, however, that the reservation of posts exclusively for nationals of the loaning banks had broken down. Under pressure of both the Chinese and nonparticipating governments, a declaration had been obtained from the Legations representative of the loaning banks to the effect that appointments to the salt revenue service would not exclude persons of nationalities other than those sharing in the loan of 1913. This guaranteed that the foreign branch of the Salt Revenue Administration would be truly international in its personnel. Thus Belgians, Portuguese, Danes, Norwegians, and even Americans were vouchsafed posts in the new administration, when qualified by a knowledge of the Chinese language and familiarity with conditions in China. Sir Richard Dane was obliged to im-

95

provise a fully staffed service on short notice. The result was that some appointees were scarcely fit to serve as colleagues of Chinese officials of high rank and personal qualifications. These mistakes were rectified by gradual elimination of the unsuitable. Dane, however, did not go as far as Hart, who created an "indoor" and "outdoor" staff in the Customs, whereby class distinctions as obtaining in Europe were rigidly preserved.

Evidently the Loan Agreement's provisions to bring the entire salt revenue of China under control and audit were inadequate. Thereby a foreign "district inspector" representing the lending banks was to be stationed in each salt producing district. It was understood that all salt revenues were collected in such centres and would thus be brought under control. This revenue was first to be deposited in the foreign "group bank" agencies. Sufficient funds were to be earmarked for interest and refunding instalments. The unused surpluses were to be returned to the Chinese government from time to time. These were harsh terms to a sovereign government.

There had been no proper accounts, however, to disclose actually what was the annual financial out-turn of the *Gabelle,* that historic French word now adopted for China's tax on salt. It might not be sufficient to take care of the Loan's service. So various safeguards for the bond-holders had been imposed. The entire revenues of certain provinces, and even unpledged Customs duties were stipulated as secondary security for the loan, in case the salt tax failed to be sufficient. But the opulence of the *Gabelle* of China was made evident when the first collections came to be accounted for. Now, surprisingly enough, millions of dollars were flowing down the Yangtze to the Shanghai bankers, from mysterious organs located in the large cities up-river, called "Salt Transportation Offices."

The Loan Agreement made no mention of these. Investigations disclosed that salt consigned from the sea-coast paid an "advance duty," equivalent to one-third of the total duty payable. This salt, transported by licensed merchants and stored in the Yangtze provinces, paid the two-thirds balance of duty, the "deferred duty," upon actual sale to the consumer. It was this previously unknown "deferred duty" which was being remitted to the foreign banks in Shanghai. Sir Richard Dane insisted upon its audit and control. The Chinese government pointed out that this was not specified in the Agreement. A compromise was reached. Mr. Chang Hu, the brilliant and experienced Chinese Vice Minister of Finance in charge of salt affairs, agreed to the appointment of a "neutral," i.e. a national other than one of the lending powers. In due course I was called to Peking to confer with Vice Minister Chang Hu and Sir Richard Dane. My appointment duly followed to one of the truly unique posts in modern public finance.

In the meantime I had retired from my post in the American consular service. Theodore Roosevelt in 1906 had completed the reforms which placed appointments (save of Minister and Ambassador) upon a compet-

96

itive examination basis and with permanent tenure of office. This had largely eliminated the "shirt sleeve diplomat," at least in the consular posts, and had begun to attract young Americans of suitable educational backgrounds. Unfortunately the reformation did not at the time go far enough. Personal fees, to which consular officers were entitled, had been abolished. (On such basis the post of Consul General at London was reputed to have been worth twenty thousand dollars a year to the incumbent.) But when the "unofficial fee" system was discontinued, the original scanty salary schedules were retained or inadequately increased. Possibly this was an overtone from the early practice of maintaining "honorary" unsalaried consuls who were free to engage in business.

American consular officers, especially in the lower brackets, fell upon evil days when meagre unofficial and personal fees were abolished by law. Less than a bare sustenance was afforded them. The young men of the consular staff at Shanghai were in particular straits. There were no free official quarters, as there were for the consular officers of other nationalities; rents and necessary representation expenses at the great metropolis were high. The vagaries of "exchange," i.e. the monthly out-turn of our American dollar salaries in local Chinese money, constantly had us worried as to whether receipts would balance budgets—which they usually did not. The passing of my second biennial examination in Chinese resulted in a small increase in salary; but it left me with fewer Chinese dollars to meet my bills than before, due to a sudden appreciation of silver on which Chinese currency was based. There was frequent recourse for salary advances and overdrafts to the Consulate "Compradore," the establishment's Chinese business agent. Old Wang retained this post largely because of the great "face" it gave him in the Chinese community. Such unsecured loans as he made us, without interest, must have been a drain on his patience, if not on his profits. Happily, after many years, this has changed. American foreign service officers are sufficiently compensated both in salaries and allowances to relieve them from anxiety. A pension system is a further inducement for well-qualified young men to adopt the foreign service as a career.

This did not come about, however, until for financial reasons many promising young officers of the service were forced to leave it. The temptation to do so was particularly strong in Shanghai where much money was being made in business. An attractive opening in one of the large American business concerns in the Far East had been offered me early in 1913. My new duties had lain in the finance and accounting department. But like most of those who have been in official life, commerce even with some improvement in financial reward soon palled upon me. When the opportunity presented itself once more to enter a government service, this time in the Chinese Salt Revenue Administration, I responded with alacrity. At the age of twenty-nine, I found myself responsible for the administration of a fiscal district with an estimated population of a hundred and seventeen millions and an annual salt tax out-turn of twenty million dollars.

The Reorganization Loan Agreement, providing for the reform of the Salt Revenue Administration with foreign advice and assistance, appeared to many patriotic Chinese to have been born under inauspicious circumstances. Some charged that "China's sovereign rights" had been sacrificed to political exigencies. It was thus the part of the foreign staff to demonstrate that our participation would be beneficial, and not detrimental to China's interests. Happily this soon became clear. The introduction of new policies under the driving force of Sir Richard Dane led to an enormous increase in salt revenue collections. Dane's administrative ability and Indian experience enabled him to perform an exceptional amount of work at the Chief Inspectorate at Peking. A rugged constitution still permitted him to make direct personal contacts in every salt district of China. He repeated the old practice of his early Punjab days of making extended tours, often undergoing hardships which even the younger men accompanying him sustained with difficulty. His example was an eye-opener to the Chinese staff. Persons in high places in China did not usually spend themselves in such directions.

My commission was issued by that Minister of Finance who had signed the Reorganization Loan Agreement, President Yuan Shih-k'ai's old friend, Mr. Chou Hsueh-hsi. My post at Hankow as Foreign Chief Auditor for the four "salt transportation offices" of Hupeh, Hunan, Kiangsi, and Anhui provinces, was thus an appointment solely at the hands of the Chinese government and not by the foreign "Group Banks." This special status continued for some time, until, with the consolidation of the service, distinctions of this sort were eliminated. All officers became employees directly of the Chinese government, and not primarily representatives or agents of the bankers of Europe.

I received my first instructions from Vice Minister Chang Hu and Sir Richard Dane, who served jointly as the Chief Inspectors of the Salt Revenue. I was to bring to audit the salt revenue operations of the Yangtze Transportation Offices from May 21, 1913, the date of effect of the loan agreement, to November 11, 1914, the day of my assumption of duty. Fortunately enough, I had little or no conception of the magnitude of the task assigned me. With the valor of ignorance I proceeded to my post.

Dane had suggested that it would be useful for me first to confer with the District Inspectors at Shanghai and Yangchow. One of these was a Russian subject formerly of the Russo-Asiatic Bank, the other an erstwhile Japanese consular officer. Both had preceded me in their appointments by something over a year and thus were able to give me the benefit of their experience. When I called upon my new Russian colleague at Shanghai, he advised me shrewdly enough in regard to the establishment of my new office at Hankow.

"Don't hesitate to ask for all you need and more too," he urged. "They will give you anything when you're new to them," referring to headquarters at Peking. He was, it was apparent, experienced in bureaucratic methods. The Japanese district officer at Yangchow courteously explained to me the intricate procedure whereby salt was supplied from the coastal regions north of the Yangtze estuary, to the vast inland consumption areas.

The province of Kiangsu is divided by the Yangtze River into a southern section and a larger northern area. This latter region in turn is known as "North of the Huai" (Huaipeh) and "South of the Huai" (Huainan). The Huai River flows between. This is a low area. A large lake, the Hung-Tze Hu, acts as a reservoir to take up the flow of the Huai which has no visible outlet to the sea. Actually the seacoast here, like the rim of a saucer, is somewhat higher than the interior. The region, thickly populated, is cut up by innumerable water-courses and is traversed by the Grand Canal, into which flood waters of the Huai and the Hungtze Lake both empty. The so-called Salt Canal furnishes transportation from the salt producing fields on the seashore to the Grand Canal and thence to the Yangtze. This avoided the longer and more dangerous route by open sea from the north coast of Kiangsu to the Yangtze valley.

The whole lowlying region of North Kiangsu province is impregnated with salt water so that pits dug even some distance from the seacoast yield brine. After a special process of preparing the salt water by "lixiviation," i.e. pouring it through ashes, the heavier brine is boiled in iron kettles. Reeds from the great marshes hereabouts are used as fuel, none other being obtainable. A reed marsh is thus a valuable income-producing property, like an American farmer's gravel-pit. The salt is packed in strong bags, woven of rushes, in weights formerly of about 140 pounds, later changed to about 110 pounds. Loaded on junks the salt was at this time shipped mostly by canal to the Yangtze Salt Stores at Shih-erh-wei.

This unique establishment was visited by me in the course of my stay at the city of Yangchow. Shih-erh-wei, "Twelve-piers," is situated on the Yangtze near the crossing made from north to south by the Grand Canal. As I crossed the enormously wide river here on a steam launch I beheld a forest of junk masts. The huge junks are built of heavy timbers. Carrying cargoes of up to six thousand bags of heavy, damp salt, they breast the strong current of the great river on their voyages to the four central Yangtze provinces. On the river-bank are salt storehouses, or mat-covered mounds of salt awaiting transportation. The area is stockaded and under strict government control, with armed "salt police" stationed about. The junks fly the pennants of their owners and upon starting on the long and hazardous voyage of several months, the ritual of gongs and firecrackers gives noise and gayety to the scene. The blood of a freshly killed cock is sprinkled on the junk's bow to appease the malevolent spirits of the river.

My first visit in November, 1914, to the ancient walled city of Yangchow remains clearly in mind. Marco Polo records that by special order of the Great Khan he acted as governor of this city, "a place of great consequence," during the space of three years.

At the time of my visit, Yangchow was a somnolent provincial city, but it still continued to be of commercial importance because of its location on the Grand Canal, immediately above the confluence of this great inland artery of trade with the Yangtze. Here the salt merchants continued to make their headquarters. With the confusion inland consequent upon the outbreak of the revolution of 1911, many of them removed their families and set up rich establishments within the protection of the foreign settlements at Shanghai.

Further up the coast is *Huaipeh,* north of the Huai River, where vast quantities of salt are produced. This is accomplished by drawing sea-water into open dyked areas or "pans." The sun and wind evaporate the water until salt in large crystals precipitates to the earthen floor of the shallow "pan." The surplus sea-water is then drawn off as certain chemical substances would spoil the salt if allowed to form by further evaporation. The layer of salt on the bottom is then raked up into piles and allowed to dry. It then awaits shipment by the inland canals to the Yangtze Salt Stores; later, with production vastly increased by the reform measures introduced by the new administration, small steamers carried most of the salt down to the Yangtze estuary and thence up-river. The Huaipeh region, long scourged by bandits, was as late as 1914 under control of a local warlord known as "the Tiger." His half-savage troops maintained a certain degree of order. Later several regiments of regular troops of the modern army, equipped and trained under German military advisers, were stationed here. Roads and bridges were constructed and measures were taken to control the devastating floods which periodically reached here through a lake region from the overflow of the Yellow River to the north. A modern port, Lao-shao-kou, was constructed. Thus, in time, facilities for the production and shipment of Huaipeh salt were greatly improved. Inland shipments were further facilitated by the extension of the continental trunkline, the Lung-hai railway, running from the coast at this point to remote Si-an city in Shensi province, in the far interior. The salt industry of Huaipeh was the object of special development.

Salt, Pillar of China's Finance

LITTLE WAS KNOWN of salt production and trade when steps were taken for the reorganization of the Salt Administration in 1914. A Roman Catholic missionary, Père Hoang, had published a monograph in French on *The Gabelle of China.* Later, in connection with the service of loans nominally secured on the salt tax in Central China, the Chinese Imperial Customs issued a *Yellow Book* in English on the salt tax in the Yangtze provinces. It was not, however, until after 1913 that the full extent and intricate character of this historic regime was disclosed in several *Red Books* issued by the Ministry of Finance.

100

My own investigations were based on the voluminous native literature on salt and its taxation, and on tours in the salt production and consumption districts. I was able to trace the origins of this oldest continuous system of public finance back to remote antiquity. According to tradition, China's "first statistician," the statesman Kuan Chung, in the seventh century B.C. devised the government control of salt for the state of Ch'i, the northeast part of modern Shantung province. Here, where salt is still produced from sea-water on a large scale, this early financier by statistical calculations demonstrated to the feudal lord of Ch'i that by controlling salt, the basic necessity of life, he could obtain a large domestic revenue; at the same time he could exercise a determining political influence over the states of the hinterland by limiting their salt supplies. Adopting the advice of his councilor, the Prince of Ch'i became rich and powerful.

But I found still earlier records than the book ascribed to old Kuan Chung which attested to the attention salt had received at the dawn of Chinese civilization. The Classic of History, parts of which I believe go back as far as the ninth century B.C., mentions in the earliest geographical description of China salt as a tribute from certain regions. Another ancient work, China's earliest constitution, *The Institutes of Chou,* probably drawn up in the fourth century before the Christian era, is a description of the political organization ascribed to China of the Chou dynasty (1122 [1049] to 256 B.C.). Salt is one of the "nine tributes." An elaborate organization of "salt officers" is described in this ancient book as taking charge of the distribution of salt.

Concurrently with my more realistic occupations in administering the salt revenue, I soon found much interest in delving into this romantic story of a tax on such a prosaic but universal commodity. Salt is the inevitable concomitant of our daily bread. It appears on our tables in America in "shakers" of various cunning forms and materials. In British territories it is generously spooned onto the plate from open dishes. In Japan, Korea and China, it disguises itself in a dark brown liquid—"soy sauce"—formed from its combination with soyabeans. In France where the *Gabelle* acquired its name as the hated salt tax, it formed a contributing ingredient of the Revolution. In India it served Gandhi and his non-cooperative followers as the symbol of revolt against the British *raj.* Its root appears in our significant word *salary*—"he isn't worth his salt." It is the basis today of our chemical engineering age. Its taxation is repugnant to Anglo-Saxon ideas as a burden on an essential food stuff. But our state and federal taxes are equally heavy on gasoline, an essential of modern life. In China the salt tax played a role of special dignity and consequence. It served as the equivalent of a poll tax. Salt is the only nation-wide commodity consumed by every citizen, who thus contributes his mite to the support of the government.

I found Chinese historical annals filled with descriptions of measures to place salt under the strictest government control. China's greatest states-

101

men are associated with such steps. Sang Hung-yang, financier and economic adviser to Emperor Chao of the Han dynasty in the first century B.C., argued the government's case for a salt tax in an historic debate with "the loyal opposition," the Confucian scholars. "Even when I sleep, statistical figures hover before my eyes," exclaimed this Alexander Hamilton of ancient China. A century earlier one Li Ping had opened the brine wells of west China in Szechuan, worked with their prototypes of the American oil-derrick constructed of huge bamboo poles lashed together. To this day Li Ping is regarded as that province's greatest patron.

That historic usurper of the throne of China and innovator of China's "new deal" at the beginning of the Christian era, Wang Mang, continued the salt impost as one of the methods of financing his extravagant socialistic measures. These schemes were imitated and extended by the unkempt but scholarly Wang An-shih in the eleventh century at a time when Popes and Emperors were struggling for supremacy in Europe. This unpopular socialist statesman extended the intervention of the government into the people's affairs beyond all precedent. Like many Americans today, the Chinese were strongly opposed to excessive official meddling in their private affairs. The administrative policies for the government control of salt by two great financiers, Liu Yen and Fan Hsiang of the T'ang (618–907) and the early Sung (960–1127) dynasties remained models at least to Nationalist China. In the last days of the Emperors of the Ming period (1368–1644) in their desperate and exhausting struggles against Mongol and Manchu invaders, orders on the government salt stores passed as a form of currency.

Thus the historic example of the Prince of Ch'i has not been lost on succeeding Chinese statesmen down to modern times. Moreover, control of salt and its rich financial out-turn always became the immediate objective of revolutionaries, rebels, brigands, and other organized malcontents in China. Where banks have been the subject of special attention by these parties in other lands, the salt revenue collecting agencies took their place in China. In fact, the more efficient salt tax collecting machinery set up after the improvements introduced in 1913 provided the sinews of war to many rebels and regional war-lords and helped to continue the anarchy of the times. This was due to the large sums of ready money concentrated in the collecting agencies under the new conditions. The gradual extension of national unification under Chiang Kai-shek after 1927 put a stop to the financial and political chaos which from 1916 on was supported by the greatly enhanced collections of the salt money.

A special interest relating to my district, the populous mid-Yangtze provinces, revolved about Marquis Tseng Kuo-fan, China's unique scholar-statesman and military strategist. He it was who directed the sanguinary campaigns which finally led to the suppression of the T'ai-p'ing rebels, who ravaged a large part of China from about 1850 to 1864.

102

With the suppression of the rebels, Marquis Tseng proceeded to reorganize the methods of salt supply and taxation for all Central China. By his system, selected monopoly merchants were authorized, by the issue of perpetual licenses, to transport salt supplies from the producing centres of the sea-coast to the consumption districts of the interior. This comprised the valley of the Yangtze as far as the borders of the far-western province of Szechuan. Here a jumble of impassable mountains formed a natural dividing line, behind which only salt manufactured at the brine wells of that province could pass into consumption.

The T'ai-p'ing rebellion in the middle of the last century had completely dislocated the supply of salt, necessity of life for a hundred million people spread over the vast inland area. In this period great ingenuity was displayed in pushing supplies into the areas threatened by "salt famine." Salt from the brine wells of West China, which had as its only exit the dangerous rapids and gorges of the upper Yangtze, was transported into Central China by great flotillas of junks and escorted by bands of heavily armed men.

Salt from the Canton area in South China was also brought northward by carriers through the mountain passes which separate Kuangtung province from Central China, to replace the customary supplies from the Huai River region on the Eastern sea-coast. Thereafter Szechuan "well-salt" and Kuangtung "sea-salt" continued to compete to some extent with "Huai" salt in these regions. But overland shipment in both cases was costly and dangerous. "Huai" salt, transported by leisurely junk up the broad Yangtze, soon regained most of its lost territory in the four central Yangtze provinces.

Marquis Tseng, a native of Hunan province, attacked the formidable problem of fiscal and economic reconstruction with the same energy and resourcefulness as had characterized his campaigns against the bloodthirsty "Long-Haired Rebels." "Licenses" were allotted to favored merchants, usually former officers of Tseng's Hunan "braves," or to generous contributors to the financing of his campaigns. Government supervisory officers were echeloned along the river ways of Central China to supervise salt cargoes. This insured that only salt which had paid the prescribed one-third "advance" duties at the point of embarkation, the Yangtze Stores, could enter the consumption districts; likewise that the "deferred," or two-thirds remaining duties would be duly liquidated in all their varying rates. These latter were calculated on the principle of a differential, increasing with the distance up river. The price of salt, including tax, could be augmented in direct ratio to the expense of "bootlegging" salt up the river which had escaped regular taxation.

An invariable question propounded to me has been "Where do the Chinese get their salt?" The detailed operation of this great food supply and fiscal mechanism gradually unfolded itself to my understanding as I made my tours and compiled my reports. It has proven, all will agree, one of the most impressive disclosures ever made of native Chinese methods. To appreciate its nation-wide application requires a detailed knowledge of the geography of China.

Following arrangements set up as early as the tenth century, the country continued to be divided into eleven salt producing districts. They were known as F'eng-t'ien (South Manchuria), Ch'ang-lu (now Ho-pei province), Shan-tung (earliest recorded producing district), Ho-tung (i.e. east of the Yellow River in its great bend in Shan-si province), Liang-huai (north and south of the Huai river, the coastal region north of the Yangtze river estuary, including most of the inland provinces of Anhui, Hupeh, Kiangsi and Hunan as consumption areas), the northeast district which includes part of Mongolia, Kansu and most of Shensi, Chekiang, Fukien and Kwangtung provinces on the seaboard, and the important salt producing inland provinces of Szechuan and Yunnan. The landlocked areas of Kuangsi and Kueichow receive salt from the seacoast.

The first district mentioned, Feng-t'ien, comprised South Manchuria seized by the Japanese in 1931. Here along the coast of the Gulf of Pei-chih-li salt is evaporated from sea water. Quantities of the commodity are shipped inland, in the summer by the Liao River, or in the winter by cart, but chiefly by the Manchurian railways. The population of the "Eastern Three Provinces," as the Chinese have named Manchuria, numbers some thirty millions, and is supplied solely by these coastal salt producing regions. Save for the midsummer months of heavy rains, the sun shines brightly and dry winds blow, forming an ideal climate for open air evaporation of salt water.

Aside from the inland producing areas of Szechuan, Ho-tung and Yunnan, salt is manufactured exclusively from sea-water. The method used has been by solar evaporation either in open-air earth "pans," or on wooden drying trays, or by boiling in iron cauldrons. In Hotung, where the Yellow River turns eastward from its north to south course, salt is derived from a small lake. This product has been so valuable that the entire lake has been surrounded by a wall.

In the far western province of Szechuan, brine has been obtained for centuries from deep bored wells. Here I have seen the prototype of all modern oilwell drilling machinery, with 40 foot derricks built entirely of giant bamboo poles lashed together. Bamboo ropes were wound over huge wooden drums, water buffaloes furnishing the "power." The drilling was done with iron-pointed bamboo drills, lifted and dropped with the necessary twisting motion. This is accomplished by the drillers alternately hopping on and off a balanced wooden beam. It has taken generations to drill some of these wells. The wells are lined with bamboo casings and the brine is drawn up, often from depths of hundreds of feet, in long bamboo buckets with movable bottoms fitting the casings.

The brine is "piped" considerable distances across the hills through large bamboo tubes, fastened together and cemented so as to be water-

104

tight. The brine of course flows only downward by gravity into reservoirs, whence it is carried in buckets to the top of the next rise to be poured into another battery of pipes. Upon reaching the evaporation plants, the brine is boiled in heavy iron cauldrons over furnaces heated by coal or natural gas. The latter fuel is often found along with underground salt deposits. Some of the salt boiled from the rich brine is left in huge round cakes, which are carried, either whole or broken into lumps, on coolies' backs throughout the wide area of Szechuan and even into Yunnan, Tibet, and Sikang. Some salt is produced in hard, dry grains for shipment packed in bags, chiefly on junks down the Yangtze. There is one area on the great River, where, when the water falls to low winter levels, salt springs appear and are worked on the exposed river bank.

In the far southwest there are salt mines and springs. Within Mongolia are salt lakes. In central China in Hupeh province, I saw a fine white salt boiled from brine which collects in deep pits from which gypsum has been mined. But the vast bulk of salt in China is derived from the sea. The Chinese use, it is estimated, about eighteen pounds of salt per person annually for eating purposes only. This is perhaps a higher average than in any other country. The lack of refrigeration methods, except in north China where ice is harvested, accounts for this. By pickling their food in brine they preserve pork, cabbage, fish, and a multitude of other food products. Chinese dishes are always well salted.

There is an enormous consumption of *chiang-yu,* known generally in the West as "soy-sauce," a blackish salty liquid, never absent from the Chinese table. For the discriminating taste of the Chinese does not permit of the sprinkling of salt on already prepared food, as with us in the West. Dishes requiring special salting when eaten are dipped into small shallow saucers of soy-sauce, which has been given body by combination with ground fermented soya beans. The process of manufacturing soy-sauce is a highly intricate one. The jars in which the manufacture is carried on are individually registered and taxed according to the salt content, like whiskey stills in America.

The ethical aspect of a salt tax, such as the Chinese *Gabelle,* has often been debated. A tax on foodstuffs has been traditionally repugnant to the Anglo-Saxon mind. The salt tax in France was a contributing factor to the popular discontent which led to the Revolution. A tax on tea furnished the first incident in the American Colonies' revolt against Great Britain—though the political principle of "no taxation without representation" was involved here. Gradually, however, fiscal needs are overcoming traditional scruples in Western lands even as in China. "Sales taxes" on foodstuffs are collected in many states. So in China, it has been argued from earliest times that the necessity of the state transcends all other considerations. Actually the incidence of the Chinese salt tax on the individual is light. The rate of taxation varies through the country, based, as stated, on the distance from the point of production. In my time the highest rate was

105

around twelve Chinese cents on 1.1 pounds of salt, or at a normal rate of exchange, about four American cents. Upon an estimated consumption of eighteen pounds *per annum,* the annual contribution of a Chinese was thus around sixty-four American cents. In the light of gasoline taxes imposed in the United States of as much as eight cents a gallon, the salt tax contribution of the Chinese populace has been well in proportion to the low economic standard prevailing.

Tale of Three Cities

AS I PREPARED to leave Yangchow after my brief visit there in the late fall of 1914, the Salt Commissioner of the two Huai Regions honored me with a farewell feast. An endless succession of deliciously prepared viands came to the table. The Commissioner, traditionally one of the most important financial officers of the realm, apologized in customary deprecatory phrases for the simplicity and crude preparation of his fare.

"This is a country place, you will realize," he complained. "It is quite impossible to obtain the ordinary products of the metropolitan centres to which the Elder-Born has been accustomed. My cook is a country fellow and knows nothing of the art of cookery."

Actually, Yangchow has always been celebrated for its *chefs;* to have a cook from Yangchow is a source of pride to hosts in other regions of China. No criticism whatever could be made of the courses: boiled "mandarin," a choice fish fresh out of the Yangtze; strips of pheasant breast plunged by the host himself into the boiling broth of a chafingdish with white chrysanthemum petals delicately scattered over the whole; the pink of boiled shrimps set off with green peas; succulent bamboo-shoots. All was accompanied by tiny silver cups of hot rice wine, and the whole concluded with bowls of steaming rice congee. The November air began to have a sharpness stimulating the appetite.

I was now to retrace the voyage I had made in early 1911, almost four years before. But I had none of the misgivings in going up the River to Hankow, already familiar to me, that I had when I left Tientsin for unknown Peking on that hot July day of 1908. The crumbling banks, the swift yellow current, the endless flocks of wild duck wintering on its never-frozen surface, drifting in clouds before the onrush of the big riversteamer, all were old friends. Phalanxes of wild greese flew high overhead to some distant sandbar. Among the reeds we knew there were tiny musk deer and ferocious wild boar with sharp upcurving tusks. Coveys of pheasants, woodcock, and quail could be flushed from the upland cover and the fallow rice stubble. The Captain's lavish table was never without these evidences of the surrounding sportsman's paradise. China's Land of Famine was far from the lush valley of the Yangtze; China's "Dust Bowl" remained well north of the Tsing-ling mountain range.

By November, 1914, the international community at Hankow was already divided by the initial bitterness of the War. For many years the

European residents of the Concessions along the river front had worked and played together in complete harmony. British, Germans, French, Americans had gathered daily on the verandahs and lawns of the Race Club for afternoon tea, followed by tennis or golf or riding. At break of day, the racing enthusiasts appeared for coffee and rolls, and to time the ponies in their early morning training. Before the late 8:30 dinner the bars of the Cercle Sportif Français and the Hankow Club hummed with conversation on the latest Reuter's news-cables. In the adjoining bridge rooms games, for considerable stakes, absorbed the players.

The Germans already had established their own separate town club. At the Race Club they gathered in isolated little groups. A few neutrals including Americans, especially naval officers, joined them. As yet the traditional *gemütlichkeit* of the Germans drew to them many who found the atmosphere of the Hankow Club "too snootily British." The *Lusitania*, with its American victims, had not yet been *spurlos versenkt,* to alter American sentiment overnight. The racial ructions which subsequently divided the world, and which especially rent the European colonies in China asunder, were already foreshadowed.

I took up my temporary residence in a *pension* maintained by a hospitable American woman. Here a group of my fellow countrymen had gathered. The German base of Tsingtao was already beset, land and sea, by the Japanese, as forecast to me by Premier T'ang Shao-yi at Shanghai on August 1st. The American Consul at the Shantung port, one of the old student interpreter group of 1908, Willys Peck, had with difficulty made his way through the lines and was now on temporary detail at Hankow.

The Hankow community represented the customary societal organization of the so-called "out-port" of those days. It was, in a word, a Shanghai on a somewhat reduced scale. The Consular Body formed the apex of the social pyramid: Consuls General for the Powers, Consuls for the lesser countries, merchant consuls for those governments requiring only occasional services. All the Powers were represented—Great Britain, the United States, France, Germany, Russia, and Japan and, less important, Italy and Belgium. Their officials were veteran officers, some having resided all their active careers in China, speaking and reading the language.

All except the American Consul General held commanding positions in their respective "Concessions," the American excepted only because he had no territorial domain. Their posts involved great dignity and influence. They guided and directed the interests of their respective nationals. At social functions they and their wives were always given the places of honor. The American Consul General, Edwin S. Cunningham, had however more to commend him than the autocracy of a tiny "Concession" six hundred miles in the interior of China. He was a seasoned career officer, with service in almost every hemisphere and climate. His forceful character and qualities of leadership were to carry him to the most important consular post in the service, Shanghai, in a term to exceed that of any of

107

his predecessors. A Consul's drawing room and dinner table play quite as important a part as the office over which the insignia of the United States hangs in its frame. American citizens in foreign parts need spiritual comfort as well as legal services. Many of us recall, with a warming of the heart, the hospitality extended us in Singapore, in Geneva or in Yokohama by some much burdened Consul and his wife. The consular helpmate may make or break a man's career. Edwin Cunningham, that stalwart Tennessean, had much to commend him, but his achievements would have fallen far short had it not been for the certain instinct, the lucid realism, and stimulating energy of Rhoda Cunningham.

There was only one impairment of the sublime position of the Consul in the microcosm of the largest up-river treaty port. This was provided by the occasional presence of the Admirals of the Powers. These brilliantly plumaged birds-of-passage appeared with their flagships when the water in the river was high enough to make navigation safe. Their visits were signalized by rounds of social functions. The navy gave color and variety to life on the Yangtze. The naval vessels of the Powers were permitted by treaty to visit for indefinite periods the various ports along the river, on grounds that they afforded the protection to foreign nationals of which the Chinese government was incapable. The duties of the naval officers consisted in time of peace in making formal calls upon the Chinese and foreign officials of the locality and in receiving and returning hospitality—luncheons, teas, receptions, and dinners. On the natal days of reigning sovereigns and the Glorious Fourth, accompanied by their flag-lieutenants and other members of their staffs, the Admirals appeared attired in gold-laced uniforms, glittering swords, beplumed hats.

As soon as they could doff their formal attire for easy togs, they hurried off to golf. Hankow, for its variety of sports, was regarded by the navies as a most desirable station. It was my good fortune to join a succession of American admirals on the Hankow golf course. My game progressively deteriorated. I assigned this to my habit of devoting an attentive ear to the spirited reminiscences of these gallant sea-dogs of the American navy. I came to suspect, for example, that in this remote corner of the world, that splendid seaman Admiral Charles B. McVay, Jr. (thrice stationed on the China coast, at length to command the Asiatic Fleet) covertly practiced upon me a special conversational technique, for later use with Congressional appropriations committees.

My more intimate contacts with admirals and lesser personages of the world's navies began at this time. Admiral Sir Edgar Alexander-Sinclair, K.C.B., M.V.O., arrived on H.M.S. *Hawkins,* an 8000 ton cruiser with a complement of over six hundred officers and men. Sir Edgar was the finest type of British naval officer. Obscurely tucked away in the wardroom was a junior officer known as Lieutenant Windsor, later to become the Duke of Kent. Prince George, youngest scion of the royal house of England, made himself extremely popular by his modesty, his assiduous devotion to every type of sport, and his grace and gallantry in the drawing room and on the dancing floor. On one occasion, when we were entertaining the British Commander at dinner, together with Admiral Henry H. Hough, U.S.N., Commander of the Yangtze Patrol, and Mrs. Hough, my wife confided to Sir Edgar that she had secretly harbored the design to include Lieutenant Windsor in the dinner party.

"My courage failed me at the last moment, however," she confessed. "After all he *is* the son of the King of Great Britain and Ireland, Emperor of India, etc., etc."

"Not at all, not at all," genially observed Sir Edgar as he looked about our palatial apartment in the Salt Revenue Building. "Lieutenant Prince George would have enjoyed nothing more than being with you here." The young Prince's democratic manner and engaging smile soon made all Hankow feel at home with him.

The Military Governor of Hupeh, General Wang Chan-yuan, gave the customary entertainment for the British Admiral and his staff at a ceremonial dinner at his *yamen* at Wuchang, the provincial capital across the river. For some undisclosed reason the General included me, an American, though Commissioner of the Chinese Salt Revenue. The elaborate Chinese feast was preceded as usual with *apéritifs* and *hors d'oeuvres* in the reception hall. The entire company then marched with great solemnity into the banquet room, the Bismarckian features of our portly host rising above the uniform of a field marshal, while the British Admiral was followed by his lean, fit staff officers. His Majesty's Consul General Herbert Goffe, C.M.G., and the Governor's personal staff were there as well. I felt both mystified and misplaced in this assembly, obviously arranged to honor Britain. My discomfort was to increase. As we stationed ourselves behind our respective chairs preparatory to being seated, the General's brass band, in the adjoining courtyard, blared forth not "Rule Britannia," but "The Star-Spangled Banner." At the moment my eyes sought the Admiral's in mute apology. The gallant sailor, who had fought his battle cruiser through Jutland, was equal to the occasion. His face never relaxed, but I fancied I saw a droop in the left eye as he gazed in my direction.

On one occasion an American Admiral hastened the six hundred miles and more up the Yangtze upon news of the murder of an American missionary by the troops of a Central China warlord. On his return from the remote river port where the tragic incident occurred, the destroyer on which the Admiral traveled "opened up" to twenty or more knots. Complaints came in later that not only had somnolent water buffaloes, taking their ease in the shallow waters of the river side, been seriously disturbed by the wash, but junks and sampans had been overturned, with considerable discomfort and danger to the river population. I was delegated to meet the distinguished naval officer with my motor car, a rare *Ford,* much in demand by friends who were not so equipped in these more primitive days in the up-river port. The reason for the accelerated return voyage was disclosed. The Admiral complained as he left his barge of an unusual attack of indigestion. He asked me to take him at once to the nearest club bar for a glass of "3 Star" brandy, the only palliative he had really found effective for such a complaint. Secretary Daniels' war-time prohibition order had left the destroyer's stores deficient in this universal panacea.

The "Comyangpat," the condensed title of the Commander of the Yangtze Patrol, was for many years in rank a senior Captain of the U. S. Navy. The "patrol" at this time consisted of a half dozen antiquated gunboats with Spanish names, indicating that they had been booty of the Manila victory of 1898. There were also two shallow-draft vessels, put together at Shanghai, the *Palos* and the *Monocassy*, and the *Helena* of the extraordinarily tall funnel. As American missionary and commercial interests grew prodigiously during the years of the World War, an officer of the rank of Rear Admiral was assigned to this post. The last of Captain's rank to hold it was an officer who had served on Dewey's fleet at the battle of Manila Bay in 1898. Consul General Cunningham duly invited a representative group of the American community to meet the Captain at a complimentary dinner. It soon transpired that the host and guest were old acquaintances. The Consul had been at sun-baked Aden on the Red Sea, his first post, twenty years before, when part of Dewey's fleet had made a brief homeward stop at that outpost of British Empire. The veterans of the two respective services recalled the enthusiastic welcome with which Dewey's men had been greeted by the British forces stationed at Kipling's "old Aden like a barrick stove." The unexpected American conquest of the Islands had relieved London of the fear that they might fall into German hands.

A gathering of distinguished American navy and army officers occurred one night in the harbor at Hankow. I was one of those invited to dine on board the U.S.S. *Isabel,* flagship of Admiral Joseph Strauss, Commander-in-Chief of the Asiatic fleet. The guest of honor was Major General William Crozier, then visiting China after a notable career as Chief of Ordnance. The eminent representatives of the two fighting services had fallen into a lively discussion on a matter of international policies involving a neighboring island nation. Their opinions differed materially. At the critical moment, there happily appeared the appeasing personality of Rear Admiral William Bullard, who had just arrived by merchant steamer from down river to assume command of the Yangtze Patrol, the first officer of flag rank assigned to that post. The threat of storms in the offing disappeared, the atmosphere cleared and arguments were forgotten in the reunion of old comrades of the two fighting services far up the Yangtze Kiang.

The American navy at Hankow, as elsewhere, was instantly prepared for battle as well as for play. The frequent civil strife of this "era of the

110

warlords" took the place of our American elections. When a general controlling a rich province had, in the opinion of his friends and associates, amassed a sufficient fortune, he would be ousted by a superior *display* of military force, marshalled by a combination of aspirants for his post. This resulted usually in much expenditure of ammunition, but little bloodshed. Sun-tzu, China's strategist of the sixth century B.C., had admonished in his *Art of War,* the skillful general "will not assert his mastery by force of arms. Such a course is sure to meet with its proper return." So machine-guns would bark, field pieces and naval guns would add to the clamor on all sides of the foreign Concessions. These affairs usually occurred in the height of summer. Added to the heat, the deafening uproar made sleep impossible. Volunteers from the nations of the various Concessions would take station on the borders of Chinese territory, in their khaki hot weather uniforms, fully equipped with rifles, revolvers, and even a couple of field pieces. The gunboats of the foreign Powers in the river would land reinforcing parties and the naval officers took general command.

While without a Concession at Hankow, the American community had its own volunteer corps as at Shanghai. The U.S. Consular premises were established in a tall and ancient edifice on the Bund, long condemned as unsafe. Here we Americans had our official headquarters. One or more U.S. gunboats, mostly the obsolete prizes of the Philippine conquest, anchored off "the Bund." As many blue-jackets as could be spared came ashore and took up station on the Consul General's verandahs. On one urgent occasion it was reported that only the chief bo'sn's mate, the Filipino cook, and the ship's mascot, an amiable bull terrier, were left on board to navigate or fight the U.S.S. *Palos.* When machine-gun fire came too close to the Concessions, the joint American forces, naval and volunteer, would send reinforcements to the menaced sectors held by British or French volunteers and naval units.

Aside from disturbance of business, these outbreaks were almost welcomed as distractions from the monotony of the long summers. On one such occasion a group of convivial Americans calling themselves the Korn-Kob-Klub were holding a ceremonial banquet at the Russian *Sobranje.* This club was a famous centre for epicures. As typically as the British abroad must have their inevitable race-track, golf course, and Gilbert & Sullivan opera, so the prosperous Russian community at Hankow provided us with excellent food, music, and the drama. Their amateur artists gave us the ballet, the opera and the theatre, as they had known it in St. Petersburg, Moscow, and Kiev. Their Consul General, M. Beltchenko, was a man of broad culture and a deep student of Chinese civilization. He had published a work on the governmental system of Imperial China just as the sweeping changes of the new Republic altered everything.

But it was in the field of gastronomics that the Russian colony of opulent Czarist days was preeminent. Their club flourished mightily in the spacious days before the Red Revolution, when the Russians still held their Concession at Hankow and the wealth of their tea merchants was proverbial. In certain streets of the Russian *enclave,* the atmosphere was redolent of tea, while the clatter of machinery making "brick tea" for the Central Asian caravan trade was deafening. With the World War and its consequences, the overland routes to Russian Asia fell into disuse; the Bolshevik government outlawed the tea-merchants as "capitalists." Their wealth was dissipated and their glory departed. Their club, however, still maintained its famous *chef.* Its well stocked cellar continued to provide for the needs of the whole foreign community, from champagne to vodka. Thus it remained a centre for festive occasions.

So, in goodly fellowship, the Korn-Kob-Klub was attacking that plenitude of cold whets known as the *Zakouska,* which consisted of caviar both black and red from the Caspian, salted ripe olives from the Crimea, smoked salmon from the Siberian littoral, cold *rabchick,* the wild grouse from North Manchuria, and the delicious pink-white meat of the Vladivostok giant spider-crab. This was a mere preliminary to *bortch,* the national cabbage soup, followed by boiled sturgeon from the Yangtze, *beef Strogonoff,* so named from a sixteenth century merchant and gourmet, and so on to *plombier,* the frozen cream which concludes the major portion of the gargantuan Russian dinner.

Suddenly the staccato of machine-guns interrupted the proceedings. Each of us, with his own official or business responsibility, and in general the military duty incumbent upon a member of the American volunteer corps, left the table. The firing was just behind the Russian Concession. We dodged across the lateral streets, exposed to whistling bullets. At last I reached my own office in the former German Concession, then under Chinese jurisdiction. Already an armed landing party of American bluejackets had taken up their positions before the building. From the left pocket of each sailor's jerkin protruded a wicked hand grenade; from the right dangled the paper medallion of the invariable "Bull-Durham," of those times. The Navy rolled its own. Report was that a great mob of infuriated Chinese had gathered at the landward entrances to the British Concession. The gates had been closed but already the rioters were tearing up the cast-iron gratings over the open street drains, hurling the jagged fragments upon the British sailors and the civilian volunteers, pressed together in the narrow road. The Concession fire-brigade was playing streams of water upon the yelling mob. But thousands still pushed forward from behind. At last the reluctant order came to fire. The mob, if it had broken in upon the handful of defenders, would have had the rich Concessions, the women and children and all of us at its mercy. Sputter of a machine-gun, a wild retreat, a few forms left upon the empty, littered street and all was quiet. The next morning I had occasion to consult a letter-file on a shelf near the open window where I had stood the night before in my office. A machine-gun bullet, embedded in the paper, fell to the floor.

112

"Hair's breadth miss is as good as ten thousand miles," sententiously observed my colleague, Mr. Cho.

The presence of the naval units on the Yangtze provided a sense of security, actual armed protection and a degree of social stimulus. In return, the foreign communities made the visits of officers and crews as agreeable as possible. The calls at Hankow of the French Admiral were rather rare. For some reason this officer, though representing a great democracy, seemed to hold a position exalted above all others. His assumed geniality was frosty; there was an air of condescension about his officers. The French naval units were based on the ports of Indo-China, a colonial possession ruled *de haute en bas*. Despite the full dress "puppet" courts of Annam and Cambodia, with kings and emperors "who reign but do not rule," the gulf between the ruling French bureaucracy and the brown-garbed peasant proletariat was wide. *Liberté, égalité, fraternité* had not appeared in the Republic's exports to her Asiatic colonies. This aloofness from intimate contact with the "native" population appeared mirrored in the deportment of the French navy on the Yangtze. The character of their relations with the civilian bureaucracy of Indo-China, too, left the French naval officers just a bit condescending to their civilian nationals of the China ports. The Admiral's rare visits were signalized by formal receptions and dinners by the local French communities.

Nothing could excel the charm and cordiality of the functions given in the French consular establishment at Hankow. This was due to the unusual personalities of M. Georges Lecomte, *Consul Général de France,* and his wife. M. Lecomte was one of those French officials to whom China was a matter of thorough scientific study and exploration. He was an adept in the language, having received his preliminary training at the feet of the great French sinologue in the School of Oriental Living Languages in Paris, Professor Edouard Chavannes. Mme. Lecomte stemmed from the substantial land owning gentry of Touraine. Receptions and dinners were arranged with the delicate attention to detail which reflected the utmost credit upon the hostess.

By an almost astral coincidence, the French diplomat, to become my most esteemed friend and colleague, had come within my consciousness even before I left America for China. While in June, 1908, I was making a farewell call upon my master in medieval studies, Professor Earle Wilbur Dow of the University of Michigan, he was reminded of the remark of an elderly lady in whose family he had resided during his student years in Paris.

"Hélas!" sighed old Mother Lecomte, *"Mon fils Georges s'occupe des pauvres bêtes Chinois."* Professor Dow provided me with a card of introduction to M. Lecomte, whom I was actually to meet "concerning himself with the poor stupid Chinese." Thus began a friendship of many years. The Quai d' Orsay ultimately recognized M. Lecomte's services in behalf of the Republic's interests in China by an assignment as Minister to the Cen-

113

tral American republics. After his retirement, he continued his Chinese studies in a cozy Paris apartment near the foreign office while Mme. Lecomte divided her time between the city and her ancestral estate in Touraine.

The British Consulate occupied a favored site on the Hankow Bund. The first British Consul reached his post shortly after the second treaty settlements with China in 1860, whereby Hankow was opened to foreign trade and residence. As a tablet in the little cemetery discloses, his career was cut short. He and his faithful Indian servant, buried on nearby Hanyang hill, succumbed as did others of the foreign community at the time to a virulent epidemic. The thought often came to our minds as to how any of the early Europeans survived plague, smallpox, typhoid, typhus, cholera and other deadly evils. We, of a much later date, assiduously resorted to vaccinations and inoculations to ward off the diseases endemic to the masses of humanity with which we were surrounded and in constant contact, through our servants and other Chinese associates.

True to type, the British Consulate at Hankow and the surrounding British Concession formed a tiny European oasis, brought out in sharp relief in its turbulent and disorderly Chinese backgrounds. Once I listened to an eminent American trained Chinese engineer, in flawless English, berate the British for developing for themselves their concessions. Chinese, he indignantly protested, were excluded from the full use and control of these *enclaves*. The answer was of course that there were some thousands of miles remaining on either bank of the Yangtze river, not as yet occupied by the British or other non-Chinese. These areas have been available to engineers like himself for the construction of similar desirable residence and business cities—if they really wanted them. No, he preferred to take on something already perfected by the labor of others. Actually, however, in the intervening years the British government, as the others, turned over its concessions to complete Chinese control.

The British consular buildings were low, cool, and comfortable, set down among green lawns, flowering shrubs, and shady trees, almost like a bit of old England. Most precious of all was the kitchen-garden which in season produced lettuce, green onions, strawberries, and such other items as could be safely eaten uncooked. An inestimable favor was to receive a basket of fresh lettuce or a bowl of strawberries from the immaculate British Consulate garden. The joy of this could only be appreciated by Occidentals living in a land where every particle of ordure, human and animal, must be returned to the soil to maintain its overworked fertility. Our Chinese cooks occasionally palmed off such desirable eatables upon us by representing the produce as having been surreptitiously bought from the Consular gardener at a fancy price (cheerfully defrayed by the employer). If the salad, strawberries, etc., had such a genuine origin, the garden's fruitfulness must have surpassed that of the traditional Garden of Eden. Undoubtedly such transactions really involved the native vege-

114

table patches which soon sprang up around the foreign settlements, but whose productiveness was maintained by the time-honored methods of fertilization employed by these "farmers of forty centuries."

Yoked to an Unbeliever

WITH MY ARRIVAL at Hankow in November of 1914, I began forthwith my duties as Chief Foreign Auditor of the Salt Revenue Administration in the Four Yangtze Provinces. So my Chinese title was translated to read. I was to be the initiator in this farflung area of the reforms contemplated in the Loan Agreement. Of equal rank and authority with me was my Chinese colleague, Mr. Cho Shao-mei. This personage, who stemmed from an ancient family of the province of Szechuan, was to prove at times a blessing, but in the end a bane. He boasted that one of his forebears had been an Imperial Grand Councillor. Medium-tall and stout, he was a man of considerable political force in official circles. Over a florid, full face, his head sloped gently upward. He was thus able to wear, for a figure of his size, a surprisingly small round silk cap with the usual red button atop. Convivial to a degree, he could absorb a bottle of "3 Star" brandy at a single sitting, and show up in the office the next morning little the worse for wear. His system did not react excessively to alcohol, it appeared.

Fortunately for us all, Mr. Cho played little part in the more technical features of administration and accounting. His activities were political and diplomatic. In these his talents for sociability could shine. To begin with, his principal role was to introduce me favorably to the Transportation Officers of the Four Provinces, to reassure them that the foreigner intended no serious impairment of their unofficial but substantial perquisites, and to reconcile them in general to this novel intervention in the affairs of the Salt Administration. The Transportation Officers, like the Shanghai *Taotai,* were largely agents for influential groups or personages in the Ministry of Finance at Peking, to whom the major profits of these lucrative offices went.

Mr. Cho entered upon his duties some weeks ahead of me. Thus when I was taken to the temporary offices of the "Chief Audit Department," in the French Concession at Hankow, I found the several rooms equipped with small, neatly varnished desks at each of which sat a member of the office's staff. Mr. Cho informed me that in order to have everything ready for an immediate reform campaign, he had taken the liberty to fill *all* posts with his own selections before my arrival. My dismay can be realized when, upon enquiry, I discovered that most of Mr. Cho's appointments had been made on a basis of family connections. While I was fully aware that nepotism was traditional in Chinese official appointments, its complete application in what was to be an establishment organized after the most advanced Occidental model was little short of appalling.

To assist in the colossal task of auditing the salt tax receipts of the Central China Transportation Offices I was provided with a Confucian scholar as "Chief Accountant." This learned man knew no foreign language, not even the Arabic numerals. Our English Secretary, the officer responsible for translations of a voluminous correspondence from Chinese into English and the reverse, proved to be an amiable gentleman of middle age, with a remote knowledge of "basic English" gained years before in a mission school. There were no typists; and no accountants for the masses of figures and statistics that must shortly be compiled in English. I made my representations to Sir Richard Dane, who fortunately visited Hankow at that moment. He cut the Gordian knot by increasing my office allowance sufficiently to enable me to hire a young Chinese who had learned typing in the German Bank at Hankow, and a secretary whose knowledge of business English was enough to make rough translations, which I in due course polished sufficiently to be intelligible. I thus foresaw that my primary duty under the Quintuple Banking Group Loan Agreement would be the tactful but inevitable replacement of Mr. Cho's eager but unqualified relatives and friends.

With this basic principle of reform in mind, I proceeded to tour my fiscal satrapy. This extended, I found, from just above Nanking on the Yangtze to the entrance of the up-river gorges at I-chang, a distance of as far as from New York to Chicago. Echeloned along the River valley were the chief "Transportation Offices." They were generally established in the provincial capitals, in the Wu-han cities (Wuchang-Hankow-Hanyang) for Hupeh, Nan-ch'ang for Kiangsi, Ch'ang-sha for Hunan. The exception was Anhui, the Transportation Office for that down-river province being established not at the province's capital city Anking, but on an island in the River. This was for greater effectiveness in controlling and checking salt-junks as they began at the nearby Yangtze Salt Stores at Shih-erh-wei their long journeys up-river.

Under each Transportation Office were numerous outlying "sub-offices," with "bonded" salt storehouses where the monopoly merchants discharged their salt upon its arrival from the seacoast. Local distributors obtained their supplies at the head- or sub-stores at a price fixed by government. The price, as notified to the public, was entirely regulated by the government. It consisted of three parts, "merchants' outlay" which comprised the original costs of the salt, transportation charges, interest on investment, and profits; the "advance duty" paid by the transporters when they obtained the salt at the government controlled stores down-river; and the "deferred duty," the consumption tax, equal to two-thirds of the gross duty payable. This was the set-up already noted as instituted by Marquis Tseng Kuo-fan after the T'ai-p'ing rebellion.

My investigations of the actual operations of this "merchant transport-government control" system disclosed many features hitherto unknown to the loan group. In the first place, the entire price obtained for salt— merchant investment and government impost—came first into the custodianship of the Transportation Officer. This placed huge sums, temporarily

116

withheld from the merchants, in the hands of a possibly rapacious and irresponsible official. In China, such sums could be put out at high interest in short term loans. I soon came to find that this was almost invariably the case. Transportation Officers held their posts for comparatively short periods. They must make hay while the sun shone, both for themselves and their higher-up political patrons. They were generally holding back sums owing both to the merchants and to the government. Their accounts were never cleared, and therefore could not be audited, until they vacated office. If their loans and investments had been successful, neither merchants nor government suffered loss. It was not always so.

Information came to me by roundabout ways that a newly appointed Transportation Officer at Hankow had placed a loan of two hundred and fifty thousand taels (about U.S. $150,000) from salt funds in his keeping, with the Golden Dragon Flour Milling Company, a concern of very dubious financial standing. Such corrupt and hazardous practices were in time largely remedied. We arranged that the merchants station their own representatives in the Transportation Offices to collect directly and at once from purchasers of their salt, the portion of the price accruing to them as "merchants' outlay" to include the already paid "advance duty." The "deferred duty" was made payable directly into the government collecting banks. The latter issued a duty receipt, presentable at the Transportation Office in lieu of cash as evidence of such duty payment.

Most astonishing was the method of calculating the "deferred duty" in the provinces. There had evidently been originally a basic salt tax, but pyramided upon this were a number of surtaxes. Thus the tax schedule on a single unit of salt might consist of a dozen items. These presented a cross section of China's history of the past half century. One item was designated, for example, "surtax for maritime-defense." This represented a levy begun prior to the Sino-Japanese war of 1894–1895, to raise funds for the construction of the navy which was so ignominiously destroyed by the Japanese at Port Arthur and Weihaiwei. Several items were entitled "indemnity surtaxes," representing, as in one instance, a levy to compensate for a murderous mob assault upon a Roman Catholic mission. Once imposed, such levies were seldom revoked, though the occasion for their collection may have ceased.

Not only was the basic "deferred duty" increased by a variety of surtaxes. Such collections were sometimes stipulated in taels (Chinese ounces) of silver, sometimes in copper cash. Rates of conversion were arbitrary and always to the advantage of the official collectors. Moreover, the taxable unit varied. Some levies were made on the "picul" as a unit, some on the "yin." The "picul" varied in different provinces in actual weight, from 133 to 140 pounds. The "yin" might consist of a "small yin" of three or a "large yin" of six piculs. Obviously this astounding and confusing variety of taxes, currencies and weights was a malignant growth. Uniformity had to be introduced, before any serious audit of the salt revenue could be

117

carried out. The whole malodorous system was swept away by a few simple expedients. The taxable unit of salt was made uniform, a "picul" of 140 pounds *avoirdupois*. Platform scales and test weights were supplied to Transportation Offices as standard checks on weights. The infinite variety of taxation schedules were reduced to a consolidated "advance duty" of one tael; the "deferred duty" of two taels.

The "tael," an ounce of silver, varied too both in weight and fineness. These variables were eliminated in due course by setting the collection of the "advance duty" at one and a half silver dollars, the "deferred duty" at three. The new Salt Administration contributed largely to the general adoption of the silver dollar as the uniform currency of China. Ultimately the use of the tael was entirely abolished by government order. The Salt Administration was thus the initiator of the long mooted reform of China's currency. Unfortunately, later advisers of the Chinese government carried the reform too far. Financial experts came from foreign parts who did not know "the peculiar circumstances of China," as Dane and the rest of us did, and proposed the divorce of the dollar from a silver to a managed-currency basis. Silver was thereupon "nationalized" by the government, following the high prices established by the silver purchase policy of the American Treasury, and exported from the country. The four hundred million Chinese were thus left in the fall of 1938 and thereafter with a continually depreciating paper currency.

The cleansing of the Augean Stables of the Salt Administration continued. With that elasticity characteristic of Oriental practices, the monopoly merchants had avoided the heavy incidence of the salt tax by the device of "surplus salt," and by less obvious methods. For decades these capitalists had caused a never ending flow of revenue to pour into the government's coffers. In times of crisis they were called upon for extra special grants-in-aid. With each incoming government, or newly installed provincial satrap, they were forced to pay new fees for "re-registration" of their perpetual licenses. The fees charged for this purpose, running into many millions of dollars, became the logical basis for the merchants to demand new concessions from the government, e.g. an increase in "tare and wastage allowances." Gifts and contributions too were necessary to insure the favor of greedy officials. The merchants must also have means to recoup themselves from frequent losses by shipwreck, as well as from official extortion. There were no facilities for insuring junks and salt cargoes. There was no appeal from the high-placed mandarin.

Two methods lay open to merchants. First, at the Yangtze Stores as the loaded junks lay out in the stream awaiting the favoring wind of departure, untaxed salt might be brought aboard. This cheat could readily be accomplished with the connivance of dishonest official underlings. The junk's papers would be apparently in order. Examinations by the numerous "checking offices" along the river were perfunctory, provided certain unofficial fees were paid without demur. When a preventive vessel under an English officer was stationed on the Yangtze River off Nanking, the seizures of smuggled salt mounted to such a figure that it became absurd to pay the full stipulated "seizure rewards" to officers and crew.

Salt, when damp, dissolves. The merchants were entitled to full tax-paid units of salt of 140 pounds upon arrival at destination. Thus special allowances for "tare" and "wastage *en route*" of as much as 9 pounds extra tax-free salt per bag, were permitted at the issuing point. Even this amount was elastic. Often the salt arrived with little or no "wastage," so that as it was weighed out at the specified weight there remained extra salt not regularly accounted for. This was designated "surplus salt" and as it had paid no advance duty, it was clear profit to the merchants. The excess salt issued without paying tax formed profitable "salvage" in the salt merchants' operations enabling them in time to recover the government's exactions with something to spare. Thus to protect the revenue, smuggling must be stopped by a disciplined and reliable "salt-police" organization on land and water. "Surplus salt," cause of contention between officials and merchants, must be regulated to just proportions and its proceeds properly accounted for.

Salt, salt, salt—for the millions. Myriads of tons of salt lay piled in glistening heaps along the China seacoast from Manchuria to Canton. Lines of coolies carried on their backs onto sampans and junks sodden bags of woven rushes. Four to six thousand picul bags of salt could be stored in the holds of the unwieldy two-masted craft, later to breast the six-knot current of the yellow Yangtze. Huge sails were hoisted to catch the favoring up-river winds. Sweating crews strained at windlasses, with long bamboo hawsers warping heavy, deep-laden hulls around treacherous river bends. Junks stranded on concealed sandbars or sunken rocks, the precious cargo dissolving as seams opened. Whole fleets anchored in sheltered bays, with bamboo matting drawn over the waist of the ship during the three-day gales which swept the river. There would be no sign of life on board as master and crew slept off the exhaustion of days of struggle against their powerful antagonist, the restless River. And finally came the triumphant entry at the distant harbor; at the Han river's mouth, or across the Po-yang Lake at walled Nan-ch'ang, or beyond the Tung-t'ing Lake and up the Hsiang to remote Ch'ang-sha. Again ant-like lines of coolies bend under heavy bags as they climb the steep planking to well-guarded salt stores on the river bank. A never-ending stream of the basic necessity, salt, has thus flowed from China's sea-coast to the remotest confines of the middle Yangtze basin, century after century since remotest antiquity.

Mandarins and Merchant Guilds

THE SALT TRANSPORTATION OFFICERS, with whom I was to be closely associated for the next dozen years and more, were men of high character by the test of traditional Chinese standards. Their positions were

119

of the greatest personal dignity and public importance, and they were recruited from the élite of the conservative Confucian mandarinate. In all my years in the Salt Revenue Administration, before the advent of the Nationalist regime in 1927, I met but one Transportation Officer who knew a foreign language. But they were able administrators, fully conversant with the historic salt revenue in all its precedents and ramifications. As I visited the various Salt Transportation Offices in Central China, I was received with much ceremony and hospitality. My mission was to introduce modern systems of administration and accounting, novel and distasteful to the conservative minds of the Transportation Officers, and more than likely to impair the personal rewards of their posts. I must testify nevertheless to the uniform courtesy of all these gentlemen of old China.

While their hospitality in lavish dinners was at times a menace to digestion, their generosity was even more embarrassing. The Oriental practice of giving presents to those whom they wish to please was a constant problem until I discovered the customary formula. Presents in China are usually sent to the prospective recipient on a showy red-lacquered litter, slung from a pole resting on the shoulders of two porters. One such appeared at my home one morning, escorted by a servant who presented the Transportation Officer's ceremonial card on red paper. On the tray were a couple of bronze ritual vessels, a pair of choice porcelain vases, several rolls of silk, and finally some bottles of Chinese wine and a few tins of cigarettes. Aghast at such an array, I bade the servant take the whole lot back to his master. The servant and his consignment, however, lingered about the premises most of the day, not daring to return and report such discourtesy on my part. The amenities would have been satisfied if I had selected a bottle of the inexpensive wine, a tin or two of cigarettes, given a fee to the servants and rejected with thanks anything further. Chinese etiquette would thereby have been perfectly served. In this particular case it was well that I had not helped myself liberally to the ancient Shang dynasty bronzes or the *Ch'ien Lung* porcelains. For the donor had his own intentions. It was that Transportation Officer who was lending out sums of salt revenue at high interest.

I had a notion to employ the celebration of my father's sixtieth birthday as a fitting occasion for returning the lavish hospitality which I had enjoyed at the hands of the Transportation Officers and the salt monopoly merchants. My colleague, Mr. Cho, brightened noticeably at a remark to this effect; but he observed meaningly that it would cost me something. With the rashness of ignorance, I proceeded to invite a dozen or so of my principal hosts of the preceding months to a dinner party at my home. Promptly my wife ordered all the office spittoons brought in and arranged about the rooms. She was apprehensive as to her rugs, for in older China there was prodigious clearing of throats and expectoration at all times and places—a practice against which the later "New Life Movement" was particularly directed.

120

IV

CENTRAL YANGTZE PROVINCES, 1914–1922

Revenue and Revolution — Implementing the Loan Agreement — Colonial Administrator — The Stratagems of Warlord Wang — Travels and Explorations — River Dragon — At Your Orders

Revenue and Revolution

WE YOUNGSTERS of the Student Interpreters corps spent one day a week at the Legation office, "the chancellery." This was to familiarize us with the applied art of diplomacy in general, and in particular wth the usually drab business of the consular offices throughout China. Questions of protection of missionaries living in the interior, disputes relating to land holdings by American citizens, native officials' attempts at illegal and extratreaty taxation, all appeared in the Legation's correspondence. We were enabled too at times to have a look into the intrigues in connection with international finance.

One afternoon in the autumn of 1909 when I was on duty in the chancellery, one of the secretaries of the Chinese Foreign Office called. He asked for an appointment for Prince Ch'ing, Imperial Grand Councillor, with Mr. William J. Calhoun, American Minister at this time. A meeting was arranged when formal request was made by the Chinese government for a "currency reform loan." Out of this grew the protracted negotiations which eventuated in the "Reorganization Loan" of 1913, for £25,000,-000, the security for which was to be the entire salt taxes of China.

But much water was to flow down the Yangtze before an actual loan contract was signed. Cable tolls between the Legation and the State Department reached such figures during the long drawn out negotiations that the Legation's Second Secretary, newly arrived from Washington, was charged with the special message to the Minister to reduce, if possible, these excessive costs.

While the diplomatic machinery of the United States was promoting the schemes of the declining Manchu Court to obtain money from America, the agents of Wall Street were also active. Willard Straight was their Peking representative. Endowed with a magnetic personality, remarkable versatility, and boundless energy, Straight had projected himself from an obscure clerkship in Sir Robert Hart's Customs service to the position of premier representative of American finance *vis-à-vis* the Government at Peking. Whether it was strumming Kipling's romantic ditties on a guitar, designing a handsome fireplace for the bachelor quarters of a Legation secretary friend, or persuading the Governor of Manchuria to balk Japanese designs on that region by the introduction of American capital, Straight was equally at home. As some might have looked upon it, he had formed an unholy alliance between himself and the American diplomatic representative at Peking.

The cautious Rockhill, who had by principle remained aloof from foreign financial intrigues in China, had now been elevated to a new post as Ambassador at St. Petersburg. His temporary successor was Henry P. Fletcher, former rough rider in Theodore Roosevelt's Spanish War regiment. Fletcher's idea of diplomacy had much of his famous Colonel's character. He was forthright and "hard-boiled." He and Straight established bachelor quarters in the Minister's luxurious residence, built from Boxer indemnity funds. They were thus able to keep in closest touch with one another, as "dollar diplomacy" unfolded its program. Straight learned that an ambitious American Consular officer stationed in Manchuria had attempted to muscle in on loans with the Chinese authorities of that region. He turned a copy of the provisional loan-contract over to Fletcher, who at once cabled a report to the State Department. The would-be financier-consul immediately received orders to report himself at Washngton. The Japanese gave out an entirely different story: the consul had been removed because he had *erroneously* reported Japanese smuggling into South Manchuria.

News leaked out from the direction of the Chinese foreign office that British, French and German banks were obtaining a concession for the construction of the Central China (*Hu-Kuang*) railways. Fletcher immediately lodged a vigorous protest demanding the admission of American interests. This demand was based upon promises made in letters to the American Minister in Peking by the Chinese Government in 1903 and 1904, guaranteeing participation of American capital in any railway construction growing out of, or contiguous to, the Canton-Hankow railway route. As far back as 1898 the Chinese Government had granted to an American firm, the American-China Development Company, a concession for the construction of this railway, but after a few miles of railway out of Canton had been built, their interest was sold to Belgians. Fletcher's protest ultimately secured for the New York capitalists a contract, signed on May 20, 1911, to build a railway of one hundred and eighty-six miles along the almost impassable gorges of the upper Yangtze, from I-chang to Kuei-chou. The first mile of rails for this line was never laid.

Out of the conference between Prince Ch'ing and Minister Calhoun grew plans for a currency reform loan. I was personally acquainted with much of the later negotiations through coding and decoding cables. It soon leaked out—inevitably, as did all highly confidential matters at Peking—that the Chinese Government was working to bring American capital into the China field. Immediately the British, French, and German banking representatives demanded their share of the business. Wall Street, apprized of this, was disposed to welcome such an arrangement.

At that time it would have been impracticable to market in America Chinese bonds to the proposed, or perhaps any, amount. We had still some distance to go before we became the world's money lender. Thus through the currency reform loan and the railway loan the "Quadruple Banking Group" was formed. But as impecunious Russia and Japan now followed up with their demands for equal participation, the original group of four nations became a "consortium" of six Powers, eager to provide China with funds on prime security. Regular receipt of the enormous Boxer Indemnity interest and refunding instalments, on a capital sum of about 330 million American dollars, to absorb for forty years the unpledged balance of Customs revenues, had convinced the Powers that China was a first class financial risk.

The state of the Chinese currency had long been a problem. For centuries, silver ingots had been the basic monetary medium of China. The Chinese early used paper money. Marco Polo repeatedly expressed his astonishment and admiration for "the secret of the alchemists," the art of producing money by cutting up mulberry-bark paper into different sizes. Nothing has been more familiar to the Chinese than a "managed currency." Silver, even salt, had at various times formed its backing. The most prized of the precious metals has been silver. Gold has been used chiefly for ornamentation, rarely as money. Cowrie-shells, copper, bronze or brass have in turn formed the subsidiary coinage.

When China showed herself an honest debtor by meeting all her outstanding debts (principally because of the efficient functioning of the foreign-officered Customs service), the currency reform loan was mooted. Although signed ultimately in April, the loan was still not floated, due to the rivalries of the various foreign banking interests, at the outbreak of the anti-dynastic Revolution of October, 1911.

Yuan Shih-k'ai, veteran servant of the Manchu house, promptly emerged in early 1912 as President of the new Republic. He had jockeyed Dr. Sun Yat-sen out of the headship of the state in the ephemeral Nanking government. The southern revolutionaries were irreconcilable to the frustration of their plans by a northern "wolf in sheep's clothing," still wielding autocratic power from behind the walls of the Forbidden City.

Thus, after the subsidence of the political earthquake which overthrew the alien Monarchy of almost three centuries' duration, the various factions prepared themselves for further conflict. The southern party, mostly recalcitrant Cantonese, the "Irish of China," prepared to complete the revolution by ousting the counter-revolutionary Yuan Shih-k'ai. This enigmatic figure at once represented the conservatism of traditional China, and a degree of selectivity in modernism. He was the first among the mandarins trained in the Confucian school of politics to display this character of compromise.

Li Hung-chang, Liu K'un-yi, Chang Chih-tung, great Viceroys of the Yangtze valley provinces, had advocated a renovated China about the time that a similar movement was under full swing in late nineteenth century Japan. How much this attitude of Chinese leaders was accounted for by events and movements in the neighboring Island Empire it is impossible to estimate. Certain it is that the cultural influences which had set so strongly from China to Japan over many centuries, in recent years have ebbed back into China. Political terminology was, for a while, generously borrowed from the Japanese. While Chinese officialdom was deeply apprehensive of resurgent Japan, it continued to look with undisguised astonishment and envy on the latter's progress.

Yuan Shih-k'ai had tested the formidable character of Japanese intrigue and power. He had represented his master, Li Hung-chang, as High Commissioner at Seoul for a decade before he was forced by the Japanese to flee in 1894. The Korean court in those years was continually subjected to Chinese, Russian, and Japanese political pressure. Successive incidents had occurred in this unscrupulous rivalry, such as the murder of Queen Min in her palace by Japanese *ronin,* and inspired rebellions by the "tonghaks," a pseudo-progressive Korean political party. Then came the trial at arms between Japan and China in the war of 1894–95. China was again completely unmasked as an effective fighting power. She lost her embryo navy, her armed forces were scattered, the rich island of Formosa was ceded to Japan. Only by the tripartite intervention of Russia, Germany, and France and an increased cash indemnity, was South Manchuria salvaged from the victor. Li Hung-chang and his High Commissioner, Yuan Shih-k'ai, were discredited. Their policies had served only to disclose China's weakness to the world. The Powers now began a demarcation of their respective spheres of influence, and their greedy scramble for concessions from 1898 onward threatened for a time the complete partition of China.

Through my boyhood years, I had heard of all this when Uncle Jim's letters from Korea were read in the family circle. Unusual enough in America, brave little Queen Min's name was a household word with us. The saddened King of Korea was an object of our very personal sympathy. Yuan Shih-k'ai became known to us in Michigan long before his name was recognizable save in high political circles close to public affairs in the Far East. His photograph, a stout personage in sable jacket and mandarin hat, adorned our parlor album.

The American-educated Chinese, whom Yuan was astute enough to patronize and include in his suite, attended Aunt Hattie's afternoon teas and tennis parties at the Korean capital. Among them were Liang Tun-yen, afterward President of the Imperial Board of Foreign Affairs and an intimate friend of Rockhill's. I used to see the two seated together and in deep converse on the Peking club verandah. Liang had lived as a school boy in the home of the Rev. Mr. Bartlett at Hartford, Connecticut. Years later he invited the two Bartlett daughters, still unmarried, to come to Peking as guest-tutors in his family. We used to see them riding on the handsome grey mounts provided by their host. T'ang Shao-yi's brilliant career began at Seoul under Yuan Shih-k'ai. M. T. Liang, Sir Chow Shun-chao, member of the Governor's Council at Hongkong, and others served their apprenticeship in diplomacy at the Korean capital.

These were some of the youngsters whom Dr. Yung Wing had taken to Hartford in the early 1870's. Though Court jealousy brought them back prematurely, their eager minds had absorbed the language and much of the spirit of America. Several of them came to be reckoned with in the earlier days of the Republic in various important roles. Blessed with long life, four of them attended an American College Club dinner in early 1937 in Shanghai's ultra-modern Park Hotel. As past president of the Club I was selected to honor them with special copies of the *University Year Book*. T'ang Shao-yi, old and feeble, cruelly hatcheted to death in 1939, was the foremost of them all as statesman, administrator, industrialist. Others played their part in the swiftly moving drama of a cycle of Cathay, a full sixty years. I sat with Mr. T'ang Shao-yi in the lobby of the Palace Hotel at Shanghai on the first day of August, 1914. All thoughts were fixed on Europe. "Japan will move on Tsingtao, and eliminate Germany from the Far East," he prophetically observed. Japan declared war on Germany before the month was out.

Whether Yuan Shih-k'ai's adherence to progress was motivated by genuine patriotism or because he discerned in it means of advancing his ambitions, is impossible to determine. Outwardly his career appeared to be that of an opportunist. He it was who disclosed to the Empress Dowager the young Emperor's reform plans in 1898. The result was her swift *coup d'état*. The Emperor's advisers, such as the Cantonese scholars K'ang Yu-wei and Liang Ch'i-ch'ao, fled. Others were executed. The thirty-seven reform edicts of the "hundred days" were rescinded and the Emperor was placed under restraint. Thereafter he played no part in public affairs from his virtual prison on an island in the Palace Lagoons. Yuan now rapidly forged ahead under the favor of the Empress Dowager and after the death of his patron, Viceroy Li Hung-chang, succeeded to his one-time authority and prestige.

Yuan was an astute politician. At his military school at Paotingfu, a sort of West Point of China, he trained young officers for his "model army." These men he held to him by ties of personal loyalty, and they in turn came to play their part in the later welter of warlordism in China. With the death of the Empress Dowager, the wrath of the kinsmen of the Emperor Kuang Hsü, whom he had betrayed, fell upon him. He was suddenly permitted to retire from the capital to his Honan estate owing to an affliction in the foot which prevented him from performing the Court ceremonies. From there Yuan sent out to his friends photographs of himself arrayed in the garb of a simple fisherman. The romance of history is inbred in the Chinese. Was there not the statesman Yen Tzu-ling of old who withdrew from active politics and became a simple fisherman on the Ch'ien-t'ang river—and thereafter represented the Izaak Walton of China?

From his central China home at Hsiang-ch'eng, Yuan continued to pull the strings. The Revolution broke. The witless Manchu Court was seized with fear and uncertainty. Yuan alone could save them. He was recalled to highest office. New honors were heaped upon him. Playing a skillful game between the frightened Court and the exultant Cantonese revolutionists, he extracted an abdication edict from the Manchus on the one hand, and, on the other, induced Sun Yat-sen to retire as first Provisional President of the Republic. Yuan not only became President, but occupied as his "White House" the sacrosanct precincts of the erstwhile Imperial Palace.

Outplayed at every point, the Cantonese revolutionaries plotted Yuan's overthrow and the effectuation of the Republic. Dr. Sun Yat-sen, professional revolutionary and so-called Father of the Republic, was actually absent in Europe during the pangs of the Republic's birth. Generals Huang Hsing, Li Yuan-hung, and other fighting men midwifed this political offspring. Hurrying back to Nanking, Dr. Sun became titular Chief Executive for a brief day and then found himself once more playing his accustomed role—that of looking in from the outside. Yuan, always a believer in money as a potent political instrument, made a grant to Sun of $25,000 monthly, to keep him quiet. Sun busied himself ostensibly in drafting grandiose schemes for a vast railway network throughout China. Actually, as Yuan well knew, he was plotting a second revolution.

Sometime in June of 1913, I had an opportunity to call on Dr. Sun in his offices located in a large building in the well protected centre of the International Settlement at Shanghai. Here he could regard himself as safer even than in London, where in fact he had once been kidnapped and held incommunicado in the Chinese Legation. The excuse for my call was to escort an old friend, an American missionary, the Rev. Dr. Loomis, who years before had befriended Sun when he was an exile in Japan. The Father of the Chinese Revolution sat in characteristic upright attitude in his *chung-shan* jacket buttoned up to the chin. His features in countless later portraits became as familiar throughout Nationalist China and in overseas Chinese colonies as the ascetic face of Lenin in Russia, the prognathic jaw of Il Duce in Italy, or the unsmiling features of the Fuehrer, with outstretched arm in Naziland. Dr. Sun's rejoinders to our remarks were remote and laconic. He appeared absorbed in those reflections which saw the light in the series of unique economic utterances and original political aphorisms which formed the *Three Peoples Principles, biblia sacra* of renascent China.

Money and yet more money was what Yuan Shih-kai required to weather the coming political storm. General Ch'en Ch'i-mei, ardent revolutionary, was planning a military *coup* from temporary general headquarters in his favorite restaurant on Shanghai's gay Foochow road. He too would seize the Kiangnan Arsenal and arm the populace. Conservative diplomats and international bankers, led by the Doyen of the Diplomatic Corps, the British Minister at Peking, Sir John Jordan, looked upon Yuan as the Strong Man of China, the only one who could curb the frothy nonsense of the southern political visionaries. Finance and trade had been sufficiently disturbed by the Revolution and its aftermath. A period of political quiet was demanded. Sir John and Yuan had been cronies at the Korean capital years before, when both were comparatively young men embarking on careers of ultimate distinction.

The representatives of the Six Nation Banking Group were hastily summoned. They lent a sympathetic ear to Yuan's pleas for cash. Interminable, and thus far fruitless, negotiations for the "Currency Reform Loan" formed a handy vehicle for the present requirements. A new agreement was drafted, this time for a "Reorganization Loan." Payments from the Customs on account of the Boxer indemnity instalments, as well as of China's several other forms of international indebtedness, had been thrown into arrears by the fiscal confusion produced by the Revolution. These would be liquidated from the proceeds of the new loan. China's debts would thus be funded in the modern manner, which would satisfy foreign requirements. Then sums from the proposed twenty-five million pounds sterling could be assigned to a variety of domestic desiderata—currency reform, disbandment of surplus troops, army reorganization or what not. At least, very considerable amounts would come into Yuan's hands for free disposal against his political commitments, without being subject to too close audit.

Thus far everything proceeded smoothly. But then arose the question of security for the loan. The Customs had been stretched to the limit by the Boxer penalties and other overseas obligations. There was left only that hoary fiscal regime, the historic salt tax of China. It had been rather casually linked to some small previous loans. But its character as a purely Chinese public administration had really never been violated. But now the exacting bankers demanded no less than *the entire salt collections* of all China as security for their loan.

"Impossible," said Yuan. "I should have all the powerful Salt Commissioners, as well as the Cantonese revolutionaries, down on me."

There are always financial "sharpshooters" about during international negotiations of such magnitude. A London City agent, named Birch Crisp, broke in on the Consortium's monopoly by advancing Yuan five million pounds with another five millions to come. This competition brought the international bankers quickly to terms with Yuan. They would make advances at once. A pliant Finance Minister signed the loan agreement at three o'clock on the morning of April 27, 1913, and China's ancient salt tax was pawned to at least partial foreign financial control.

Willard Straight, wearied of the interminable wrangling at Peking, had long ago departed for New York. Straight had made a brave enough fanfare of his leaving despite the lack of success of his activities. All of the American Legation folk were at the station, as was most of Peking "society," to see him off in his private car, where his office staff continued busily at work. He had, it is true, signed on behalf of his Wall Street principals the Hu-Kuang railway loan. But none of the railways projected, despite considerable expenses for preliminaries, were completed until Chiang K'ai-shek's young American-trained engineers extended the line in the late 1930's through from Changsha to Canton in anticipation of the war with Japan.

New York, it seems, felt it could place its funds at least as profitably and certainly more safely at home. When Straight's enthusiasm waned, Messers. J. P. Morgan, his principals, lost interest as well. So much had been spent in the maintenance of their representatives at Peking, that the American bankers were loth to withdraw completely, and thus be compelled to write off their losses. They counseled with the State Department, now in the charge of Secretary of State Bryan. President Wilson was introduced into the picture. The idealists concerted on a policy of nonsupport of the loan on grounds that it involved "the pledging of particular taxes, some of them antiquated and burdensome," and also "the administration of those taxes by foreign agents;" and that anyway support of our bankers in an international loan to China "might conceivably go to the length in some unhappy contingency of forcible interference in the financial, and even the political, affairs of that great Oriental State, just now awakening to a consciousness of its power and of its obligations to its people." This pronouncement was delivered on March 18, 1913, to the press by the White House, and not by the Department of State the regular channel for such releases.

The American bankers now left it to their British, French, German, Russian, and Japanese associates to consummate the loans. Belgium, "jackal to France's lion," appeared also in the financial picture. Wall Street seemed glad of an excuse to withdraw from the China field, what a banker later described to me as a "financial headache." The political squeamishness of the U. S. Government did not last long. Later in the Wilson administration, at the request of the State Department, American interests again entered the international banking consortium. But for the time being, European bankers were thoroughly satisfied. They had secured a strangle-hold on China's remaining "pillar of finance," the Salt Gabelle, second only to the foreign administered Customs service. They saw no reason for regretting the loss of the Americans who anyhow never played the game of financial imperialism as they conceived it should be played.

On that 26th of April, 1913, a forlorn figure sat out the night on the

128

stone steps of the British Hongkong & Shanghai Banking Corporation premises on Peking's Legation Street. China's historic salt tax was being signed over to foreign control. The lone protestant was my young Chinese friend of Ann Arbor, "C. T." Wang.

Implementing the Loan Agreement

SWEEPING CHANGES, the most far-reaching in the two thousand years of the recorded history of China's salt tax, were now to be carried out in association with foreign experts. A Chief Inspectorate of Salt Revenue was created at Peking, represented in the provinces by District Inspectorates and in the "Yangtze transportation offices" by the Audit offices of the Salt Revenue. In each salt producing district, the Chinese and the Foreign District Inspectors, under authority of the Chief Inspectors at Peking became jointly responsible for collection and deposit of the salt revenue and for the issuance of permits for the release of salt from the Government-supervised stores.

The amount of thirteen million taels (twenty million Chinese silver dollars * approximately) generally agreed upon as the net sum obtained by the Central Government prior to the reorganization, now swelled rapidly to $60,409,976 in 1914, and by 1922 reached as high as $84,789,049. These results were attained by the consolidation of heterogeneous taxes, dues, and even "voluntary contributions." Such results were made possible by the centralized control of the strong military organization of President Yuan Shih-k'ai.

An important reform was the restoration of a principle known to have been operative as far back as the T'ang era (618–907 A.D.). This required that the salt tax be paid in full when salt supplies were purchased by wholesale distributors at the place of manufacture. The procedure was now revived, copying the modern British operated salt administration of India. Some necessary exceptions to this rule continued, however, as in the Yangtze provinces, where, as will be later described, part of the salt tax was paid by the ultimate consumer. Measures were taken, only partially successful, to abolish official and private salt monopolies, found to be the most expensive and unsatisfactory method of raising revenue. The monopoly merchants who supplied the Central Yangtze provinces were left undisturbed. These powerful traders were responsible for regular shipments of salt from the sea coast to the interior consuming districts and for the payment of the full duty thereon. The government could not risk disturbing these revenues by precipitate "reforms." The salt works in the various producing districts, operated by private interests, were brought under more effective government control. Smuggling of untaxed salt was greatly curtailed.

---

* All figures given, unless otherwise noted, are in Chinese silver dollars, which ranged in value from as high as par with the American dollar (in 1919–20), or even higher, to as low as forty-two cents, or less.

129

A standard unit for taxing salt was a further useful innovation in a trade involving as many standards of weight as there were districts. Administrative economies were introduced wherever possible. The fruits of the reorganization became at once apparent in the production of large surpluses of salt revenue over the amounts required for the service of loans, and at the free disposal of the Chinese Government reaching as high as $78,861,-682 in 1922. Later under inflationary conditions, the "dollar figures" of these sums were infinitely increased.

Thus after payment of all operating expenses, and interest and amortization charges on foreign loans, the Chinese treasury was enjoying almost four times as much *net* revenue as the whole reported collection when the reorganization of the salt revenue administration with the assistance of foreign officers began in May, 1913.

The new administrative regime reached a high point in 1922. After this year a serious decline in income ensued, due, not to any inherent defect in the administration, but to the increasing political chaos of the succeeding years. By 1926 a sum of only $8,868,828 was actually remitted into the central treasury. Province after province resumed local control over salt. Regional governors, defying Peking, were quick to turn their attention to the salt revenue collectorates, whose ready funds served to finance and perpetuate civil war. The result was, by 1926, a virtual collapse of the Administration. At the end of that year, the Associate (foreign) Chief Inspector, in a note to the British, French, and Japanese banks which still retained an interest in the Reorganization Loan, pointed out that almost no fresh funds were being received for the service of the loans secured on the salt tax.

The consolidation of the Nationalist Government in 1927 under General Chiang K'ai-shek and its recognition by the Powers enabled the salt administration to enter upon a new phase. Dr. T. V. Soong, in his capacity as Minister of Finance, announced through the press in February, 1928, that in the service of loans, responsibility for payments would be assumed by the Ministry itself. The original loan terms provided that all salt revenue collections should first be deposited in the China agencies of the foreign lending banks. Only when all payments due to the banks and the bond-holders had been made by the banks, was the remaining surplus to be handed over to the Chinese government. To this new arrangement the foreign banking interests agreed, thereby countenancing the infraction of the specific terms of the loan. This they did, however, on the grounds that the new proposals, originating with the Minister of Finance, offered better prospects of payments to holders of bonds secured on the salt revenue.

After the restoration of the Inspectorate to its full functioning at the end of 1928, a striking program of progress raised the gross collections of salt revenue to $125 millions in 1932. The seizure of Manchuria by Japan in 1932 caused a net setback of some $20 millions; but the upward trend

130

continued to reach its maximum in 1936, when $201 millions were accounted for to the Chinese treasury. Between 1929 and 1935 China's annual salt revenue collection was increased by almost 117 per cent. This was a far cry from the record of the first year of the Inspectorate, twenty-two years before, $19,044,200. The possibilities of the Chinese salt tax under efficient administration were thus strikingly exemplified.

The duty on salt had been increased in the meantime, to be sure, both by actual increase in rates and by the reduction in size of the taxable unit of salt to the so-called metric picul of 50 kilograms or 110.23 pounds. This was incidental to the general introduction of standard metric weights to replace the varying customary standards used throughout China. As in the case of our own *avoirdupois, troy* and *apothecary* weights, so the Chinese have had a variety of standards of weights. The number of these however has been legion, differing in many localities and with various commodities.

The achievements of the Salt Revenue Administration after the reorganization measures following 1928 were notable in the history of public finance in China. These measures were to concentrate all functions within the modernized Inspectorate itself, to eradicate ancient practices involving personal sources of profit to the Salt Administration staff, to reorganize along lines of greater efficiency the salt revenue guards whose duty it was to prevent smuggling, to construct Government salt depots in the great producing districts, and to effect better conrol of the salt works themselves.

The primary concern of the foreign public, the service of foreign loans secured directly upon the salt revenue collections, was satisfactorily answered. Service of the Anglo-French, "Crisp" and Hukuang Railway Loans was met from the "loan quotas" imposed upon each salt revenue collecting District. At the same time, substantial progress was made in clearing up arrears in these loans. The credit of China so far as foreign loans secured on the salt revenue are concerned, was maintained at an enviable point, despite financial pressure sustained by the loss of the Manchurian revenues, distress caused by disastrous Yangtze River floods, the military operations of 1931 about Shanghai, and recalcitrant peripheral provincial authorities who diverted salt revenue collections to their own local uses.

The modern civil service arrangement set up for the salt administration proved an example to other organs of the Chinese government. The strict maintenance of civil service ideals, involving reasonable compensation for employees, resulted in promoting efficiency and *esprit de corps* in this Service. It was hoped that rather than permit any impairment of these principles governing a great civil service, a constructive policy would continue to be followed whereby they would be extended to most other branches of the Chinese government.

SIR RICHARD MORRIS DANE, Knight Commander of the Star of India, was not a newcomer to China when he was invited to take charge of the reform of the Salt Gabelle, under the terms of the Reorganization Loan of 1913. Sir Richard had made a name for himself when he visited Canton with Lord Brassey's Royal Commission on opium in the early 1890's. He had marshalled the evidence for the Government of India in a monograph on the history of the drug in India and China which "knocked the bottom out of the case of the anti-opiumists that the Indian Government was responsible for the opium habit in China by pressing the Indian product on that country."

I used occasionally to walk with Sir Richard from his quarters near Legation Street to his office in the Central Salt Administration Building. This was after I had joined the salt service in 1914. I was frequently called from my headquarters at Hankow for conference at Peking. Our way would take us on to the broad thoroughfare known as the Ch'ang An Chieh, "The Street of Prolonged Tranquility," which skirts the vermilion walls of the Forbidden City just north of the old British Legation *glaçis*. Yuan Shih-k'ai was President of the Republic and we could see above the walls the yellow tiled roofs of the quondam Imperial palace where he now resided. Sir Richard's ricksha puller would trail behind, as we walked along. When the old gentleman felt himself becoming a bit warm from the exertion, he would climb into the two-wheeled vehicle and be trundled on to his office. If I happened to walk on his right, he would order me to the left which was his good-ear side. He limped somewhat—an old injury from some big game hunt in India, Africa, or Borneo. His eyesight too was weak. Back in 1878–79 when he spent a short spell in the Foreign Department of the Government of India, an opposing player in a polo match at Lahore nearly knocked his right eye out with a backhander. The eye was saved but he was disfigured for life. Thenceforth he shot his lions, tigers, bears, bison, rhinoceroses, and smaller game, from the left shoulder.

He used to talk to me with keen satisfaction about those early researches he made on the spot at Canton for his opium report. His humour was robust but always kindly.

"Without a sense of humour in China, we'd have to give it all up," he used to say.

One day when I had heard that he might be retiring to England, I made bold to ask him for his photograph as a memento of our association.

"Tut, tut," said the old man as a grim smile overspread his rugged features. "It's not so handsome. You can't make a silk purse out of a sow's ear."

Sir Richard was of that stalwart race of British administrators who held India for so many generations. The Danes were a versatile family. Sir Louis, the younger brother, was a Lieutenant-Governor of the Punjab, and one of several unlucky Anglo-Indian administrators who were wounded by the revolver of an Indian patriot in Caxton Hall when General O'Dwyer was shot down. This was a belated echo of the tragedy at Amritsar when British troops fired on an Indian mob, killing 100 and wounding 1200. O'Dwyer was Lieutenant-Governor of the Punjab at the time and strongly supported General Dyer, the officer responsible for the command to fire. The East has a long memory!

Upon the hasty conclusion of the Reorganization Loan Agreement on April 26, 1913, the practical question arose at once of the reform of the system of collecting the salt tax. As early as 1898 the revenue derived from salt had been designated as security, in part or in whole, for loans contracted by the Chinese government with foreign bankers. The payment of principal and interest upon these and other subsequent loans such as the Anglo-French and the Hu-Kuang (Central China) railway loans, had been so prompt and uninterrupted that no interference with the collection of the salt tax had been necessary by the foreign lenders. It was not until the conclusion of the "Reorganization Loan" of 1913 that China "engaged to take immediate steps for the reorganization of the collection of the salt revenue."

The problem was to secure a taxation expert to advise and assist the Chinese government in its task. From which of the nationalities making the loan, should the foreign "Chief Inspector" be appointed? Should he be a person familiar with China, one of the senior foreign Commissioners of Customs, or should he be a specialist in public finance from overseas? The Chinese government selected an able Dane with a long career behind him in the Chinese Customs, Mr. J. F. Oiesen. (Oiesen later became his country's Minister to China.) As Mr. Oiesen informed me years after, his appointment as director of the salt tax reorganization was actually gazetted, but immediately protested by the French Minister at the (doubtless personally regretted) instigation of his life-long friend the British Minister, Sir John Jordan. The Quintuple Banking Group would have none of him, a "neutral." Finally a bargain was struck. A British subject would be appointed Associate (i.e. foreign) Chief Inspector of Salt Revenue, a German as his principal deputy, while a Russian and a Frenchman were each given high advisory posts in the Bureau of Audit. The Danish candidate of the Chinese government was summarily jettisoned. "Due compensation" was thus found for all the Powers represented save Japan. The latter did not, it appeared, demand posts for its nationals, for, as in the case of Russia, Japan had no money to lend China. These two floated their shares of the loan on the Paris and London bourses. Japanese nationals, it appeared, were to head the principal salt tax collecting districts, a matter of no small satisfaction and advantage. This arrangement was based on an undertaking that in the award of appointments the nationals of the loaning powers not given positions in the government at Peking, should find compensation elsewhere, viz., in district inspectorates.

133

Of course, no provision was made for the employment of American citizens as the American government had withdrawn its support from the Reorganization Loan on March 18, 1913.

British interests as usual were able to produce an admirably qualified expert for the colossal task of reforming the system of collecting the salt tax of China. During his many years in India, Sir Richard Dane had served successively as an under-secretary to the Government of the Punjab, as a boundary settlement officer in Central India, and as an assistant-commissioner for the Indian States. As far back as 1890, he had served as commissioner of excise and inspector-general of registration. He established his reputation as an excise officer with his notable report on India's opium trade with China. Thereafter his advancement had been rapid. Following service as secretary in the Finance and Commerce Department, he became Commissioner of Salt Revenue for Northern India in 1898— a welcome post for so keen a big-game sportsman, but one which had before been regarded as something of a sinecure. He took up the commissionership with his accustomed zeal and changed it into a live appointment. He had a bluff and hearty manner, and in his constant touring of all parts of the Punjab he endeared himself to the people. In 1907 he was made the first Inspector General of Excise and Salt for India. When he retired in 1909, he was awarded the Knight Commandership of the Star of India.

No other nation has equaled the British in its type of colonial administrator. The far-flung Empire provided unparalleled training for its favored sons. As in the case of the mandarins of old China, a "classical" education had been all that was required. Competitive selection, upon either the basis of the Confucian writings, or the Greek and Latin classics, produced, respectively, China's and England's great public servants, a Tseng Kuofan, civilian-military genius of the T'ai-p'ing rebellion, or a Lord Cromer, rehabilitator of a bankrupt and demoralized Egypt. The two apparently disparate types of mental discipline, memorizing Confucius or conning Horace, were identical at least in enabling talent to disclose itself. Sir Robert Hart, Sir John Jordan, Sir Richard Dane were all products of this system and their services to their country and to China were notable.

The experience of Dane in India adapted him admirably to the final and greatest task of his career in a new field, China. The criticisms ultimately advanced against him involved the very virtues he had displayed in his fiscal activities in India. His reforms showed that economy and efficiency go hand in hand. One day he remarked to me in his pithy manner.

"China is virtually a bankrupt government, yet it can unconcernedly indulge in any extravagance that comes to the mind of its officials. India's public finance is on a sound foundation; yet any uncommon expenditure is very carefully considered beforehand."

If the British and other bankers anticipated a pliant tool in their selection, they were disappointed. Dane's honesty and independence of char-

134

acter led him to oppose oppressive measures by the foreign banks upon the Chinese, as well as to wage relentless warfare against corrupt Chinese officials.

The Paris government sought to force China to pay certain claims which were under dispute, on penalty of withholding surplus salt revenue balances held in the French official agency, the Banque de l'Indo Chine, to the credit of the necessitous Chinese treasury. Sir Richard Dane immediately declared this illegal and unfair and demanded the release to China of the impounded funds, under threat of resignation. The Quai d'Orsay yielded. . . . A certain General Soong demanded a preposterous sum for the upkeep of his salt-guard battalions. His demands were accompanied with the insinuation usual in such cases that unless the money were forthcoming, he would be unable to restrain his starving soldiers from looting the salt store-houses. Sir Richard proceeded forthwith to the General's headquarters and suggested an immediate review on the parade ground of the General's entire active forces. A sorry scattering of ragamuffins was all the General could muster. The General's allowance was correspondingly scaled down.

The veteran of council room and *safari* retired after six years' service. He was awarded high Chinese decorations to add to those won in the Indian service. He had earned the respect of both bankers and mandarins. A high Chinese official declared that there were three foreigners who had really helped the Chinese, General "Chinese" Gordon, Robert Hart, and Richard Dane—and to Dane they owed most. Discounting Oriental hyperbole, there was much truth in this encomium. Like all colonial Britons, he had looked forward to the years of retirement, the life of slippered ease at home. There I found him in truth in the winter of 1937, on his beloved Hereford estate, Morney Cross. Though an octogenarian, he was still fishing the Wye for salmon. In his old vigorous style he wrote me a cordial note to come and visit him and tell him all about China.

*   *   *

Mr. Cho had ideas of my father's sixtieth birthday far transcending my own. This event is the first great congratulatory milestone in life among the Chinese. It is the "Cycle of Cathay." Happy is he who passes this "thousand autumns" on the steepening pathway of life. Happier is he who in filial gratitude is privileged reverently to celebrate such an auspicious occasion in his father's honor. Thus, unknown to me, word was sent up and down the Yangtze Valley. For days before, large red satin scrolls, on which were emblazoned congratulatory sentiments in golden letters, silver cups and vases inscribed appropriately to mark the occasion, came to the house at Hankow in swelling volume. Each was brought by a special messenger and in the custom of China must be acknowledged by a gratuity to the bearer in proportion to the value of the gift. These cash gratuities promised to run into considerable money.

On the day itself guests began to arrive from near and far. The original feast prepared was wholly inadequate. Chinese restaurants, which will send out whole meals of many courses, served piping hot, were called upon to provide for the overflow. Additional tables were set up in the drawing room, in the hallway. My wife arranged for the Chinese ladies in the bedrooms above. The overflow reached the office, while hungry guests still poured in.

All first made obeisance before my father's festively red-draped portrait in the large hallway. When that sturdy Aberdeen Scotsman, John Gale, and his Pennsylvania-born wife, Miami Bradt, on a stony hillside farm up in mid-Ontario, contemplated on a chilly first day of November, 1855, their third child and second son whom they were to call Hugh McLaren, nothing could have been so far from their expectations as that precisely sixty years thence this obscure occasion would be celebrated in Central China with all the ceremoniousness of twenty centuries of Confucian ritual.

*   *   *

It was about this time that we were honored with a visit by Chang Hu, Vice Minister of Finance, Chief of the Central Salt Administration and colleague to Sir Richard Dane in the Chief Inspectorate of Salt Revenue at Peking. Mr. Chang had been responsible for my appointment as an American to the important Yangtze Transportation Offices. The Vice Minister knew no foreign languages, save perhaps Japanese, which, especially in written form, is readily enough learned by Chinese. Yet he appeared to be extraordinarily well informed. When I first called upon him at Peking he was gracious enough to make favorable comment upon my command of Chinese. At a subsequent well appointed dinner which he gave in my honor, a burned-out fuse suddenly plunged the large party in darkness. Our host, with the poise which characterizes the Chinese gentleman, continued the conversation as undisturbed as though nothing had happened. Mr. Chang was a brilliant and versatile administrator and enjoyed the full confidence and respect of Sir Richard Dane. Upon his arrival at Hankow I arranged a call on the American Consul General, Edwin S. Cunningham, whom the Vice Minister had expressed a desire to meet. At the ensuing interview, the experienced Chinese official impressed upon the Consul General the desirability of using official channels only as a last resort. Informal adjustment of matters in controversy between American and Chinese interests, made settlements the more easy.

Upon the occasion of the Vice Minister's visit, the ancient and honorable, the Salt Merchants Guild, provided sumptuous entertainment for President Yuan Shih-K'ai's powerful Vice Minister. The merchant guilds of China antedate those similar venerable organizations in England by many years. The most respected London bankers and merchants vie for membership in the Liveried Companies, the Pepperers, the Salters, and the

136

Fish-mongers Guild. Time and again these organizations have sturdily banded with others to deny "forced contributions" to an exiguous British Crown. Similarly the salt merchants guilds of China were designed, among other mutually beneficial purposes, to withstand the exactions of oppressive officialdom. Even the most rapacious Transportation Officer has been obliged to moderate his demands when faced by the united front of the Yangtze guilds. On the other hand, Chinese governments, Imperial, Republican or Nationalist, have turned to the salt merchants when their needs were greatest. For the salt monopoly merchants of the Yangtze valley have been the wealthiest capitalists of all China. Their houses date back for generations. Like the widow's cruse, the salt merchants' coffers were never empty.

The salt monopoly merchants of the Yangtze valley, I found, were formed of two interlocking groups. One group was made up of actual license owners. It is they who held the original certificates granting their privileges. These documents entitled the holders each to transport a specified quantity of salt, according to a stated numerical or rotationary order, to a designated provincial area in Central China. Some, or most of these license holders had long ceased to play an active part in the business. They accordingly leased their shipping rights to transporting merchants. The latter actually operated the salt trade between the salt manufacturers on the sea coast, and the wholesale distributors in the up-river consumption districts. The Transportation Officers supervised all these operations to insure the payment of the salt tax. The system has been known as one of "merchant-transportation, government-supervision," truly one of the most ingenious fiscal systems in the world.

My own relations with the salt merchants guilds of the central Yangtze valley were constant and intimate. In times of stress when the armies of rival warlords were commandeering junks on the waterways the merchants would call upon me to aid in the recovery of their argosies. When impecunious governments at Peking increased their pressure for "benevolences," or sought to raise the salt tax to heights curtailing public consumption, they appealed to my good offices. They were men of substance, their word was as good as their bond.

The merchants controlled fleets of river junks, all of which were registered with the government. Their captains and crews were hard bitten, weather-tanned, accustomed to daily risks of ship and cargo, and often life, on the yellow torrent against which they constantly strove. Stranding or wrecking of salt junks was immediately reported to the nearest Audit Office for the dispatch of official investigators to verify the loss. Thereby not only might the owner of the cargo secure a new consignment of salt free of advance duty, but the deferred duty payable on the lost shipment would be waived. When I happened to be in the vicinity of a reported wreck, I would make a point of visiting the scene of the disaster. There, to be sure, the naked masts of the foundered junk would appear above

137

the water, perhaps also the partly submerged hull, while piled up on the nearby bank would be hundreds of empty rush bags as witness to the doleful story.

But all was not prosaic business or stark tragedy in the Salt Merchants Guilds. Their lofty incense-scented guild-halls—where fragrant sticks burned before the shrine to patron god of salt and sail—were scenes of jovial feasts and merry theatricals. At the head of the table sat the venerable chairman of the guild, old and wise in the ways of crafty mandarins and dishonest junkmen. The feasts were dignified enough until the hot rice wine had made its several rounds. Tongues were then loosed; markets and money formed the invariable topics of conversation until the last of the score of courses had been tasted. All then withdrew to the stiff ebony-wood chairs along the side walls to sip tea from covered porcelain bowls.

I frequently visited Changsha headquarters as the guest of the U.S. Consul. One invitation of the Salt Merchants Guild to dinner led to another. It was not long before I succumbed to the continued diet of rich viands. To preserve an already overtaxed digestion, I made my escape by taking the first river-steamer back to Hankow. A constitution notoriously impervious to all gastronomic assaults enabled Consul Johnson, future Ambassador to China, to outwear even the hardy salt merchants themselves.

Consul Johnson and I often deserted the conventional comforts of his official establishment to sleep on hot nights on camp-cots set up among the cool rockeries of the adjacent garden, a memorial to Tso Tsung-t'ang, one of China's greatest military figures. Fellow provincial of Tseng Kuo-fan, with whom he cooperated in the suppression of the T'ai-ping rebels, General Tso was sent on to pacify the Mohammedan areas in the extreme western marches of China which in the 1870's seethed with rebellion under their chieftain Yakub Beg. Tso's method, leading to the victorious issue of his protracted campaigns, was to occupy a region with his troops long enough to grow a crop, then proceed to farther territories in turn. This was the celebrated "military-field" system of garrisoning, and ultimately settling outlying lands, devised by the ancient Chinese in expanding the Empire.

The Stratagems of Warlord Wang

IT HAD BECOME my duty to cross the River from Hankow to the provincial capital, the walled city of Wuchang, to remonstrate with the Military Governor of Hupeh, General Wang Chan-yuan. Peking had instructed me to lodge a "vigorous protest" with this provincial Warlord for his interference with the smooth working of the national salt tax in his territories. Wang was guilty of the unauthorized introduction into the province's markets of a couple of steamerloads of salt as a private venture of His Excellency, to the disturbance of the legitimate monopoly-merchants' trade and profits. Furthermore the Provincial Treasurer, because of the stress of securing funds for Warlord Wang's numerous official *entourage,* had added a local "surtax" upon the already heavy salt duties.

This was the period of "China under the *tuchüns*" or military governors. After President Yuan Shih-k'ai's death in June 1916, his military regime was perpetuated. The principal feature of Yuan's tenure of office had been a temporary consolidation of the government under his army chiefs whom he had appointed to head the different provinces. There soon ensued a struggle between himself and the fledgeling parliamentarians as to whether the executive or legislative branches should dominate. To support his regime, the cash proceeds of the "Crisp" and the "Reorganization" loans negotiated on the security of the salt tax, had been devoted. It was in Yuan's presidency that the World War and Japan's seizure of Germany's holdings in Shantung occurred. The presentation of the notorious "Twenty One Demands" in 1915 foreshadowed Japan's later policy of encroachment on China's sovereignty. I happened at the time to be in Peking on some special work. Daily I watched the departure of the emissaries of Japan from their headquarters at the Grand Hotel des Wagons-Lits to demand President Yuan's acceptance of these disastrous terms. Only partially accepted then, the attempt was made anew twenty-four years later, to put them into effect in a "New Order" in East Asia.

Yuan closed his career in June, 1916, with the tragic attempt to restore the monarchy, with himself as the first of a new dynasty. His political legacy to his country was to leave his former army henchmen as military governors in control of the provinces. These *tuchüns* were without loyalty to the state, but primarily concerned with their own personal power and the enrichment of their families and supporters. The period from 1913 to 1927 retarded China's modernization until it came almost too late.

Tuchün Wang, his detractors said, had originally been Yuan Shih-k'ai's head chair-bearer. Whenever I confronted Warlord Wang I actually felt, despite an assumed stern exterior, a bit shamefaced. For the Military Governor of Hupeh put me in mind of my maternal grandfather, William Henry McDowell. There was, I fancied, an unmistakable physical and spiritual resemblance. Both were tall and ruggedly built. Both had small piercing eyes. To be sure, General Wang's were of a peculiar hazel, found in China only among certain warlike people of Shantung province, whence the General hailed. My grandfather's were a steely grey, after the Ulster manner. Both wore sparse grey beards. Both inspired me with awe, if not fear, for there could be a latent fighting quality about them indicated by a menacing gleam of the eyes.

With these secret impressions in mind, certainly unsuspected by the *Tuchün,* I gathered myself together and delivered in my best classic Chinese the burden of the Central Salt Administration's grievances against the local authorities.

Warlord Wang in turn assuming the manner that the old time Chinese official was adept at, and in the simplest colloquial, invited me.

"Let's sit down and have a chat. How is the health of my highly esteemed friend, your honorable country's Consul General, Mr. Cunningham?"

Under the disarming influence of this friendly greeting, how could I not become even more loathe to disturb such an ideal relationship by the introduction of a sharply worded "protest." I finally handed the *Tuchün* without further oral explanation a previously prepared *aide-mémoire,* written of course in Chinese characters. He mildly took it in his hands, adjusted his huge horn-rimmed spectacles, and scrutinized the document upside down. The mighty Warlord was completely illiterate in his own, as well as in all other languages. After an appropriate interval of careful perusal, he ended the solemn make-believe by handing the paper to his waiting secretary. The business part of the interview ended with assurances that there must be some misunderstanding on the part of the Peking government as of course the authorities of his province would never, never do anything out of harmony with the Capital's wishes. If certain irresponsible underlings had exceeded their authority, they would be duly punished. An invitation to join him and his staff at lunch followed.

The ensuing luncheon was an informal and sociable affair. His Excellency, after politely assigning me the place of honor in China, which is the left, seated himself at the table. With us was the gubernatorial staff— the harried provincial Treasurer, the Colonel in command of the Governor's body guard, the Chief Secretary and others. *Tuchün* Wang directed at me certain questions of a personal, though in Chinese etiquette, highly courteous nature. What was my salary; did I have much money put away? How many sons did I have (question *re* daughters usually waived)? Were my parents living? How happy I must be that my venerable father had just celebrated his "sixth-decade" birthday. Conversation, which was largely monopolized by the host, then became reminiscent. The general related the hardships he had undergone when the Chinese fortress at Port Arthur in south Manchuria was besieged back in 1894 in the Sino-Japanese war. As a young officer in the garrison he with his comrades had been reduced to the extremity of eating nothing but boiled millet, with not a grain of rice available.

As the reward of a long military career, and after several years tenure as governor of this rich central China province of Hupeh, General Wang was credited with having amassed a fortune of some twenty million silver dollars. For greater security this was for the most part stored away in the vaults of the foreign banks at Shanghai. Now the Chinese believe in moderation in all things. It is the Confucian doctrine, adumbrated in the famous classic the *Doctrine of the Mean,* memorized by all Chinese school boys. Thus several impecunious military governors of the neighboring but less opulent provinces felt that the time had come for General Wang to retire and enjoy the leisure that a life full of war's alarums entitled him to. The commanders of the armies in nearby Hunan, General Chang Ching-

140

yao in control of the central region, and General Feng Yü-hsiang in the west, thereupon moved upon Wuchang.

Opposition to the clinging to an office for an excessive period against good sense and tradition, is not confined to any one country. Officials in China too are expected to "play cricket." It is the unsatisfied political adherents who usually force their successful but tired leader to continue in office. General Wang could muster little support against his poor but vigorous adversaries. He was, therefore, prepared to vacate his post. Only one consideration delayed action. If he could hold out until the tenth of the coming month, he might collect once more the "military subsidy" of $100,000. He had blackmailed the Peking authorities to agree to this subsidy by veiled threats that his otherwise "unpaid" troops might seize all the salt taxes of his province.

I had been given complete discretionary authority as to signing and issuing on the tenth of each month the cheque upon the Salt Revenue's bank account for the *Tuchün's* $100,000. The armies of Generals Chang and Feng were known to be marching on the virtually undefended provincial capital. The tenth was rapidly approaching and General Wang became more and more apprehensive of being shut out of the final payment. I, on my part, had information that another strong and well equipped force was hurrying north, to share in the spoils of Wu-ch'ang. Its commander was General Wu Pei-fu, whose strategy doubtless was to carry off the whole prize, while General Chang and General Feng fought over it. The Hupeh governor's Provincial Treasurer repeatedly called on me, urging on various grounds the immediate issue of the subsidy. The hostile armies and the fateful tenth of the month loomed over us. At length a messenger direct from the *Tuchün* sought me out privately in my home. "His Excellency," the special deputy confided, "proposes to provide you with his sealed receipt for the full hundred thousand dollars, but will himself be satisfied with a cheque for fifty thousand." I begged to be excused, on grounds that the necessary telegraphic instructions from Peking for the issue of the current month's military subvention had not yet reached me.

Noblesse oblige is a well understood aphorism in China. When the inevitable moment of retirement came as superior forces closed in, an avenue of retreat was noticeably left open. General Wang was permitted to withdraw in good order and with most of his possessions intact. The succeeding generals knew that the day would come when they too would find themselves in a similar predicament. They too would desire the consideration of the conquerer. "Woe to the conquered" finds no counterpart in the Chinese vocabulary; rather as the old military philosopher Sun-tzu said in his *Art of War*. "Do not press your enemy too closely."

By the tenth, General Wu had skillfully manoeuvered himself into the provincial capital, while Generals Chang and Feng had retired to their original positions. The cheque for the full hundred thousand dollars was issued to the victor.

141

THE SUMMER HEAT of Hankow is proverbial. Hence in the days before artificial ice, food and especially meats could be kept only with difficulty. Contrary to the Confucian maxim "Taste not the flesh of the creature whose dying cry you've heard," the squawk of the live chicken in the kitchen preceded its appearance *à la Maryland* in the dining-room by only a brief interval. In earlier days, even vegetables were scarce. Thus a heat-exhausted wit one evening in the Club bar was moved to describe summer Hankow as "an island of chicken-and-rice wholly surrounded by Scotch-and-soda."

Occidental residents of the three Wu-han cities sought refuge from summer's rigors in nearby mountain resorts. Missionaries and teachers left early for the cool heights. Families of business men and consular officials did also; but their men-folk could spare only occasional fortnights or prolonged week-ends.

The principal refuge in central China's torrid season was the fairly lofty Lu range where an extensive summer colony grew up. With customary enterprise, it was a group of British and American missionaries who had first seen the possibilities of this site, four thousand feet above the steaming river valley. Foremost among them was Edward S. Little, an extraordinarily versatile Australian, who later developed the distribution of chemical fertilizers to enormous magnitude in China; and an Englishman, John Berkin, who during a long lifetime devoted himself to the promotion of the great hill resort. At a point known as Ku-ling, "Ox-ridge," the pioneers marked out roads and lots and established a local self-governing council. In time scores of substantial stone bungalows dotted the verdured hills. The creek which ran through the mountain-top valley was trained and bridged. Dams impounding the water for swimming pools were constructed, tennis courts laid out; church, library, hospital, assembly-hall were built. Eminent divines from overseas were invited for summer "Chatauqua" lectures and conventions. Enterprising Chinese tradesmen—butcher, baker, builder, tin-smith, grocer, tailor—all set up shop in "the Gap," the populous Chinese village at the entrance to the foreign settlement. Within a couple of decades this mountain-top eyrie became one of the most flourishing European colonies in China, vieing with the gay seaside summer cottage resort of Peitaiho in North China, and Tsingtao with its hotels and villas on the Shantung beaches.

After torrid weeks when the mercury inexorably climbed day after day to the hundred mark, and a tennis match on the Race Club courts wrung all the liquid out of one, the vacationer boarded the 9:30 evening steamer for the down river port of Kiukiang. A holiday spirit reinvigorated the wilted group of European and American males who gathered in the first-class smoking room. Early next morning the big steamer swung in the swift current alongside the landing hulk at Kiukiang's riverside. This was

142

the black painted hull of an ancient fiddle-bow clipper, once the pride of the seas, now ingloriously moored out in deep water with heavy chains fore and aft, her anchors forever in the bottomless silt of the Yangtze. Manila cigars were briskly lighted after a hearty breakfast; the mere sight of the cloud wrapped ridge of the Lu-shan energized the party for their day long, hot journey. Accompanying a few belated up river missionary families, we would all cross the long planking leading from the hulk to the "Bund." This was the usual shaded thoroughfare along the river front, onto which faced the various consular buildings and the principal British shipping firms. Kiukiang was one of the "ports" opened by the 1858–1860 series of treaties. It had its neat British Concession, a minute replica of the one at Hankow, built adjacent to the sprawling native city with its narrow shop-lined streets and lack of sanitary services.

In secular no less than spiritual matters, the British and American missionaries excelled. Here at the annual landing port each summer for several thousand whites—men, women, and children—they had set up a rest house and transport office. The journey in the earlier days was entirely by sedan chair, carried by lean bearers who swung swiftly along the first eleven miles across the super-heated plain to the foothills. Here the bearers were changed for the arduous climb—up, up thousands of rough stone steps, until the cool misty heights above were reached. The transport office arranged for all this, rent of chairs, hire of porters and baggage coolies, even to the rate of "cumsha," or customary tips. Without such organization there would have been pandemonium among the thousands of coolies, heated controversies over rates of payment, and infinite delays in getting on with the journey.

In later years a road was built across the plain, bridges were reinforced, and motor cars carried passengers speedily to the foothills. But the sure-footed, sinewy chair-coolies still plodded upward with their heavy burdens, to frequently changing the carrying poles from one aching shoulder to another just as the chair might be swinging out over a dizzy height or yawning chasm, but with never a mishap on record. Patient plodding specimens of humanity, thin to bone and muscle, clad in a few cents' worth of blue denim, straw sandals to save their weary feet from the bruising stones of the pathway; and at the end of hours of toil of draught animals, a few coppers for a bowl of rice and vegetable! Such has been the yellow man's burden in cruel Asia!

*   *   *

"As sure as the gods made little apples," observed my host sententiously but with a twinkle in his blue Nordic eyes, "you have ruined a most excellent wine."

I had stupidly enough taken a vintage Burgundy for an ordinary table claret, and had diluted it with water from my glass. We were lunching together in the comfortable bungalow at Ku-ling assigned to the Hankow

143

Commissioner of Customs for his use during the hot weather. A bell was clanging from the nearby Assembly Hall. Noon-day service was proceeding, with refrains of Moody and Sankey's stirring gospel hymns. Commissioner of Customs Oiesen and I had had a long walk that morning. We had scaled the ridges which commanded, from a 4000 foot elevation, magnificent views of the Yangtze far below, swollen with its ochre-colored summer flood. The Great River meandered eastward across the plains on the way to the far distant Yellow Sea. River steamers, looking like tiny toys from our height, could be seen making their way up or down, or manoeuvering in the swift current to tie up to the Kiukiang hulks.

Commissioner J. F. Oiesen was all things to all men. Of Danish birth, he had lived much of his boyhood in the United States. His spoken American was absolutely excellent; English he enunciated with a perfect accent. Like most natives of the smaller North European countries, he also had a fluent command of French and German. A sojourn of forty years in China had enabled him to speak various dialects. Unlike the famed Von Moltke who could remain silent in seven languages, Oiesen was a delightful conversationalist in them all. *"Plus catholique que le pape, plus royaliste que le roi,"* he would characterize some individual given to extremes. The recollection of my associations with him, either in the Customs Commissioner's house on the Bund at Hankow, or in long rambles over the hills at Ku-ling, I prize highly. His fund of anecdote and incident, particularly relating to Sir Robert Hart and other prominent figures in the Customs service, was inexhaustible. His attitude towards his old chief, the "I.G.," shared both adulation and good natured cynicism.

I had first heard of Oiesen's urbane personality through my family connections in Korea. Innumerable stories were told of "J.F."—his generosity, his social *savoir faire,* his meticulous household arrangements whereby he maintained all the amenities even in the lonely, east-coast port of Wonsan in Korea where Hart had exiled him for many years. How, as he stayed on well over calling time one afternoon, Aunt Hattie had been obliged to invite him to dinner, knowing full well that only meagre preparations had been made for the family. Her mystification was boundless when they all sat down to an ample repast, including prime roast ribs of beef, unobtainable save on special order in the refrigerator of a steamer from distant Shanghai or Russian Vladivostok. Excusing herself as soon as possible, she breathlessly interrogated the Korean cook in the kitchen. The latter, unruffled, observed that when he had heard of the guest's remaining, he had sent over to the "Great Man's" own house for the complete dinner already awaiting him there.

As a young Customs assistant at Canton, Oiesen had fallen grievously ill. When foreign medical science seemed about to fail, his nurse, a young Cantonese woman, finally had recourse to those medicaments upon which two thousand years of empiric medicine have taught the Chinese to pin their faith. Miraculously he recovered—whether due to the wisdom of the

144

Great Herbal, the record sayeth not. The usual "nurse plus grateful patient" *dénouement* ensued. Mrs. Oiesen, who remained modestly in the background, but whose guiding hand was discernable in all her lord's domestic affairs, was a person of dignity, and of that good sense so characteristic of Chinese womanhood. Through my Aunt Hattie's good offices their children enjoyed the education in Europe which she provided for her own. One child, unusually gifted, was first in her class in a foremost woman's college in New England and displayed an organizing and directional talent which called her ultimately to Geneva to establish the Maison Internationale des Etudiants. At times the East and West *do* meet.

North of Hankow was "Cock's comb-hill." Here too were elaborate villas and more modest bungalows which served as summer retreats from the parching heat above the Honan plain. Chi-kung-shan was reached not by water, as its counterpart Ku-ling, but by the Peking-Hankow railway line, convenient to the innumerable mission stations in north central China; as well as for Hankow residents. The difficulty was that in the constant conflicts of ambitious warlords, the railway was often interrupted and the community cut off from transportation facilities.

A warlord's predatory army was returning to the north, one hot July, after thoroughly looting the province of Hunan. Trains were being commandeered by the troops. A number of us set forth from Hankow to reach the isolated mountain-top community, made up mostly of women and children. The long passenger train left Hankow for Peking, six hundred miles north, exactly on time. But when it reached the top of the pass crossing the Tsing-ling mountains which divide the Yangtze valley from north China, we were informed that it would proceed no farther. We expostulated with the train officials, pointing out that we had paid for tickets to take us to "Newmarket," the station at the foot of "Cock's-comb-hill." No use; if our fine express train once crossed the divide, it would be instantly commandeered by General Chang Ching-yao's unruly braves. There is, however, no situation in China so desperate that it is not amenable to compromise. The locomotive was uncoupled. Our special party clambered up onto it, some in the cab, some on the running board along the locomotive's side to cling to rods so hot as to be grasped only for a few moments with one hand while the other cooled off. Dan Wilson of the China-American Lumber Co. perched precariously with me on the engine's "cow-catcher." As it puffed up the steep gradient to the top of the pass and plunged with a shriek of the whistle into the darkness of the tunnel, chilly drops of water beat upon us from the living rock above.

We emerged to come to a full stop on the north side, for here the line was blocked with long strings of cars, freight and passenger, and an occasional locomotive. All the rolling stock in sight had been seized by the warlord for the use of his troops. Running ahead of our locomotive, we found a train just pulling out northward. We jumped into the open side-door of a freight car. It was full of armed soldiers. They carried their commissariat with them in the shape of bags of rice, and they lounged about on these, taking their ease as the train rolled along. I asked a leering "non-com" to what unit he belonged, "To the 1st Battalion of the 4th Route army."

"Let's get out of here," I whispered to Dan Wilson, "They're the band of cut-throats that shot down poor Ekval, the Norwegian-American missionary at Yochow, as he stood his ground in the gateway of his Chinese girls' school."

The train pulled up at "Newmarket" to water the locomotive. It took us but a moment to drop out of the freight-car's side door—and without delaying to say good-bye to our truculent fellow travelers.

*   *   *

The actual business of the Salt Administration took me far afield in the spacious Yangtze provinces. For a time, the balances of unremitted salt taxes at Ch'ang-sha, the Transportation Office for Hunan, continued to grow. Eight hundred thousand dollars, nine hundred thousand, a million! It was time I visited the provincial capital to make personal investigations. The political situation was critical; President Yuan Shih-k'ai was launching his scheme to restore the monarchy, with himself as the first of the new dynasty of *Hung Hsien*, "Expanding Constitutionalism." He was meeting with widespread opposition, especially in the south. General Ts'ai Ao, ardent republican patriot, had raised the standard of revolt, safely enough, in remote southwest Yunnan. In my travels were no local foreign-style hotels, where I could put up. In Ch'ang-sha there was, of course, the hospitable American Consulate.

And then there were the Brownell Gages, the Edward Humes, the "B.B." Branches, the Dickson Leavenses, the William Hails, and many others. The most charming people imaginable were to be found at Yale-in-China, that remarkable American college of the liberal arts and medicine set down through American munificence in this ancient walled city. Its influence upon modern China was already spreading far and wide. Not one, but all these doors were wide open to the wayfarer. We whose occasions took us about China away from the "treaty-ports," in a land as devoid of modern hostelries as Livingstone's darkest Africa, recall with a warming of the heart the hospitality of our friends of inland college and mission station. Their homes were oases of American culture and comfort, in a world where the Spartan living of the upper classes was as unaccustomed to an American as a Roman atrium, and where the common inns must be shared with pigs and chickens and worse. An ill-fated friend, professed to find no menace in sharing the life of the people among whom he lived. While serving as Vice Consul at Chungking, he made a journey through the mountainous country to the south-west, living in native inns. He died of confluent small-pox.

The Transportation Officer at Ch'ang-sha, a Mr. Liu, wore colored spec-

146

tacles. These were of such opaqueness that it was impossible to watch his eyes as he talked. Moreover he had an amazing impediment at times in his speech. While obviously straining to make things clear, one felt only the more bewildered as one followed his explanations. The reasons for the failure to remit the growing revenue balances from Ch'ang-sha continued to be but vaguely understood. One afternoon, however, as Elizabeth Johnson poured tea for her brother and myself in the comfortable drawing room of the Consulate, an official communication in large blue and white envelope with a great red seal affixed, was handed the Consul by a special messenger. It was from the Military Governor. Reading the Chinese text readily as he did, Consul Johnson translated to us the startling announcement that President Yuan Shih-k'ai was dead. This had occurred on June 6, 1916.

Unofficial word was that, balked in his elaborate scheme for making himself Emperor of China, he had "lost face and died of chagrin." The Chinese know human nature if not pathology! His German doctor of course more scientifically diagnosed the President's death as due to uremia. Shortly, word was brought to me that the outstanding balances of salt revenue, hitherto retained, would be reduced by the immediate transfer of at least eight hundred thousand dollars to the receiving banks at Shanghai. President Yuan could no longer make use of the nation's revenues to further his personal political ambitions. From Caesar to the present it is ever "the people's voice" that drafts a reluctant ruler. Yuan had forgotten his boyhood lessons in Mencius, China's "Second sage" of antiquity. The most important element in the state is the people said this early political scientist. "Heaven itself does not speak ... Heaven sees according as my people see; Heaven hears according as my people hear."

*   *   *

The occasion now seemed propitious for a long anticipated tour of south Hunan. In the mountainous areas on the Kuangtung-Hunan border, salt from the Canton regions was consumed instead of that made on the seacoast north of the Yangtze, as for the rest of Hunan. A "transit tax" was levied on this salt which came up on shallow draft boats by the North River, and thence was carried by porters across the mountain passes. Neither the rates of the taxes nor the amounts of the collections were clearly known. My arrangements for the expedition, which would involve the recovery for the central government of large sums of revenue, were made with due attention to comfort and safety. A roomy, rattan armchair was securely fastened to long, resilient chair-poles. Eight tall surefooted bearers were hired for the journey, as well as a sufficient number of coolies to carry our baggage and food supplies. A dozen variously uniformed salt-police, duly armed with antiquated muskets and freshly oiled paper umbrellas, were assigned to me as escort. They turned out to be invaluable for kitchen-police work, such as washing dishes, making fires, etc.

147

Accountants and secretaries were included in the investigating personnel. My colleague, Mr. Cho, explained that one of us at least must remain at Hankow headquarters to deal with emergencies. So he begged to be excused from the journey. As I contemplated his rotund figure I concluded that a period of relative abstinence and physical workout would have done him no harm. My chief technical aid, Ts'ai Hua-chieh, a well trained and experienced auditor, substituted for Mr. Cho on the journey. Mr. Fu likewise accompanied us in secretarial capacity. Despite his Confucian erudition and lack of acquaintance with even the Arabic numerals, Mr. Fu, it had to be admitted, was deeply versed in Chinese salt affairs.

I had secured a well-recommended "traveling boy" who also could qualify as cook. When asked what special equipment he required, he asked permission to purchase for a nominal sum two empty five-gallon kerosene tins. These he had rebuilt into roasters—sort of "fireless cookers." With them, and a couple of cast-iron charcoal pots, he performed miracles in the culinary art. On the subsequent twenty-three days' journeyings into one of China's most primitive regions, he produced at the close of each day with only an hour or so of preparation, full course dinners—soup, broiled fish, roast pork (edible white Hunan pig), baked potatoes, hot biscuits, and puddings in commendable variety. Our box of stores was placed in charge of two specially trustworthy porters, for I apprehended that we would sooner or later reach an area where decent food would be unprocurable. Actually the cook-boy's resourcefulness in obtaining locally almost all that we required made it scarcely necessary to broach our tinned food *cache*. My well-founded gratitude to this good provider later had domestic repercussions. Upon my return to Hankow, I proposed that he be permanently installed in our kitchen. My wife, however, could not dissuade him from using her best Irish linen table-napkins as dish-rags and dust-cloths. When too, she found him exercising in the kitchen by tossing gleaming butcher knives, three at a time, into the air, she delivered the ultimatum. Recalling the hardships and dangers of the long journey we had shared, cook and I parted only short of tears.

Our expedition at length strung its way out of the Consular compound at Hunan's capital to commence a more than seven hundred mile journey due south. Consul Johnson handed me books to beguile the time as I lolled in my comfortable "sedan-chair." Among these was *Ruggles of Red Gap*. While the journey progressed I chuckled over that grotesque animal, quaintly called the "high-behind," and Harry Leon Wilson's other absurdities. The gaunt chair-bearers would glance furtively at the foreigner making strange noises. They doubtless thought the hardships of the journey were driving him mad.

Day after day we plodded along, following a course southward, but up the north-flowing Hsiang river. At Heng-shan, Messrs. Ts'ai, Fu and I ascended this, one of China's five sacred mountains, and visited the gorgeously decorated temples at its base. It was from these shrines, tradition

148

holds, that the Buddhist patriarchs set out when they introduced the Indian-born religion into Japan. By night, we bivouaced in spacious "ancestral halls." These edifices, the property of wealthy clan-families, were built in the form of high, windowless rectangles, with inner, partially roofed galleries, facing onto open courtyards. Untenanted, save as places of refuge in time of bandit-raids or civil commotion, they provided clean and airy camping places. The squalid inns were quite impossible. Mr. Fu's stertorous snores, reverberating intermittently from wall to wall were the only disturbances to peaceful slumber in the ancestral halls. When, later, even these stopping places failed us, we resorted to the salt tax offices themselves. In these without too much ceremony, we preempted after a long day's journey, the best rooms to be had. The day's march began each morning as soon as there was light enough for the chair-bearers to see where to place their feet on the narrow path.

The wealth of this little-known region of China was made apparent to us as we visited the salt tax offices, situated strategically along the waterways. Unlike the deforested slopes of central and north China, the hills were covered with vigorous stands of firs. The trees are carefully cut to be used as building poles and are floated in great rafts down the rivers and across the Tung-t'ing lake to the Yangtze, and then down-river even to Shanghai, hundreds of miles away. Reforestation is carefully practiced. This region, too, is a vast rice granary, the hills being terraced with paddy-fields to their very tops. The rare, but essential minerals, antimony and tungsten, are found in this region, tin farther west in Yunnan. As our path wound up into the higher ranges of the great Che-ling Pass, we found the roadway cut through outcroppings of coal measures. Armies of porters passed us continually, some coming northward with baskets of sea-salt slung on carrying poles; others going southward with the same baskets filled with chickens, ducks and even small pigs—a lively example of a barter economy. In the squalid mountain villages were to be seen occasional Miao-tze, remnants of the aboriginal tribes of south-west China, now largely replaced by the Yellow River race of Chinese.

At last we marched up the broad, flag-paved Imperial highway which, crossing the top of the pass, formed through the centuries the road between Peking, distant capital more than a thousand miles to the north, and the teeming city of Canton, in the south. Beyond us southward we could see a wild jumble of mountains and gorges. A rapid descent brought us to P'ingshih, "Flat-stone," a shipping town at the headwaters of the North River. Here we paid off the sturdy, sure-footed chair-bearers, the baggage coolies, and the valiant escort. Our impedimenta, including voluminous notes and statistics on the inter-provincial salt trade and its taxation, were stored in two long flat-bottomed sampans on which our remaining party were to travel. A thrilling two days' voyage ensued as we shot the swift rapids, the boatmen with long bow-sweeps skillfully steering us clear of jutting rocks and boiling reefs. On either side towered magnificent cliffs.

149

At length the river broadened into a wide sluggish current, leaving the mountains behind. We glided past the town of Loch'ang, half hidden behind huge banyan trees, and on to Shaochow. Here was the railhead, the only visible evidence of the quickly abandoned American attempt, at the beginning of the century, to introduce railways into China. After a few hours we came by the back door, into Canton, to that enormous aggregation of humanity, where the foreign trader and later the missionary first breached China's centuries of isolation. The Cantonese—turbulent, artistic, enterprising—are to their fellow-countrymen the "Irish" of China when at home, and to the outer world "the Chinese" when abroad.

It had taken me twenty-three days to make this journey overland and by river from Changsha to Canton; nowadays, on the railway constructed over the same route that I traversed in 1916, it takes as many hours.

River Dragon

SHORTLY AFTER assuming my duties at Hankow, I acquired the handsome motor house-boat, the *Tso An* as we named it, appropriately enough meaning "Saline Tranquility." In June, 1915, when the melting snows of the Tibetan ranges join the rainy season below to fill the wide channel of the Yangtze river, I undertook a voyage down stream. My ultimate destination was Tat'ung, the seat of the Salt Transportation Office for Anhui province. I was accompanied by Chief Accountant Fu, and several other Chinese secretaries and clerks.

The *Tso An* rode lightly as her two twenty-six horse-power Gardiner motors churned the current with twin propellers. Down stream we surged, passing innumerable villages and towns. We watched the swift torrent gnaw out great chunks of overhanging soil from the high river banks which dropped from time to time with thunderous splash into the river. Steamers, junks and sampans passed in a never ending procession, up and down. Fishermen on the banks drew up their wide, square nets, balanced on weighted poles like an old-fashioned well sweep. Water-buffaloes, wallowing in river-side shallows to shake off swarms of stinging insects, gazed at us stolidly. By night we anchored in sheltered harbors, always, at Mr. Fu's suggestion, in the company of "gun-boats," for river-pirates might be about. The gun-boats were native wooden house-boats, brightly varnished and flying gay pennants. On the forward deck of these thirty-foot craft was mounted on wooden blocks a small smooth-bore cannon of very ancient vintage. The protection afforded was purely symbolic.

One evening, when we anchored in the little bay of P'eng-tze, Mr. Fu was in thoughtful mood. In this picturesque village, he observed, with its encircling wall running up the hill-side and its quaint kiosk gates, one of China's greatest poets used to be the magistrate.

"Where is he now?" I asked absent-mindedly. "Oh he flourished in the Chin dynasty (third century A.D.)," was Mr. Fu's reply!

150

To the timeless Chinese, history is a mirror in which they view the remotest past with the most lively sense of actuality.

"The poet T'ao Ch'ien, whose nickname was Yuan-ming," Mr. Fu continued, "disdained official life. When a superior officer came to inspect his magistracy at this little town, he threw in his resignation. 'Why, he exclaimed, should a poet crook the back to an ignorant politician for a salary of a few pecks of rice a month?' Tao, when he returned to the family farm," Mr. Fu went on, "composed one of the greatest poems of all time on the joy of living at home again, and once more being among his fields and gardens."

Our conversation entered the realm of ornithology.

"How do you account for the sudden appearance of all the wild ducks and geese on the Great River as soon as winter comes?" I asked.

"Such birds" was Mr. Fu's reply, "emerge in the late autumn from the deep mud of the marshes, like certain insects do in the spring. Our song-birds, which are with us all the year round, are produced from eggs in nests which you can see." Curiously, such close observers of nature as the Chinese have been, had never followed migratory fowl to their breeding grounds in Siberia.

Such placid evenings were often followed by days of risk and adventure on the treacherous river. The journey ended at Wuhu, one of the small, old Yangtze treaty-ports, which had been opened to foreign residence and trade after the signing of the treaties of 1858–1860.

Our return journey, commenced from Wuhu, was tedious, difficult and dangerous. The *Laodah,* the launch's captain, was a skilled navigator, thoroughly familiar with the river's tricks. With the utmost caution he navigated his vessel along the quieter reaches, rarely venturing out against the stream's full force. Finally we came to Ma-tang Bluff. Here, athwart the stream, a massive rocky spur juts out, against which the down-coming current strikes furiously, to be deflected sharply in a swirling mass to the left, clear across the mile-wide river.

Immediately below and behind the rock, the water is dead calm. Bringing the launch through this backwater, the steersman drove the broad, shallow-draft craft into the transverse current at full speed ahead. Unapprized of the navigational feat we were about to attempt, Mr. Fu and I had been quietly sitting on camp chairs on the forward deck. The launch careened at an alarming angle. Our chairs toppled beneath us and we clutched the rail to keep from going overboard. I saw the *Laodah* furiously spinning the wheel in the pilothouse, but to no avail. Away we shot across the stream, at the mercy of the current. We dropped anchor in quiet water a mile from the rock. The *Laodah* reported that at the critical moment a rudder-chain had snapped, leaving the craft without steering apparatus and helpless. Mr. Fu and I caught a *very large* river-steamer at the next port, leaving the *Tso An* to find its leisurely way up river and back home without our company.

151

The end of the handsome motor house-boat "Saline Tranquility" was indeed a tragic one, in which I myself and all on board narrowly escaped sharing in the holocaust. This was in the late autumn of 1915. At the suggestion of an American friend who had a visitor from Boston, I had made up a party of four, including a British friend in the Customs, for some duck shooting. We left for down-river late in the afternoon on the *Tso An*. This fifty-six foot, twin-screw British built craft, was equipped with two powerful internal combustion kerosene engines. The hull was strongly constructed of teak-wood over steel frames. There was a 17-foot cabin, with stationary and folding bunks, and a bath, with hot and cold water laid on. The kitchen galley separated us from the engine-room aft. Over the cabin was a roomy deck-space covered with canvas awning. This comfortable craft had been built originally for the use of the British engineers surveying the line of the railway under construction to Hunan.

We cast anchor out in the stream in the Seven-mile Creek, deep and swift, which pours into the Yangtze some distance below Hankow. A long line was made fast to the bank. After a brief hunt in the reeds for duck, our party returned on board. We had dinner served us by my house-hold cook whom we had brought along; and having divested ourselves of heavy boots and warm shooting clothes, we were settled down to a leisurely game of bridge. A sudden tumult broke out in the motor-room. A Chinese boy-helper rushed in on us, his cotton clothing aflame. We quickly wrapped a steamer-rug around him, smothering the fire. By this time the stern quarters were a roaring mass of flames, which soon reached the canvas awning above and rapidly spread forward. The Chinese crew crowded in and we all huddled together on the forward deck.

Between us and the shore were many yards of black, swift-flowing water. The flaming launch grotesquely lighted up the high reeds along the river-bank. By luck a fisherman had tied his *sampan* to our stern. The *Laodah,* the plucky Chinese captain of the *Tso An,* managed to creep back along the gunwale of the launch, avoding the flames with difficulty, and pull the little boat forward to the bow. There we all, some dozen or more souls, hunters and crew, scrambled into the frail craft. With only an inch or two of free-board above the water, we cautiously pulled ourselves ashore, hand over hand, by the line which had luckily been attached to the bank. We stood helpless as our handsome launch burned to the water's edge.

Scantily clothed as we were in bed-room slippers or other light foot-gear, and with dressing gowns flapping in the sharp November wind, we at last made our way through the reed marshes to a government operated paper-mill some miles away. We had managed to save the guns, except for a valuable London fowling-piece which was missing. Knocking at the door of the residence of the American manager of the mill, we had considerable difficulty in persuading this fellow-countryman of ours that "All men are brothers" and that we were not as in the famous Chinese romance, an

152

armed bandit horde.... The explosion of a blow-torch in the motor-room had caused the fire. The second engineer, his clothes aflame, had leaped into the river. He was swept out into the Yangtze and seen no more.

This, however, was only one of my near-escapes on the malevolent river. There is indeed justification for the innumerable tiny lighted tapers floated out by the river people onto the stream at dusk on the Feast of Hungry Ghosts for the souls of persons drowned. Just above the city of I-chang, the Yangtze pours an enormous volume of water out of the two hundred miles of alternate rapids and gorges between Hupeh and Szechuan provinces. On one occasion I happened to arrive at I-chang on a holiday. The entire foreign community of the port were to gather at the Glen of the Three Friends. Here they would witness the start of boat races between the local Customs out-door staff and the crew of the *Moorhen*, a small British gunboat in port. Most of the men-folk had gone up earlier. Dan Wilson of the China-American Lumber Company had arranged to bring on a boat load of women and children later. I joined him. The large open motor-boat sped up stream with its merry party. We were just entering the swift water below the mouth of the I-chang Gorge, a great cleft in the mountains through which the river finally emerges. Ominous whirlpools appeared, quickly sucking down any small floatage.

Suddenly the launch began to turn—in ever-narrowing circles. A heavy list brought the water close up under the gunwale. The chatter and laughter ceased; instead there were suppressed shrieks from the women. The tiller-rope had broken and the rudder had swung to. We were on the point of capsizing, while the motor continued to run at full speed. Nobody seemed to know how to shut it off. Calmly enough the Chinese steersman stepped down into the hatch where the motor was chugging away and jerked the ignition wire loose. The racing propeller stopped. Caught in the current we drifted swiftly down stream, until a Customs launch threw us a line and towed us to the landing jetty. . . . Once again the River Dragon had missed its prey.

At Your Orders—Zu Befehl

FRAU MARGARETE VON LIPKE, whom I never saw, was said to have been a lady-in-waiting to the Kaiserin. Herr Erich von Lipke, her husband, thus had influence at court. He seems first to have appeared in China with the belated arrival of the German punitive expedition against the Boxers in 1900. It was chiefly Germany who started that row two years earlier by her seizure of the Bay at Kiaochow and its port Tsingtao, as reparation for the murder of German missionaries in the interior of Shantung province. Berlin's Minister at Peking, the courageous Baron von Ketteler, had been shot down by a Chinese soldier just before the siege of the Legations commenced. Nevertheless the Kaiser's well armed expeditionary force was the last of all to reach North China.

In fact, all was practically over by the time the troops took up quarters

153

in the spacious grounds of the Temple of Heaven. The British, French, Japanese, Russians, and Americans had already done all of the fighting and most of the looting. Thus time hung heavily on the hands of Kaiser Wilhelm's troops, except for occasional punitive expeditions when some peaceful village alleged to harbor Boxers was burned, or, "to mark the offense," a pagoda was dynamited—some picturesque local landmark which had stood since the fifth or sixth centuries.

Herr Kapitan von Lipke had looked out over the China horizon and had liked the prospect. There was little or nothing to take him back to his native Weimar, where Goethe once sang, and not far away too from where Luther had nailed his ninety-five theses on the Wittenberg church doors. The natural thing for the young German aristocrat was a post in China's International Customs service, but not as for all the other Europeans and Americans—to begin at the bottom. The German Legation exerted due pressure and a higher-up post was discovered conveniently vacant. On grounds of Germany's limited representation in the Customs personnel, which was claimed to be quite disproportionate to her rapidly mounting share in China's trade, von Lipke found himself within a few years promoted to be a full-fledged "Commissioner of Customs." Such a high post could not be attained by a member of another nationality, not even the favored British, until after many years' service, spent largely in the "outports," remote from the amenities of European life.

With the £25,000,000 "Five Power Loan" to China in 1913, secured on the salt tax of all China and which the German bankers shared with Great Britain, France, Russia, and Japan, the moment seemed to have come when that still potent influence at Potsdam could be brought helpfully to bear. Herr von Lipke at the time had been strategically relegated by the British directors of the Customs to distant Chungking, 1200 miles up the Yangtze, a squalid up-river town.

Arrangements had now been completed for an entire foreign official hierarchy for the about-to-be reorganized salt tax administration of China —an Associate (Foreign) Chief Inspector, Financial Secretary, Secretary General, Chief Accountant, and Adviser to the Revenue Guards, with a numerous international corps of assistants. The German Legation, however, firmly pointed out a serious oversight. No provision had been made for a "Deputy Associate Chief Inspector." The *Kaiserliche Gesandschaft zu Pekin* had however, just the officer in mind for such a post, to wit, Herr Erich von Lipke. Thus was this gentleman pitchforked into the Chinese salt revenue administration.

The World War broke in 1914 shortly after Herr von Lipke assumed his duties at the Chief Inspectorate of salt revenue at Peking. The Associate Chief Inspector was now British, as was the Secretary General; the Financial Secretary was French. Even the latter's assistant was a Belgian. Thus von Lipke found himself without negotiable relations with his principal European colleagues. To be sure there was a Swiss in the accounting

154

department; but he was bad-tempered and inclined to take advantage of von Lipke's uncomfortable position.

There was nothing for von Lipke to do but to go off into the interior of the country on protracted "tours of investigation." For two reasons he chose my district as a corridor for his excursions which brought me into direct contact with him. First, as an American citizen I was at the time still a neutral and he could linger in Hankow in my company without embarrassment or friction. Secondly, my offices were on the route to Chungking city in Szechuan province, which he favored for his tours, both because of his former official familiarity with this region as its one time Commissioner of Customs, and because of that province's famous salt wells, and the large volume of the salt tax collected there.

He wrote me when he would arrive at Hankow over the railway from Peking, and that he would be glad of my company on the way up river as far as the town of I-chang. He stipulated that we should make the several hundred miles' journey by one of the salt administration's own vessels. The reason became clear when I was reminded that as an "enemy national" he could not secure passage on the regular up-river steamship lines, which flew the British or Japanese flags. The salt revenue service possessed a numerous and miscellaneous fleet of small steamers used ordinarily for patrol purposes. One such had a small cabin forward, which might accommodate us for a few days without too much discomfort.

Herr von Lipke dallied in Hankow for some time before giving the word to set sail. As in duty bound, we provided entertainment for our distinguished visitor. This however met with difficulties, again due to the War. Aside from the American Consul General and his wife, the usual official guests, represented especially by the Consuls of the allied powers, could not be invited to a complimentary dinner. Luckily, the Commissioner of Customs hailed from Memphis, Tennessee. He and his wife helped us at length to make up a dinner party. Herr von Lipke, tall, steely, and Prussian, charmed us all with his courtly manner, the smart click of the heels, the swift jack-knife bow from the waist, and the light touch of the lips on the hands of the ladies.

The day to cast off came at length—or rather the eve. For we did not get out into the stream until after the darkness of an early winter nightfall. As we sat in the little cabin, the steady throb of the triple expansion cylinders, with various appropriate hissing sounds as of escaping steam, and the swish of the water from the vessel's bow, assured us that we were under way. We stretched out for the night on the short and narrow seats, with our blankets tucked about us. Next morning, up early, I expected to see the town of Ch'eng-ling where we were to pass the entrance of the Tung-t'ing Lake. Instead, we had reached only a small village less than half way. I perceived a heavy native lighter lashed alongside. Calling the *Laodah,* the native skipper of our small steamer, I asked for explanations. With a deprecatory grin, the fellow disclosed that his brother kept a coal-

155

yard at the river town of "New-dyke" and had persuaded him to bring up a consignment of the fuel. This accounted for our belated departure in the concealing darkness of the night before. There was nothing to do but carry on, while the double load was costing us an extra day's steaming, at least.

Between "New-dyke" and "Sandmarket," or as known by their Chinese names, Sinti and Shasi, we ran into one of those three days' blows which descend upon the Yangtze valley, with cold driving gusts of wind and rain. All living creatures seek shelter, including the river boatmen, and the whole world hibernates. Astonishingly large waves are whipped up in the broad reaches of the mighty river, and woe to the junk or sampan that risks such seas.

We tied up in a sheltered cove by a high bank. Von Lipke, impatient to get on, and made highly irritable by the unfavorable trend of the war news, paced the roof of the cabin all day and much of the night. The steady footfalls above drove me to distraction.

"What a beastly land," he would ejaculate as he regarded the dripping yellow-clay river bank, and the scudding clouds overhead.

"Do you see those?" He pointed out a string of steel lighters, which despite the storm were being towed down-stream by a powerful tug. "They are carrying antimony from the mines in Hunan for the American munition factories, to be used against *my* country," he commented sourly.

When we went for a tramp ashore, wrapped in rain coats and with heavy shoes for the mud, village dogs dashed out to bark at us. Enraged at this, von Lipke with upraised stick pursued one mangy cur into a courtyard. An old woman protruded her head from a door. Noting it was a foreigner, she shrieked vituperations at him, until he fled beyond the range of her shrill, cracked voice.

"The sky's clearing. Up steam and cast off," commanded von Lipke when we returned to our dismal quarters on board. "Sorry, Master," reported the *Laodah*. "Engine-man say leaking pipe in boiler blow out and no can get up steam to make headway against seven-knot current. Engine-man try make repair."

"How far is Shasi?" demanded the impatient von Lipke.

"Ten hours ordinary steaming."

"Send a man overland," I intervened. "There's an American Oil Company agency there, and they'll send a motor-launch for us."

The messenger departed at a dog trot. Within an hour or two, during which much hammering was heard in the engine room, the *Laodah* reported, "Have fix engine."

"How did they do it?"

"Have put wooden plug in boiler-pipe."

Laodah liked to use his "pidgin English." It gave him much "face" with his crew.

We heard the engines turn over and soon the regular drive of the pistons. We proceeded cautiously, taking advantage of every eddy and back-

156

water. *Whish* went the escaping steam. We silently awaited the grand catastrophe! But in China machinery adapts itself to the most remarkable improvisations. In due course we reached Shasi under our own power. The rescuing American Oil Company's launch was all ready to start.

We were in time to attend a birthday feast. Real "manhattans" took the last of the river's chill out of us. Even von Lipke seemed to thaw in the jovial American atmosphere, for our hosts of the oil company had called in as reinforcements the North Carolinians from the Tobacco Company's mess. What a celebration for this tiny outpost of Western commercial penetration! The occasion was made memorable in the annals of the almost forgotten treaty-port by the unanticipated arrival of the two personages from the outside world.

By next morning the Oil Company's mechanics had patched up the leaking boiler-tube. Herr von Lipke and I bade our hospitable hosts good-bye. We were soon debarking at the city of I-chang just below the great gorges of the Yangtze. Von Lipke put up at the German consulate, where I, as well, was invited to dinner the night of our arrival. About the table sat a half dozen guests, all Germans except myself. I had never seen any of the party before save for von Lipke and the host, Consul Bracklo, who had been one of the guests at the Shanghai Mixed Court Magistrates' dinner years before.

As the good Rhein-wine circulated, tongues were loosed and strange tales of remote parts of Asia were told. One man, his face burned to a dark red by the winds of the Pamir passes, told of the part he had played in Afghanistan. His intrigues against the Indian *raj* at the Ameer's court had almost succeeded, until alert British agents thwarted them. He had barely escaped, to march across "the roof of the world" into Tibet and to the Szechuan border. He had then continued his journey down the rapids of the Yangtze in a swift "red-boat." His plans were to get to America.

The flushed faces glowed with optimism. The one *Auslander* at the table was forgotten—though the familiar tongue of the Lutheran parochial school in far away Michigan made every boast clear enough to him. "Sieg heil" the company shouted in chorus as they lifted their glasses time and again.

The next day my *compagnon de voyage* and I parted at the I-chang bund with definite relief, at least on my part, though with some regret as well. Together we had braved the hazards of a winter voyage up the river. Von Lipke boarded a junk which would, by sail and trackers, and if fate were kind, weeks hence bring him up the rapids and through the whirlpools to Chungking. There was a heavy mist in the I-chang gorge that morning. As it moved up river to the noise of sputtering fire-crackers and the beating of gongs, the big junk could soon be seen only in vague outline. But the chant of the forty men of the crew straining at the long sweeps, led by the grizzled *lao-dah* at the tiller, long after came back to us.

I never saw von Lipke again.

157

V

MANCHURIA, 1922–1924

Change and Decay — Manchurian Tiger — Baronial Keep — Railway Empire

Change and Decay

I RETURNED to Peking at the end of 1922 from a six months furlough in the United States. Even in that short interval important changes had occurred. Political disorganization had increased. The officers of Yuan Shih-k'ai's old Praetorian Guard, the provincial Warlords, were working their will on the unfortunate country. They sat astride the new national railways, commandeering freight cars and even the luxurious new American-made all-steel "Blue Express" coaches, as barracks for their troops, draining away traffic receipts for their support. The devoted railway operating staffs did miracles in upkeep and maintenance without adequate funds.

Nevertheless, in China's international relations, despite the domestic chaos, progress was being made. Young Chinese, educated abroad, were turning the tables upon their erstwhile mentors of the Occident. They had acquired erudition in international law and political science by way of Columbia, Michigan, California, and other universities. At Versailles and at Washington, Alfred Saoke Sze, V. K. Wellington Koo, Cheng-t'ing Thomas Wang, and lesser lights had displayed those forensic and disputative talents native to the Chinese mind. Oratory has been called the fatal gift of the Oriental.

For a while the Warlords themselves had tried their hands at international politics. Marshal Tuan Ch'i-jui, senior militarist of Yuan Shih-k'ai's old group, headed the "Anfu" party, so-called because it held its meetings in an obscure Peking lane of that name. They had shown themselves subservient to Japan in return for vast sums of money, said to have amounted in the single year 1918 to two hundred and fifty million yen, lavished on them as "loans" through a semi-official agent, one mysterious Nishihara. There had been, however, such violent popular reactions, whereby certain of these venal politicians had received painful hurts at the hands of indignant Peking students, that the Warlords had to turn their attention to the more immediately profitable and time-honored "squeezing" of the inarticulate Chinese people. This promised less reaction on the

159

ground that it was "old custom." Besides, save for loans from Japan, there was little money to be derived from the field of international relations.

Young China was more astute. The new generation of officials perceived illimitable possibilities. There was, for example, prospective "Customs autonomy" whereby the extremely low 5% to 7½% *ad valorum* import duties as set by the treaties could, once in China's control, be elevated to the extravagant heights, say, of the United States tariff. The abolition of "extraterritoriality" would result in the turning over to Chinese disposal of the taxation potentialities of the rich foreign administered *enclaves* at Hankow, Tientsin, and particularly at Shanghai. All this was promised at Washington. In fact an international Tariff Conference met in Peking in October of 1925. American Minister J. V. A. MacMurray was a conspicuous protagonist for China in her battle for tariff autonomy, until he realized that the increased receipts would be largely frittered away in paying the Japanese for the corrupt Nishihara loans. After many disappointments China did at last win the right to set her own tariff rates, but only after the successful Nationalist Revolution in 1928, even Japan agreeing thereto in 1930.

There had followed in January 1926 a Commission on Extraterritoriality. Lawyer Silas Strawn of Chicago was its Chairman, and Dr. Wang Ch'ung-hui D.C.L. (Yale), barrister-at-law (Middle Temple), authority on international law, its chief Chinese representative. This Commission was convened to abolish the exemption of foreign nationals from Chinese law, provided by that astute Newburyport, Massachusetts, lawyer, Caleb Cushing, in the Sino-American treaty of 1844. The Chinese case against "extrality" was presented by American-educated young Chinese as "an infringement upon China's sovereignty." This latter phrase had likewise been learned in American college lecture rooms. Before the beginning of our Christian era, swashbuckling generals of the Han dynasty had extended China's "protective custody" to considerable portions of Central and South Asia. The early Manchu Emperors, too, had "consolidated the Empire" by their expeditions against recalcitrant Eleuths and others. None of these empire builders had been governed by such political concepts. *Mutatis mutandis,* Europe and Japan had ignored basic principles of international law in a century of encroachment upon China's territories.

Moreover, pointed out China's young advocates, with British and American supreme courts in China, with Japan's and France's respective appeals of litigation in China to higher tribunals at Nagasaki and Saigon, and our own United States District Court of Appeals in California as a tribunal of higher resort from the U. S. Court for China, with Consular Courts and Mixed Courts, there was vast confusion of jurisdiction and laws and frequent miscarriages of justice. As illustrated in the case of the defaulting clerk of the American Legation at Peking, there was no system of extradition whereby escaping criminals could be brought back to China. When a prominent American official in Shanghai unlawfully converted large

160

amounts of other people's property to his own use, and managed to reach the United States, he lived happily ever after. Finally the foreign Concessions and Settlements brazenly gave asylum to Chinese political refugees on Chinese soil. The argument against the foreign Concessions was advanced always by the Chinese party in power, never by those temporarily under a political cloud, to whom these ready "funkholes" offered safe refuge from pursuing enemies.

In 1908, I had shared a study-table in the history seminar room of the University of Michigan Library with a bright young Chinese student. Early in the summer of 1913 this friend called on me unannounced at my home in the International Settlement at Shanghai. Would I, he implored, secure a permit from the American Consul General to enable him to take the first outward bound steamer? His story was that he had joined the revolutionary party at Nanking. Ardor for the cause had rapidly cooled when he became better acquainted with the professional revolutionaries of that era. He thereupon purchased a railway ticket from Nanking to the safe retreat of Shanghai, taking a return coupon to throw suspicion off the scent. With consternation he found that the Revolutionary government had induced the Shanghai consuls to place the International Settlement temporarily out of bounds for political refugees. He would thus be liable to arrest by the Municipal Police to be handed back on demand to his Nanking "friends." I arranged for his sailing from Shanghai that afternoon, never to return, from that day to this, to his native land. For through all the political vicissitudes of the succeeding years he served his country abroad from the safe distance of a Chinese Embassy. Such is the role that extraterritorial "Concessions" have played in Chinese domestic politics.

Much time would elapse, it had been expected in 1925, before the work of the Tariff Conference and the Commission on Extraterritoriality could be put into effect. A platonic resolution favoring tariff autonomy for China was adopted, followed by suspension of the Conference because of a violent outbreak of civil war among the military leaders, who were only remotely interested. These doughty warriors agreed, of course, that the treaty limitations of the existing tariffs provided insufficient revenue for the needs of the country; moreover, such low duties failed to protect native industries. But there were more expeditious ways of raising revenue for immediate needs—seizure of railways, unconscionable increases in the salt tax, forced contributions from chambers of commerce on pain of looting cities, etc.

Even of less interest to the Warlords were the deliberations of the "Extrality" Commission. This Commission had stipulated that Chinese administration of justice must be "effectively protected against any unwarranted interference by the executive or other branches of the government (e.g. the Warlords)." There should be marked improvements in respect to codes, laws, procedure, prisons. The foreign courts functioning on China's soil should administer Chinese law as far as possible, and do

161

away with abuses, "pending the abolition of extraterritoriality." Thenceforth the Chinese government issued an impressive succession of "Provisional Constitutions," of civil and criminal codes, of Presidential mandates and Ministerial orders filling volumes and employing for the purpose the foreign-trained legal talent of the land. Underneath all the adaptations of Occidental law lay the basic Confucian political and legal concepts, the deep down experience of a people millenniums old in the conduct of human relationships, conditioning at all points the veneer of Western legalism.

During this stirring period I spent many "moments in Peking," of greater—like my friend Lin Yu-t'ang's novel—or lesser length. A kaleidoscopic procession of foreign Chief Inspectors of Salt Revenue had succeeded the pioneering regime of Sir Richard Dane. With characteristic good sense, he had retired. Following the eclipse of his powerful patron Yuan Shih-k'ai, he foresaw the inevitable decay of the central government's authority and the consequent independence of regional authorities. This boded ill for the efficient administration of the salt tax as a federal organ.

Sir Reginald Gamble succeeded Dane. This amiable British colonial administrator, son of a Governor of Barbados (where he was born), was brought in from the Indian Finance Department. No longer backed up by the British *raj* to impose an iron authority on a supine populace, Gamble found himself in daily contest with an astute, hydra-headed, recalcitrant Chinese bureaucracy that fought every measure, however commendable, that threatened its privileges and prerogatives. Glad of release at the end of three years, he declined to renew his contract and retired, presumably to the idyllic, if obscure, life of an English country gentleman of ample fortune.

Next came Sir Ernest Wilton, a British consular official who in early years had gained the notice of Lord Curzon while serving as Chinese interpreter to Sir Francis Younghusband's expedition in 1904 to Lassa, the hitherto unapproachable capital of Tibet. Wilton found the unaccustomed duties of his new post irksome in the extreme, for he too in a previous career as Consul in China and Minister to the Baltic States had his Majesty's government to support him. After the expiration of his stipulated three years term of office, he gladly shook the dust of China from his feet to reemerge for a moment in the public eye as post-war President of the Saar Government Commission.

Sir Ernest Wilton was a man of much polish, a charming *raconteur*. It was while on a walk at Peking, with him and the Dutch *chargé d'affaires,* M. Oudendyk (later "Sir William," for his services to British interests while Dutch Minister to Moscow during the Soviet Revolution), that I learned that Count Carlo Sforza, brilliant young Italian Minister to China, belonged not to the senior, but to a *cadet* branch of the Renaissance Milan family. Years later, Count Sforza, self exiled to America from the repugnant fascist regime, my wife and I were having tea together in an art

162

store in Ann Arbor. "A relation of mine," exclaimed Sforza. He was looking up at Guido Reni's famous, if disputed, portrait of Beatrice Cenci displayed on the wall by the dealer. Count Sforza scrawled his name on the back of Beatrice's portrait, which I have kept as a memento of the distinguished statesman. The same signature appeared as Italy's plenipotentiary on the Treaty of Rapallo with Yugoslavia (1920).

Meanwhile members of the permanent foreign staff fiercely struggled for the coveted Chief Inspectorship, as it fell from the grasp of a succession of valetudinarians. The historic rivalry between Horatio Nelson Lay, Thomas Wade and Robert Hart, in the middle of the last century, for the post of Inspector General of the Chinese Maritime Customs was reenacted. A brilliant Cambridge matriculate, as English Secretary, was the administrative *deus ex machina* during this era of *fainéant* chiefs. When frustrated in his ambition to succeed Dane owing to Chinese dislike of his dictatorial manner, he took leave of absence. He fell from a boat in Lake Louise, Canada, and was drowned—so word came back to us. The mysterious disappearance of high officials, temporarily under a cloud for some reason or other, had occurred before in British annals. A vigorous type of British commoner in the service cherished similar ambitions until the socially fastidious Sir Ernest Wilton introduced as English Secretary his own candidate and presumptive official heir, a British consular officer of Cambridge provenience. An American had the termerity to scheme for the exalted Chief Inspectorship. He was promptly cashiered by a hastily arranged drum-head court-martial, presided over by a temporary officiating British *locum tenens* and a compliant Chinese colleague.

While the ambitious *majors domo* of the failing Merovingian house of foreign Chief Inspectors were fighting for the crown, the Chinese were recovering the authority virtually surrendered during the vigorous regime of Sir Richard Dane. Chinese Chief Inspectors, too, came and went with bewildering frequency as one warlord after another assumed temporary control of the Capital. Nevertheless Chinese influence gained in the interval.

At length the intrigues for the succession by the junior foreign staff were terminated by the unexpected appointment of a British subject, approval of whose appointment by his own Legation at Peking was not previously sought by the Chinese government. This person had had a brief career in the Customs service, followed by a congenial assignment as Secretary of the Haiho Conservancy Board at Tientsin. His duties had involved the organization of parties of prominent Chinese and foreign residents of North China, whom he escorted to the scenes of dredging and other conservancy works on the tortuous river which provided the artery of traffic between the great North China *entrepôt* and the sea. The Chairman of the Conservancy Commission was a onetime minister of finance, generally known as the lobbyist at the Capital for the vast merchant salt interests of my own district of Central China. The connection was obvious. It was desired to secure the appointment of a compliant foreign Chief

163

Inspector of the Salt Revenue who would be indebted for his post to his "Boss." Thus does politics operate, in China as well as in Newark or Chicago.

*   *   *

A distinguished luncheon party had just been seated in the dining room of the spacious Chinese villa, occupied by his Excellency the Minister of Foreign Affairs, Dr. V. K. Wellington Koo. Service plates were of gold; at either end of the room hung priceless scrolls by the thirteenth century landscapists. Our hostess had just reached Peking from Paris. She complained wearily of the task of superintending the unpacking of some forty trunks and boxes. A personal elegance in costume, coiffure, complexion, and manicure, indicated that every facility offered by an ample fortune and the fashion-centre of the world had been availed of.

Our hostess carried an insolent Pekingese lolling over her arm. I spoke my admiration for the handsome little creature's points as I seated myself beside Mme. Koo, remarking appropriately that my wife, too, was very fond of her "Na T'ung" and "Pu Lun," named after two Manchu princes.

"We never do that," said the exquisite Madame Koo, frostily. "In China we never give dogs people's names," Mme. Koo emphasized.

"Oh we often do," I hastily rejoined. "I have a large Airedale that I call 'Beatty,' after the hero of Jutland," I went on.

I was extricating myself from a conversation that lay at the bases of two cultural points of view. Mme. Koo despite her Parisian makeup and almost complete overseas background, still harbored ineradicable racial sentiments.

The previous day, upon my arrival at the Capital, from Hankow, I had paid my respects to Dr. Koo at the *Wai-chiao-pu,* China's Downing Street and Quai d'Orsey combined. The rambling, immense, foreign style building was one of the first of its incongruous kind in Peking. It had been designed by that American architect whose palace dogs had kept me awake my first hot night in Peking. It was already dusk when I entered the spacious chamber which constituted the Minister's office. I could just discern in the relative gloom, a brightly lighted desk in a distant corner. It seemed to take me many minutes to cross the length of the room. Behind piles of documents sat His Excellency, a distinguished if rather smallish personage. I was in the presence of the Paladin, the knight in shining armour, of the American "returned student."

A graduate of St. John's, the American Church Mission College at Shanghai, young Wellington Koo had acquitted himself brilliantly in political science and international law at Columbia. His Ph.D. thesis was a masterly study of the legal status of aliens in China. When still under thirty, he was already China's Minister to the United States. To be sure, his father-in-law had been the powerful elder statesman T'ang Shao-yi. Almost the first of the late western trained school to burgeon into political

164

prominence, he presented his country's demands at the post-War conferences at Paris and Washington with such eloquence and learning that he confounded his relatively inarticulate Japanese adversaries. At the moment of my call, the Minister was carefully editing what appeared to be a draft of a state document written in classic Chinese ideographs. There fell upon me a consuming admiration for the Chinese mind which can equally master the cultures of two hemispheres! My call was purely social and personal.

The day before, I had taken a limbering-up walk, after a six hundred-mile train journey from Hankow. My way had led out the gate next the British Legation where a part of the old fortified brick wall was still standing. It was pock-marked with bullet holes from the Boxer siege of 1900; on it was painted in fading black letters "Lest We Forget." I crossed the glaçis, the wide defence space beyond the loop-holed walls which surrounded the entire Legation Quarter, to the broad avenue called the Ch'ang-An-Chieh, Avenue of Prolonged Peace. A tall figure approached me, walking nervously and rapidly, with the aid of a stout stick. When we passed, despite the dark sun-glasses he wore, I recognized Sir Francis Aglen, Sir Robert Hart's substantive successor as Inspector General of Customs. Sir Francis hurried on without even a nod of recognition. He was staring straight before him; his usually ruddy complexion seemed even more flushed that day. I learned in due course that the little man in the great room at the Foreign Office had just summarily dismissed the "I.G.," an unheard of sacrilege. Frank Aglen for years had served the Chinese government to the great enhancement of China's international credit. He had even accepted the onerous trusteeship of her domestic loans, secured on the Customs surplus revenues. His merits were great.

The whole story was told me at Shanghai in the autumn of 1939 by Sir Frederick Maze, Aglen's successor as Inspector General of Customs, when, following a Sunday afternoon game of croquet, we sat at tea in his drawing room.

"Aglen ruined his chances," observed Sir Frederick of his predecessor, "and was dismissed for adopting the same attitude as Horatio Nelson Lay, away back in 1863. He felt himself independent and outside the Chinese government. Aglen wrote a letter to Atkinson, non-Resident Secretary of the Customs in London. The Chinese got hold of it; I have a copy of it in my safe. He as much as said that the Customs was an *imperium in imperio,* independent of China, and depending on the Powers. Now I myself," Sir Frederick continued, "follow the policy of Sir Robert Hart, who always remained in the background, although in the absence of a trained Chinese diplomatic personnel Hart was responsible for almost all China's moves in his time. Lay and Aglen made the mistake of thrusting themselves forward and putting the Chinese in the background."

By way of *obiter dicta,* Sir Frederick spoke on of his Uncle, the "old I.G.," Sir Robert Hart:

165

"Hart's diary runs into seventy volumes, but it must be carefully edited as it contains all sorts of entries. J. O. P. Bland was to be entrusted with writing Hart's biography, and he would have done it well. However, when he had read the diary, he concluded to make a very special approach. He would write of Hart, not as the administrator of China's Customs for a half century, but as a poet, theologian, and philosopher. The diary was largely taken up with matters such as these, as well as letters to lady friends."

The fundamental difficulty with Aglen was, in my own opinion, that he was English and not an Irishman. It took an Ulsterman to get his way with the Chinese! Jordan, Hart, Dane, and Maze, Britain's outstanding diplomats and administrators in China, all hailed from Belfast!

Manchurian Tiger

IT WAS IN NOVEMBER, 1922, that I undertook the reorganization of the salt transportation offices of China's most northerly provinces, Ki-rin (Chi-lin) and Hei-lung-kiang. These, usually referred to in the jargon of the salt revenue service as "Ki-Hei," made up, with the southerly province of Feng-t'ien, the "Eastern Three Provinces," as the Chinese denominate Manchuria. After a six months' furlough in America, I had returned to China outfitted for the sub-tropical Yangtze valley. Years of continuous service in Central China had, it seemed to me, almost established my prescriptive right to be stationed at Hankow. Moreover, the international political circumstances of my appointment to this region which was unrecognized in the formal Loan Agreement, appeared to attach me permanently to the salt administration of the Yangtze valley. The prospects of residence in a desolate, near-Siberian region were not inviting. I had had ears and nose too often frost-bitten in my native Michigan's sub-arctic winters to regard ice and snow as sporting. However, out of regard to the Chinese government's needs in the region, diplomatic and fiscal, my wife settled the question by pronouncing that "there was more *for* accepting the assignment than *against*."

"The North Manchurian government salt monopoly is in an appalling mess; we'd like you to go up and try your hand at straightening things out. Besides," added the hard-bitten little British colonel temporarily in charge of salt affairs at Peking, with a malicious twinkle in his cold grey eyes, "they say there's quite a good cemetery at the Ch'ang-ch'un headquarters."

Whereupon we proceeded to those same Peking outfitters that had served me fourteen years before, when I prepared for my first Manchurian winter. Our light clothing was packed safely away. We went in for whip-cord riding-breeches, fleece-lined underwear, corduroys and heaviest woolen stockings. Furs could await acquisition in Manchuria itself, chief fur market of the world. My wife went south to gather up our household effects which were still at Hankow, and to bring up Amah and her husband Chang who were to serve us loyally in the ensuing years. Na T'ung

166

and P'u Lun, proud "Peeks" bearing princely Manchu names, were to be included in the family *hegira*. I left for the north, traversing the route of that almost forgotten journey of the end of 1908.

Ch'ang-ch'un, Eternal Spring as the Chinese had euphemistically named this strange urban hybrid, was an agglomeration of three cities. It lay sprawled about the northern end of the Japanese controlled South-Manchuria Railway zone, and at the terminus of the southern spur of the Russian built Chinese-Eastern Railway. The railway systems of Manchuria at this time described an enormous letter T. We were about midway on the upright stroke beginning at Dairen and Port Arthur on the famed Liaotung Peninsula. The transverse part of the letter crossed North Manchuria from the Siberian border to the Maritime Province on the way to the Pacific port of Vladivostok.

The oldest of our three cities was the original walled Chinese town. Here the streets were narrow and ill-paved. Russian-style carriages drawn by two or three shaggy Mongol ponies, crowded the streets. Shops did a thriving business in furs, cloth, grains, and spirits. Nearby was the Japanese railway town, laid out in broad avenues, spacious parks and hybrid Eurasian dwellings and office buildings. Over this section by night blazed electric lights, giving the town an outward air of intense activity. But all was strangely subdued; there was a feeling of repression as there is wherever the Japanese are, in contrast to the noise and hub-bub of a Chinese city. Even in sub-zero weather, figures wrapped only in cotton *kimonos* with straw sandals on their feet, would be seen flitting homeward from super-heated public baths. In the Japanese town were elaborate *geisha* houses, cabarets in the Nipponese style. From these emerged the hesitant, staccato notes of the Japanese *samisan* and the hilarious laughter of Japan's pioneering *filles de joie*. The Yamato Hotel supplied the traveler with musty, near-European accommodations. Everything was controlled by the South Manchuria Railway, which, octopus-like, occupied its special railway zone, a right of way extending seventeen miles on either side of the roadbed.

Some miles beyond the Japanese and Chinese settlements lay the old Russian railway-town of Kuan-ch'eng-tze. This was made up, like a Siberian settlement, of low, one-storied log-houses. In fenced-in yards gay-colored petunias and large fleshy begonias grew in the summer; in the winter the cotton-stuffed double windows blazed with red and pink geraniums. There was the inevitable "sobranje," the communal club, where amateur music, the ballet, and the drama flourished. Here in warm weather small tables were set out in the garden and exceptionally good meals were served. It was a rich land, with plenty of food, warm furs and felt and wadded clothing, and the heavy drinking of *kaoliang, saké,* and *vodka* in all their alcoholic intensity.

But hidden away on a back street, we were to find the antithesis of all this hearty living. In a flimsy, foreign-style building scores of wounded

167

Russian officers were lying, the remnants of Merkuloff's White Brigade which had been forced out of Vladivostok by the triumphant Bolshevik forces and driven across the Manchurian border. Like the trek of a Tartar tribe, they had come with their families across the plains or through the forests in carts or on horseback. Their few possessions had rapidly melted away. Confronted with a novel problem, the Chinese authorities had housed the strange host in barracks for a year or more, until most of the able-bodied men had drifted southward to the China port cities. Many of the women came to be found in the cafés and cabarets which from Harbin to Hongkong catered alike to whites and Orientals. It was part of a vast ethnic movement, first of the tragic procession of refugees out of Europe to reluctantly hospitable lands. Culture transfers of the most far-reaching influence were to follow. Russian ideas of food, clothing, hair-dressing, even high-heeled shoes for the women, came to be popular in Chinese and Japanese circles. Even more significant was the blow to the white man's prestige at this spectacle of indigent Europeans, wandering helplessly along the Asiatic coast.

The last backwash of this miserable host were found in our midst, the hopelessly incapacitated, huddled together, freezing and starving. Promptly we wrote south and east. Money came in from the Red Cross in Korea and clothing from Hankow and Shanghai. A soup kitchen was organized. Bread and meat were issued daily on ration-cards. The local transport agent of the ever-present American Oil Company, an English-speaking Russian half-breed, administered the philanthropy for us. The gratitude of these people and their dependents was expressed as they could—in due course a concert was given in our honor. To this day we can hear the magnificent tones of the Cossack chorus. When at length we left Ch'ang-ch'un for good, our *protégés* crowded the railway station platform and tears coursed down bearded faces.

*   *   *

My chief Chinese associate in the "Ki-Hei" Salt Transportation Office was one Mr. Yen, a Chinese politician of ability and experience. Whatever his origins, and there were whispers that they were none too exalted, he had cultivated a suavity of manner and a force of expression, which left no doubt of his qualities of vigorous leadership. His attainments in public finance, learned in no formal school, were of a high order. He had thus been selected by the powerful ruler of Manchuria, Marshal Chang Tso-lin, for the most productive of all provincial revenue posts, the Ki-Hei salt monopoly.

Mr. Yen had built himself a solid, four-square house behind my own in the Ch'ang-ch'un headquarters compound. It was of concrete, one storey, and of a peculiar layout. The entrance led into a large hall, with ante-rooms on either side, where conferences could be held. From the hall one passed on, if he so wished, to a strange enough room. One could perceive

168

that it had no windows, and hence no natural light or ventilation. In the deep dusk there were tiny lamps burning on a large *k'ang,* or brick dais, which went all around the sides of the room. There was a heavy, sickening odor about. Mr. Yen, and his many visitors, would disappear for a few moments into this room. Later emerging to rejoin a dinner party or the council table, their eyes would flash, their tongues would wag, in an atmosphere of high animation and well-being. Gradually eyes would dull, tongues would cease to wag; the life of the party would die down. One after the other, they would excuse themselves, dive into the murk of the windowless room, to emerge later for a repetition of the previous performance. This apparently went on all day and most of the night. . . . North Manchuria's opium production has been one of the greatest in all of China.

One sunny but intensely cold morning shortly after my arrival, I was informed that a tiger had been shot by soldiers up north on the Sungari river, and that it was now temporarily on display in the town. We drove in at once, for I had often heard of, but had never seen a specimen of *tigris filis longipilus,* the long-haired Manchurian tiger. Sure enough, on a table in an outhouse, a magnificent male tiger reared up in frozen semblance of his ferocious living self. He measured fourteen feet from bewhiskered muzzle to tip of tail. Great yellowed fangs snarled from his frosted lips; his enormous paws concealed strong retractile claws. The fur on him was very long and so light in color that the familiar deep orange-and-black stripes, characteristic of his lithe Bengal cousin, were scarcely discernible.

"What is to be done with this magnificent beast," I asked.

"He will be sent to Mukden for presentation to Marshal Chang Tso-lin, our dauntless Warlord of Manchuria," I was informed by the soldier on guard. "His Excellency will hold a grand feast for his generals. As the tiger is the fiercest of all beasts, so its strength and ferocity are imparted to those who eat of its liver and other vital organs."

Mr. Yen advised me that it was high time to make my official call upon General Chang Tso-lin, absolute ruler of 380,000 square miles of territory and thirty million people. A date for the audience was set and we proceeded the two hundred miles southward on the Japanese railway to the provincial capital, Mukden. Despite a varied and fairly successful experience with truculent warlords, I approached my present ordeal with some trepidation. I had heard that my predecessor, a New Zealander, had once called upon the Manchurian Generalissimo with his Chinese colleague, a Mr. Miao. The latter had displayed unusual temerity. Mr. Miao had "spoken out of turn" on the subject of His Excellency's retention of an undue proportion of the national salt revenues for his own purposes. A cloud had gathered on the brow of the warrior chieftain whose *franc tireur* forces had so harried the Russian armies in the late war as to earn Japan's gratitude and subsequent support. The New Zealander's well-placed kicks

169

delivered from beneath the intervening council-table only just in time reminded the intrepid Miao that his head was in jeopardy.

Our three-horse droshky dashed through the crumbling gate-tower of Mukden's Manchu city, halting at length before a red-painted gateway. Soldiers in dog-fur caps and sheepskin overcoats held their rifles at business-like attention along the brick-paved walks. There was an alertness about the entrance to the Palace unusual in Chinese military circles. Mr. Yen's secretary, who accompanied us, explained to the Captain of the Guard that we had a prearranged audience. We were escorted inside. Thereupon Mr. Yen, with an air of great familiarity, led the way towards an ornate, ginger-bread like building of grey brick with green painted verandahs.

We ascended the steps. The door swung open. A small Chinese person in plain blue silk gown, with close-cropped head, nodded to us, and we silently followed him down a corridor and into a room furnished in heavy black-wood, marble-inlaid furniture. There on a dais crouched my recent acquaintance, the long-haired Manchurian tiger, grinning horribly as the local taxidermist had arranged him. The whole setting was designed to impress a visitor with the risks he ran in venturing into the presence of the ex-bandit chieftain of Manchuria. Our mild little man motioned us to seat ourselves at a round table. He himself took the opposite chair.

"I am always glad to welcome Americans. My son Hsueh-liang plays tennis at the local American Y.M.C.A.," he observed, without looking directly at me. My astonishment closed my mouth to any reply for some seconds. This was the notorious Chang Tso-lin in person.

When I recovered from the shock of my close-up of reputedly one of the most formidable figures of China's swashbuckling warlord era, I proceeded to state my business. Under orders of the recognized central government of China, I had assumed my duties as Auditor-General of the North Manchuria salt monopoly. This far-flung organization, with more than forty offices distributing salt from below the Sungari river up as far as the Amur, lay within the domains of Marshall Chang. Moreover, the enormous quantities of salt purchased by the government monopoly came from his Southern seacoast, where it paid the salt tax like any private purchaser.

"But His Excellency would recall," I ventured to point out, "that the entire salt revenues of China had been pledged as security for the service of the Reorganization Loan of 1913 with the foreign banks. It was my official duty, as well as personal interest, to do everything in my power to maintain China's credit in the money markets of the world. Hence, I must insist that the operations of the monopoly be brought to audit and the net profits duly covered into the national treasury in accordance with the terms of the loan contract."

Instantly there was a change. The little man snapped up straight as a

170

ramrod, his eyes blazed, he drew back his lips so as to show his teeth like a snarling animal.

"Not a copper cash of my Manchurian revenues shall fall into the hands of the traitorous and usurping gang at Peking. Generals Wu and Feng may dominate Peking but they shall not use my own money to fight against me."

The fire in his eyes died down.

"As for Elder Brother Guy-lo (my name rendered in Chinese), though he is an American, I note that he expresses his sentiments in the language of our country with great elegance. We are friendly with your honorable countrymen for they have no designs upon China. They do much good to our people, through their missionaries and teachers. My own personal adviser, Mr. Carleton Baker, is an American. You are only doing your duty and *I shall keep that in mind*," he concluded mildly enough.

When I proposed to visit Peking at the end of the year, Mr. Yen entrusted me with a bank draft for $250,000, silver.

"The Generalissimo wishes you to hand this to his friend, the Minister of Finance Chang Hu, as a personal accommodation to help him tide over the innumerable demands made upon the government with the approaching New Year," explained my colleague. "But he wants it clearly understood that it is no gesture of friendship to Generals Feng and Wu."

This was the first remittance of salt revenue to Peking since Chang Tso-lin had a few months earlier in 1922 declared the independence of the Three Eastern Provinces from the warlord-dominated Peking regime.... The Generalissimo thus kept his promise and gave his American friend much "face" with the high Peking authorities.

Baronial Keep

SOFT FURRY PAWS concealed the sharp claws of the tiger. April, 1923, arrived. All through the winter, over the iron-hard crust of Manchuria's frozen plains, the salt-carts had carried their precious cargoes to the remotest confines of Kirin and Heilung-chiang, even into Barga, and outer Mongolia. Now the disappearing frost, following torrential rains, turned the rich black soil into a bottomless quagmire. As far as the eye could see from the still solid railway embankments, thousands of square miles of giant millet soon would wave, food for man and beast. Between the seven-foot stalks of *kaoliang* would grow tons of soya beans for Europe. The Salt Monopoly at its headquarters at Ch'ang-ch'un showed a handsome net trading profit of over two million dollars on its winter operations. In addition, large sums in salt taxes had been paid at the Feng-t'ien salt works on the sea-coast to the south. I was recovering from a sharp attack of pneumonia which had nearly placed at my disposal the cemetery at Ch'ang-ch'un, which my Peking colleague, the little British Colonel, had recommended.

171

Word came that Mr. Yen would see me. I received him as I sat in a well cushioned invalid's chair in my residence.

The salt monopoly head-offices were situated in a baronial establishment, just within the borders of former Inner Mongolia. Here on an elevation some ten acres were enclosed by a fourteen-foot castellated brick wall, with rounded "martello-towers" at each angle. These were pierced with loop-holes for rifles or machine guns, commanding all approaches. The only ordinary ingress was by the main gates, guarded day and night. The road crossed a bridge over the creek at the foot of the hill, up whose steep incline horse-drawn carriages or motor-cars raced furiously to keep up momentum until safely through the gates above.

A garrison of several companies of "salt guards," cavalry and infantry, patrolled the dozen long red-painted wooden warehouses in which thousands of bags of valuable salt were constantly stored—the "ever-normal storage" applied to salt and rice against dearth and high prices, since time immemorial in China. In freezing weather when the deep-rutted roads were negotiable, the yards were filled with heavy iron-tired two-wheeled carts drawn by straining horses and mules, treated with sadistic brutality by a race of half-savage carters. Frequently enough the alarm was given that the dreaded bandits, the almost fabulously ferocious "Red Beards," were about to descend upon us. Excited guards would let their rifles go, bang! bang! and sometimes bullets would whistle across our house roof.

A spur of the South Manchuria railway reached us from the Japanese town of Ch'ang-ch'un which was visible from our height, especially by night when it appeared as a distant glow of electric lights.

Our own residence was a long low bungalow, with glassed-in verandah, to gather as far as possible the brilliant rays of the near Siberian winter sun. The latitude, 45 degrees north, was precisely that of my own native Huron County, Michigan. Luxuriant vegetable- and flower-gardens, tennis courts, and a tea-house in Chinese style, provided amusement and recreation in the summer. Here the Chinese office force—for my wife and I were the only non-Chinese among the several hundred souls within our well-guarded castle—gathered for tea and tennis. Marushka, the jersey cow, furnished a twice-daily serio-comedy when Chang, the house-boy, exercised his talent, rare indeed for a Chinese, for milking. When the time came, a charming pastoral would be enacted: Chang, displaying for once on his bland expressionless face a weight of great responsibility, was arrayed in spotless white apron. Under his arm he carried the milk pan. Behind him stumping along on tiny bound feet his wife, Amah, followed with the wooden milking-stool. The dignified "Peeks," Na T'ung and P'u Lun, participated in the ceremonies with equal solemnity. Last came Old Du, the gardener, carrying a pail of warm water with which to lave Marushka as necessary. He alone failed to maintain that standard of importance and dignity demanded by this ritual. The Chinese disdain for dairy products was ill-concealed upon his usually good-humored face. He was

172

allotted, too, the least dignified role, that of holding fast Marushka's tail during the milking.

The pedigreed stock of the American Oil Company's manager at Mukden provided our flock of White Leghorns. In the stables champed a *quadriga* of coal-black Russian stallions which Mr. Yen affected in his carriage turn-outs. One or two wild drives behind these maddened beasts reduced us to the uninterrupted use of the Ford sedan. Our chauffeur, Krijanoffsky, salvaged from the least helpless of the Merkuloff wounded cavalry officers, found a riding horse for me. "Cossack" under my hands was a simple hack. When Krijanoffsky mounted the old war-horse, together they performed feats of equestrianism, both rider and steed seeming as one in the recollection of parade-ground and battlefield.

In the garage there reposed most of the time on flattened tires an antique Hudson limousine. It glistened in plate-glass and shining brass, in the manner of motor cars especially constructed for Oriental potentates. Mr. Yen, my colleague, usually remained close to his powerful patron, Marshal Chang Tso-lin, at Mukden. Whenever he came up to Ch'ang-ch'un, word preceded him, and the Hudson juggernaut was trundled out. Russian mechanics from Kuan-ch'eng-tze were brought in, new inner-tubes fitted, the motor overhauled. At last the motor would turn over of its own accord, and the car would make its way with startling explosions down the hill and over the two miles to the railway station. By some further engineering legerdemain, the machine reached home again, triumphantly bearing Mr. Yen to his official residence. Once more it stood silently in the garage until Mr. Yen chose to proceed to the railway station for the return journey to Mukden. After successive repair bills for these brief excursions had been presented, my attention was called to the several hundred dollars, silver, expended on each occasion of Mr. Yen's movements. I more than suspected that Mr. Yen's chauffeur, a tall bandit-looking fellow, always accompanied by a small satellite, customarily exaggerated the need for repairs, and padded the bill.

While walking past the garage on the way home from my office one evening, I noted a light inside. I stepped in and found the two chauffeurs tinkering with the motor. I rather unwisely demanded of the big fellow an explanation for recent heavy repair bills. He turned on me, and in surly fashion told me in effect that it was none of my business. He was employed by Mr. Yen! In the face of such a disrespectful attitude, I stepped closer to him and in vigorous Chinese told the fellow off, adding that Mr. Yen would indeed hear of this. The man withdrew a step or two, while looking meaningly beyond and behind me. I turned quickly, just in time to catch sight of the satellite with a long sharp steel file in his hand, which he had held upraised over my back. Both men disappeared that night into Manchuria's wilds.

*   *   *

173

Mr. Yen's formally announced call was succeeded by his appearance. He apologized charmingly for thus disturbing me during my convalescence from an illness he only now realized had been of far greater gravity than he had been led to suppose. His sympathetic expressions were profuse but sincere; Mr. Yen had engaging qualities. But, he went on, he had an urgent message from the Marshal at Mukden. The tri-provincial government was in pressing need of military funds. There was suspicious activity on the part of the Russians on the northern boundary, especially across the Amur at Blagovestchensk; the Mongols had been none to tractable lately in the face of further advances of the Chinese cultivators into their grass lands. Then, too, the Marshal had to keep his fences mended down at the Sea-and-Mountain Pass, the bottle-neck along the narrow corridor from Manchuria to North China. Generals Wu and Feng were concentrating troops there. Machines for his arsenal at Mukden, and warm leather jerkins for his troops, were about to arrive from America, and must be paid for, without delay, etc., etc. The point was that the provincial financial commissioner was urgently expecting me to sign a cheque for one million eight hundred thousand dollars, silver, for the Marshal's account. This was the major portion of the winter's profits of the salt monopoly.

I explained meticulously to Mr. Yen the new arrangements about the salt revenue. It must all be paid first into the foreign banks which had made the big loan to China; these in turn, after retaining such portions as were required for the interest-coupons and the amortization tables, would pay over any remaining surplus to the Central Government at Peking. Thus, if the Marshal required funds for the defence of his province, he should apply directly to the Ministry of Finance at the national capital. As for myself, while personally I should like nothing better than to accommodate His Excellency at Mukden, I would of course have to report the matter first to the Inspectors-General at Peking and obtain their approval. Mr. Yen listened patiently, repeated his request and thereupon bade me good-bye.

Shortly after, a brusque note was handed me from Chin, Mr. Yen's secretary. Composed in discourteous carelessness, demand was made upon me to sign a cheque forthwith in the required amount for the Marshal's financial deputy. Or else.... It is customary for high Chinese officials to maintain an agent, a sort of *alter ego,* who cheerfully and efficiently assumes all unpleasant duties on behalf of his patron. This maintains the big politician's reputation for amiability and keeps his own skirts clear in case of mishap. Such was Chief Secretary Chin's relationship to urbane Mr. Yen. I at once wired the Chief Inspectors of salt revenue at Peking for instructions as to how to proceed. Pressure on me by written note or special emissary continued. While still awaiting my orders from Peking I was being held *incommunicado* until I surrendered. Finally an ultimatum reached me. I must sign the cheque within three days when the Special

174

Finance Deputy would return to Mukden, for Marshal Chang would brook no further delay.…

Serious as all this seemed, it was really fine play-acting. Marshal Chang Tso-lin had long before ordered that all funds of the North Manchuria salt monopoly should be deposited in his own provincial Bank of the Three Provinces. He could help himself at will as he already had. The curious Chinese insistence upon observance of proper form had led to all this by play about my signing a cheque. I continued the game on my part until the last moment when as the ultimatum was about to expire, a telegram from Peking arrived granting me authority to sign "subject to the Peking Government's reservation of all rights and interests in the Manchurian salt revenues, now and henceforth, as prescribed by the terms of the Reorganization Loan Agreement."

Railway Empire

WHEN, at the end of 1922, I made my first visit to Harbin, capital of Russia's North Manchurian empire, John F. Stevens was packing up to leave for good. I called promptly on the famous railway builder, who had had a wider experience in his field than any other American, or, for that matter, anybody else. He had had an active engineering career, beginning in Minneapolis as far back as 1874, and had been president or general-manager of most of our north-west trunk lines. His career was to culminate as chief engineer of the Panama Canal and Chairman of the Isthmian Canal Commission. The abortive Siberian expedition of the World War allies, in which the Japanese stole the show by sending in ten times the troops of the other expeditionaries, had gradually dissolved. It had at least enabled the Czechoslovakian contingent, which had been trapped by the Revolution in Bolshevik Russia, to withdraw across Siberia to Vladivostok. Then, so a Russian officer sourly informed me, they loaded steamers with various little souvenirs picked up along the way, such as pianos, paintings, dining-room suites, gold-framed ikons and other knickknacks. The vestigial remainder of this unhappy international effort, which was being liquidated at the time of my appearance, was the "Inter-Allied Technical Board for the Supervision of Siberian Railways." The latter included the Chinese Eastern Railway extension across North Manchuria. Burly old John F. Stevens was President of the Board.

The Russian advance upon the virtually empty spaces of Eastern Asia is one of the epics of history. In the sixteenth century the great mercantile house of Strogonoff sent their agent, the sturdy Yermak, across the Urals into unoccupied Siberia. Within half a century Yakoutsk was founded on the Lena river, and the sea of Okhotsk was reached. The great Amur, Black Dragon River to the Chinese, was explored and Albazin was founded by Khabarov, who gave his name to the settlement at the junction of the Amur and the Sungari, Khabarovsk. The Chinese knew the Russians longer than they had any other white people, for the Asiatic boundaries of

175

the two countries were contiguous for thousands of miles. The treaty of Nerchinsk was concluded in 1689, "the longest lived treaty on record." Russia exchanged broad-cloth for China's silk, tea and cotton. By diplomacy so astute that it remained the model for Japan in later years, the Russians secured the Maritime Province, the Primorsk on the Pacific, in 1860, and at length overran Manchuria. Had it not been for the Russo-Japanese war of 1904–5, Russia's territories would have embraced Korea and perhaps much of North China as well.

That disastrous encounter, followed by the complete absorption of the nation in its decades of internal political ferment terminating in the Bolshevik Revolution, deflected the "bear that walks like a man" from its Far Eastern venture. When I reached Harbin in 1922, Russian interests had but a tenuous hold on railway and region. The Inter-Allied Technical Board had provided a prop for the tottering Russian management; while the Chinese for so many years the "sleeping partner" in the immensely lucrative railway, had at length awakened to their opportunities. Across the Siberian borders of the two termini—Manchuli and Pogranitchnaya—Red Soldiers watched for the day when the order would be given to swoop down upon the small band of White refugees who momentarily operated the line, and to take over all the agencies, political and commercial, which it comprised. For the Railway was the ruling power of North Manchuria.

Boris Ostroumoff's technical qualifications for the post of General Manager of the Chinese Eastern Railway were superb. He was an Oriental-featured person who had gained distinction from the building of railways in Central Asia. For one thing, at an early date he had adopted the aeroplane for rapidly reconnoitering difficult terrain, for despatching staff-personnel to distant points, and even for distributing much needed supplies over the vast spaces traversed by the new strategic Turk-Sib railway. Along the glistening Manchurian line the little autocrat was now in constant motion, and everyone personally felt his generous praise or sharp blame, from track-walker to district engineer. He had gathered about him a group of Tzarist Russia's outstanding railway technicians. All was set for one of the most ably managed and profitable lines in the world. But alas, the railway began nowhere and ended nowhere, and its managers were men without a country. The Russian borders were virtually closed to traffic and the connecting Japanese South Manchuria railway sought to deflect all traffic from the north over its own line to the ice free port of Dairen.

It was now twenty-five years since the breaking of the first sod for the "C.E.R." Li Hung-chang had paid the price of Russia's intervention in 1895 against Japan by the grant of sweeping railway concessions in Manchuria. It was when the great Mandarin was on his way home from St. Petersburg, after effectuating this settlement, that I had had that thrilling glimpse of him at Toronto. In 1923 when the quarter-centennial of the Railway's establishment was celebrated, all was outwardly serene. Behind

176

the scenes there were mounting deficits in operating expenses, and the Chinese authorities were seeking an excuse to take over the line. Red Russia had particularly excluded, in its self-denying treaty with China, renunciation of its claims in the old Imperial railway domain. This and the Persian caviar fisheries in the Caspian sea, even the proletarians of Russia could not bring themselves to forego.

My own official relations with the Railway were extensive. It was the vehicle whereby many tens of thousands of bags of salt were distributed throughout the far-flung North Manchurian provinces. Our monthly freight bill was probably the only prompt and substantial resource of the line. Thus as Auditor General of the North Manchuria Government Salt Monopoly offices I was favored with a special invitation to attend the festivities marking the Railway's quarter-centennial. My brother-in-law, Charles J. Carroll, was Engineer-in-Chief of the American section of the Hu-Kuang railways of Central China, American participation in which had been secured by the forceful representations of energetic American *chargé d'affaires* Henry P. Fletcher, when I had been in the Peking Legation back in 1909. Carroll had been placed in charge, too, of the German section of the projected line running from Hankow to I-chang, when China entered the War. His work in China followed years of trans-continental railway building in Mexico, and was to be succeeded by one of the last great railway construction achievements, the linking by rail of the Persian Gulf with the Caspian Sea. Engineer Carroll was one of those eminent railway men brought to Harbin to give distinction to the celebration of the line's quarter centennial.

The tradition of Czarist opulence still flourished under the open-handed regime of Boris Ostroumoff. From early morning breakfast to the lavish state banquets of the evenings, caviar, cold meats and fowl, smoked sturgeon and salmon, *aspics,* salads, sausages, cheeses in infinite variety, and countless bottles of champagne were set out. The luxurious coaches of the *Compagnie Internationale des Wagons Lits,* stranded here from their erstwhile trans-Siberian functions, were placed at the disposal of the Railway's guests, night and day. Special trains were run from Harbin to the east and west terminals. On the eastern section we passed through hills well wooded with birch and larch, to stop at the charmingly laid-out flower gardens of the Railway at the little town of Imienpo.

To the westward of Harbin, the road crossed slightly rolling prairie-land, fertile but untilled, on which roamed a few nomads of the Solon tribe. These broad, empty acres, equal to Canada's western plains, could provide foodstuffs for millions. Beyond came the Hingan mountains, part of the ranges which spring from the T'ien-shan, the great ridges of Central Asia, and project north-eastward as far as the frozen sea of Okhotsk. We stopped at Cha-lan-t'un, a *station climatérique,* provided for the health of its employees by the paternalistic Railway. Perfectly appointed meals were served us in the *Kursaal,* while an excellent orchestra played.

177

A lovely crystal stream, the Yal, flowed past, teeming with trout, a fisherman's paradise. Mountain trails for riding led in all directions.

Knowing his guests needed exercise after so much hospitality, the energetic Ostroumoff organized a riding party. Some twenty or more of us, ladies and gentlemen, joined him. A Cossack escort insured our safety from marauding bands of Mongols. Off we cantered on a variety of mounts, from tall Russian horses to diminutive ponies. Our route took us up and across the valley of the Yal. Within an hour or two black clouds suddenly appeared about the neighboring peaks.

"A mountain storm," shouted Ostroumoff. "We must return."

So down the pass we cantered, the party gathering speed as the cloud masses on the hills drew nearer. I was recuperating from the attack of pneumonia at Ch'ang-ch'un that spring. My tall, angular mount, named Vasili, bounced me about until I began to feel the sharp twinges of scarcely healed pulmonary lesions. These effects remained with me for some days, as well as the more customary tender spots which remind a rider of the need for more regular sorties a-horseback.

In the meantime our party had reached the ford where we had previously crossed the Yal. The stream was rising rapidly with the heavy rains in the near-by mountains.

"Hurry" Ostroumoff interpreted our Cossack leader's admonitions "or we shan't be able to get across."

The horses plunged in with great splashing. Suddenly we heard a call from Lady Philips, wife of the British Consul General at Harbin, an excellent horsewoman, who was riding a small white pony. The swift current, already up against the animal's body, had gradually forced it down stream to a point where the ford shelved off into deep water. The pony floundered, while Lady Philips was using her spurs vigorously to urge it back against the current. Two Cossacks dashed to her aid and seizing the pony's bridle from their tall mounts, hauled it half floating from its precarious position into shallow water and finally to the bank. Lady Philips took her narrow escape with complete calm.

*   *   *

The policing of the extensive territories appertaining to the Chinese Eastern Railway involved the expenditure of considerable sums of money, extensive patronage and a minimum of technological skills. Thus this field appeared to Ostroumoff and his colleagues as the most suitable to surrender to the Chinese pressures. General Chu Ching-lan, an old-style military mandarin, was placed in command of the Railway Police Battalion. Years later when, with swollen money bags, he had taken up a leisurely retirement in the Shanghai International Settlement, he was usually referred to as "the well-known philanthropist, General Chu." This was a role that most of his retired warlord colleagues assumed. General Chu Ching-lan's chief of staff at Harbin was Colonel Wen Ying-hsing. The

178

latter differed considerably, both physically and temperamentally, from his ponderous chief. Colonel Wen had graduated from West Point. Less than five feet six in height, he affected a natty uniform such as was rarely seen in those days on a Chinese military officer. Uniforms were made usually with such amplitude as to enable them to be worn in cold weather over voluminous padded underclothing.

The ceremonies attending the twenty-fifth anniversary of the Chinese Eastern Railway had reached a point where a formal visitation was made upon the Russian *gymnasium* or technical high school. This like almost everything else, drew its support from the Railway. The group of visiting guests, including General Chu, Colonel Wen and their staff, reached the doorway to the school. The Director, a scientist distinguished for his achievements in education in pre-revolutionary Russia, greeted us. The July sun beat down with all the brief intensity of the summer in high latitudes. All, except the Chinese officers in their heavy olive-drab uniforms, were in whites.

Suddenly a Chinese voice was raised, *Pu kuei-chü, pu kuei-chü*—"Such discourtesy, such discourtesy." In the heat, the school Director wore a "Barrymore" collar to his shirt, open at the neck, without tie or coat. It happened that the "comrades" in Russia had adopted generally such an undress mode.

Everything instantly was at a standstill. The Chinese refused to enter until a stiffly dressed representative of the school's faculty had made profuse apologies. This indeed was a new order when the descendants of Count Muravieff-Amursky, who had a half century earlier gained all Eastern Siberia for Russia, could be humbled in public by the contemned Khitaians. It pretold unmistakably that powerful Marshal Chang Tso-lin at Mukden—now that the last support of the Railway had been withdrawn (rugged old John F. Stevens and his Inter-Allied Railway Board)—was preparing the way for a *coup* that would place the Railway exclusively in Chinese hands. Not long afterward, in fact, one Ivanov came over from Moscow. With the cooperation of the Manchurian authorities, he replaced the erstwhile Tzarist group headed by Ostroumoff.

The U. S. Minister came up to Harbin to exercise his good offices in the acrimonious railway dispute proceeding between Ostroumoff and the Chinese. No representative of the United States ever commanded, from Burlingame to Rockhill, I take it, greater respect among the Chinese than Jacob Gould Schurman, distinguished President of Cornell University, Member of the first Philippine Commission, and at this time American Minister Plenipotentiary to China. His finished public addresses, his ripe diplomatic experience, his recognized scholarship, all commended him to a nation which has ever placed intellect above all else. I joined Dr. Schurman's special train at Ch'ang-ch'un and accompanied him upon his return as far as Mukden. I marveled how lightly the veteran educator and diplomat bore his sixty-five years. After the fatigue of a long day, fol-

179

lowing an early morning start from Harbin, with uninterrupted conferences with argumentive Russian and disputatious Chinese, he reached
Mukden as fresh in spirit and vigorous in body as if the day had been
devoted to rest and recreation. But the fate of the Railway Empire in
North Manchuria was in the end to rest with neither Manchu nor Mus-
covite. In 1926 Ivanov himself was placed under arrest by the Chinese
who continued to control the Railway until the seizure of Manchuria by
the Japanese in 1931. Ultimately the railway was bought over from the
residual Russian interests by Japan.

My relations with the Japanese-owned South Manchuria Railway were
also fairly close. All salt for the Ki-Hei Monopoly must be brought from
the sea-coast in the south over that railway as far as Ch'ang-ch'un. These
shipments accounted for a considerable portion of the railway's freight.
Periodical negotiations were held to readjust freight rates, based upon
annual maximum and minimum salt shipments. For such purposes I visited the head offices of the Railway at Dairen in 1923 to discuss a new
contract with the general traffic manager of the Railway, and, by way of
preliminary, with the president. The line impressed me as operated with
great efficiency, largely after American standards of rolling stock, both
freight and passenger, and in trackage and gauge. The Russian railway
used such a broad gauge that all bothways freight, including salt, had to be
transhipped at Ch'ang-ch'un at great cost and waste of time. Its wood-
burning locomotives, moreover, with inverted cone shaped smokestack,
and old-fashioned "spark-catcher," reminded one of the Hollywood dram-
atizations of the first Union Pacific trains to cross the American continent.

Count Kodama, scion of a distinguished family, was for the time being
Governor of the Kuantung leased territory, the Japanese controlled peninsula at the southern extremity of Manchuria. During a prolonged official
visit at Harbin, he and his suite were extensively entertained by the management of the Chinese Eastern Railway. Escorted by his hosts back to
the terminus of the Russian line, Count Kodama returned the courtesies
he had received in the form of an elaborate banquet in Japanese style at
the largest *geisha* house in Ch'ang-ch'un. The Japanese Consul who was in
charge of the local arrangements, included me in this colorful function as
a member of Ch'ang-ch'un official family. The hosts and guests, all Japanese or Russian save myself, were seated *à la Japonaise* on the floor of
the spacious but austerely simple dining-hall of the restaurant. We were
made comfortable by the soft *tatami,* the cushioned matting with which the
floor was covered. Our host sat at the top of the long room, the President
and Vice-President of the Chinese Eastern Railway sitting at his left and
right, the others ranged along both sides of the long hall. A special wait-
ress placed a low table before each individual. Separate trays were brought
in for each course. On them were lacquer bowls and dishes containing
clear fish-soup, fried sea-weed and prawns, raw fish which with a sort of
horse-radish sauce was surprisingly palatable, a cold, sweetened omelette,

180

and other less readily identifiable dainties. The banquet was punctuated by the ceremonious drinking of tiny cups of *saké,* the Japanese rice-wine, immediately refilled by the attentive little *neisan* who ministered to each of us.

Just before our departure from Ch'ang-ch'un, a function no less sociable, but with more hidden portent, was given. For three days the representatives of the two railway lines had vigorously negotiated over the renewal of joint freight tariffs. The Japanese insisted that the rates on the southbound Harbin-Ch'ang-ch'un line be reduced to a point where shipments would be deflected to their railway and thence to Dairen, instead of to the competing Vladivostok line. Russians are the most skillful of all diplomats. Not until the elaborate dinner, which concluded the proceedings, served on General Manager Ostroumoff's special train, was it disclosed that the anti-Red management at Harbin had all along desired to turn away freight from their hated compatriots in the Maritime Province. From the beginning, they were more than ready to offer inducements to shippers to turn their freight over to the southern Japanese line. It had been deemed advisable, however, to carry to the end the farce of negotiations. Throughout the banquet, quantities of wine were consumed in never ending pledges of *Za-vashe-zdorovye's* and answering *Banzai's.* Boris Ostroumoff met these demands by draining his glass repeatedly. Astonished at such capacity for apparently one so frail, I looked closer behind the floral arrangement at his plate. Unnoticed by his challengers, half hidden by the flowers, was a tea-pot from whose amber liquid, stimulating but not inebriating, he constantly replenished his wine glass.

*   *   *

"More for it than against it," my wife had tersely decided when our North Manchuria assignment had been broached to me by the little Colonel at Peking in late 1922. The words had been prophetic. The Manchuria we had spent our two years in was a land of clashing racial interests, full of the vigorous pioneering spirit of our own West. But that highly recommended cemetery at Ch'ang-ch'un had almost proved its utility. So before the harsh sub-Arctic winter closed in on us again, we were off to the familiar scenes of central China, once more to be at Wu-han's three cities.

VI

NATIONALIST CHINA, 1924–1939

China Typhoon — Academic Interlude — Streamlined
Dragon — Retreat from China — Fate of a Nation

China Typhoon

THE THREE-THOUSAND-TON China-coaster *Fengtien* steamed out of Weihaiwei Bay precisely at midnight. Out late hosts, the Harry Pearces, had
brought us out to the ship by motor launch from their spacious beach
bungalow. For the past fortnight, we had swum in the warm salt water of
this exclusive North China summer-resort, or fished for sea-bass at the
harbor's entrance. That August night of 1926 the full moon swung high.
The Yellow Sea was as glass. A long white cruiser, H.M.S. *Kent,* lay at
anchor off the British naval station on Liu-kung-tao island. Her after-deck
was covered with awnings, and lights of many colors sparkled. The home-
ward-bound pennant floated from her foremast. One of Britain's tiniest
crown colonies was paying its homage by a farewell party on board for
"Lieutenant Windsor." Tanned by the Eastern sun, and familiarized with
the most distant parts of his father's dominions, Prince George had completed his tour of sea duty, and was returning to his royal duties in England.

It was almost too hot, that still August night, to turn in. There were
odors of oil and dried fish, and the sickening smell of sugar cargo. Yet
the first-class quarters of the little steamer were clean and ship-shape as
British seamanship maintains its sailing craft the world over. Sleep at
length overpowered us...In a single bound I was out of my berth and
holding up my wife's ward-robe trunk which stood open on end swaying
backward and forward. In the nearby serving-pantry there was a crash of
falling pans and dishes. I hastily put on a silk *kimono* over my pyjamas
and managed to get out into the ship's saloon. The little steamer was
pitching and tossing under the combined onslaught of wind and waves.

"Another typhoon up from that infernal island of Yap", shouted
Macauley, the first officer, as by main force he pushed the saloon door
shut against the wind. He was dripping water from his oil skins. I looked
out the porthole into a haze of rain and spray carried along by furious
gusts. The yellow water roared and splashed about us.

183

"Man, but it's terrible," continued the mate. "Pity the poor folks ashore on a night like this."

I could have exchanged with alacrity this bounding steamer for the risks of *terra firma.*

The swirling mass of heated air up from the tropics lashed the China coast from Ningpo northward. Even big trans-Pacific liners *en route* from Kobe or Nagasaki to Shanghai lost their bearings in the narrow seas and found themselves off their course. The staunch little Clyde-built *Fengtien* bobbed about like a cork. At last the skipper shaped her course out to sea.

"We're getting into shallow water, too near the coast."

Most of the passengers were in their berths, clutching the side boards. I sat clutching the saloon table with eyes glued to the pages of an old *National Geographic Magazine,* but actually little conscious of the gaudy photographs of tuilp-beds in Holland, or the stirring account of the Society's expedition up Alaska's highest volcano.

The third morning found the sun shining brightly. As we neared the familiar Saddle Islands in the Yangtze estuary, the sea rapidly subsided and we glided up that deep tidal river, the Whangpoo, which leads to Shanghai's busy wharves.

"Worse storms over Central China; you'll have to hurry back to your post," announced Consul General Edwin S. Cunningham as he greeted us at the Customs jetty. "The armies of Chiang K'ai-shek, with Soviet military and political advisers, have marched overland from Canton. Wu-ch'ang is now under attack."

We were off again on the night river-steamer. At Kiukiang I escorted my wife up to K'u-ling, a dramatic night journey, with flaming torches to light us up the mountain. It was still the worst heat of the "summer tiger"; women are best out of the way when machine-guns chatter.

The uproar at the Wu-han cities was deafening. Shut up in the walled city of Wu-ch'ang, Warlord Ch'en Chia-mou's troops maintained a barrage of small arms and artillery fire in the general direction in which the attacking forces were believed to be. Gun-boats patrolled the river, the reverberations of their guns shaking the buildings along the Bund. As customary, activity increased with night-fall, making sleep impossible. One pleasing feature was that *Tuchün* Ch'en at sundown had innumerable lighted lanterns festooned along his beleaguered city's wall, so as to be able to discern at once any force daring enough to attempt an assault. These lights twinkled festively as we viewed them across the Yangtze.

In this warfare the aeroplane figured in China for the first time, but not seriously. Chiefly, pamphlets were scattered in great numbers from the skies, calling upon the populace to abandon their reactionary leaders, and join the people's movement. A few small bombs were dropped upon Wu-ch'ang. Shut up in the city were American and British missionaries and their native adherents. The close siege soon began to tell. Foodstuffs were running low. Expeditions were organized in Hankow to enter the city

184

with supplies. At length *Tuchün* Ch'en decided to observe the Tertullian maxim, "He who fights and runs away. . . ." He was carefully let down over the high wall in a basket. Although he had changed his field-marshal's uniform for the blue denim of a common coolie, the alert besetting forces promptly spotted him; his pock-marked features were readily recognizable. In due course he was paraded through the streets of his capital in a wooden cage, the only living Chinese warlord in captivity.

Meanwhile, the foreign community at Hankow were in a state of trepidation. The invading "Nationalist" forces were well supplied by Michael Borodin and other Soviet advisers, including, it was said, the noted Red General Galen. Day by day reports were circulated that the foreign "Concessions" of which only the British, French, and Japanese had survived the settlements of the World War, would be taken over by force. This applied particularly to the British. A few of the Powers' men-of-war were anchored in the River, capable of laying down a heavy barrage or landing armed parties. Admiral Henry H. Hough, U.S.N., was in alert touch with American Consul General Frank Lockhart. The dilemma presented was that overt action at Hankow against the Chinese might bring reprisals upon defenseless missionaries in the interior. The situation was perplexingly delicate. The British and American Volunteer Corps were on duty day and night. The Japanese in their more distant Concession remained quiet, probably better informed than any of us. The French Concession was defended by a few Annamite colonials as well as by civilian volunteers.

As we were preparing to return to America on a periodical furlough, I called at the British Consulate the morning of January 3, 1927, to secure visas for our passports through British territories, against our anticipated voyage *via* the Suez Canal route. His Majesty's Consul General, Herbert Goffe, C.M.G., met me. He was freshly shaven and immaculately dressed in well pressed tweeds. A carnation blushed in his lapel, and he was smoking a fine Manila cigar. But his features were glum.

"It's all over," he sighed enigmatically . . . He had received instructions from Downing Street *via* the Peking Legation—no resistance to the revolutionaries.

That evening we sat on cushions on the floor in the apartment of our friends, the Hugo Seitzs'; this was on the former Russian, now Chinese Bund overlooking the British Concession. Our hostess was preparing *sukiaki,* a light Japanese chafing dish preparation of chopped beef and vegetables, served with plenty of rice. The men were in the khaki uniforms of the American Volunteer Company. Our commander Captain Raymond Mackay burst in.

"The British Concession has been rushed by the Nationalists, the Volunteer Corps disarmed and the British naval landing force withdrawn to the ships."

Despite its actual seriousness, it still seemed all a part of the hilarious unreality of life at Hankow.

185

The "psychological assault" continued against both the Chinese "capitalists" and foreign "imperialists" (the latter consisting of American business men of the dangerous type met with at Rotary luncheons, or British dealers in Manchester printed calicos). With the date of my sabbatical leave approaching (after five years' absence from America), the salt merchants, harried though they were by the troops commandeering their junks up and down the river and causing them enormous losses, courteously invited me to a farewell feast. We sat in a restaurant in the street dividing the British Concession from the Chinese city of Hankow. On the way to the restaurant, I had driven my *Detroit Electric* past a long procession of Wu-han's proletariat. Assembled for the purpose, they had been taught to shout the usual slogans—"down with the foreign imperialists," "death to the running-dogs of the foreigners," the latter presumed to be Chinese in foreign employ or otherwise associated with Westerners. Waving banners were inscribed with equally felicitous injunctions. Individuals were mounted here and there along the streets on boxes, carts or even rickshas haranguing gaping crowds of wharf-coolies.

As the venerable chairman of the Huai Salt Merchants Guild was in the midst of a complimentary speech, extolling the fairness of my administration and the very present aid I had proven in the existing confusion and turmoil, a shot rang out. There was an involuntary, but quickly suppressed movement on the part of hosts and guests to exchange their chairs for the relative safety beneath the table. All remained rigidly awaiting the next event. The head waiter rushed in to reassure us. It was only the bodyguard of a military officer feasting in an adjacent compartment, who had accidently let off his Mauser pistol.

A final effort against Warlord Sun Ch'uan-fang was made at Shanghai—China was launched on a program of fundamental reform and progress. *Western educated* young China was at last in control.

Academic Interlude

UPON MY RETURN to America from distracted China in 1927 I found myself foot-loose in the homeland and available for an academic interlude. I accordingly accepted an invitation by my alma mater to spend a year at Ann Arbor as visiting lecturer on the history of the Far East. This unexpected commitment projected me into the beginnings of a vigorous movement to promote and develop Chinese and Japanese studies in the United States along scientific lines, but with American objectives. From the University of Michigan I was called to the University of California where for four years I served as chairman of the department of the Chinese and Japanese languages.

Twenty years earlier "Duke" Neville disclosed to me the possibility for the first time of learning these Far Eastern languages (as well as Turkish and Arabic at the American Embassy at Constantinople) under government auspices. I was then perhaps as familiar with existing facilities for

186

foreign language training in the United States as most people. My own linguistic exploits to that date had not been inconsiderable for the average American. The *pater* was an M.D. C.M., degrees obtained at McGill University in Anglo-French Montreal. Of almost pure Scotch origin, he had a decided flair for languages. Besides a fairly thorough training in the convential classics, Greek and Latin, he had necessarily acquired French in his university days. He took up German sufficiently to have a good working knowledge for his later fifty years' general practice in a polyglot Michigan community—both North and South Germans, French Canadians from over the border, a large Polish *bloc,* and a rapidly increasing Jewish settlement. He had me reading the Bible in French before I went to school; and then instead of the regular public schools, I found myself inserted into one *Evangelische Lutherische Bethels Schule,* a German parochial institution.

Here came my first linguistic adventures, long later to be continued in distant Asia. My school-mates were all from German immigrant families, bilingual after a manner, speaking German in the home and English with their fellows on the playground. *"Wie heist du,"* a visiting teacher asked me one day, not having been informed of my non-German provenience. I stared at my interrogator blankly. He repeated the question. I stubbornly remained silent and was promptly "thrashed." Later, on the playground, the boys crowded around me.

"Why didn't you tell him your name?"

"Oh was that what he asked me," I observed ruefully rubbing my tender spots.

Latin, and then Greek, obtained my enthusiastic devotion in the local high-school, with a minor accompaniment of German and French. There were good teachers in the "primitive" high-schools of those days, before heavy bond issues provided palatial buildings as at present. "Professor" R. Henri Gauthier provided most excellent instruction in the purest Parisian French routed in *via* the Quebec seminaries. Mrs. Stonebreaker taught the language of Goethe and Schiller. Neither had many hours of "education" or perhaps for that matter any "teaching diplomas"; but both had authentic accents and deep feeling for the great literatures they taught. My appetite for languages was further whetted at the University of Michigan. Here and there I sampled the linguistic feast—"Silver" Latin, Old French, Anglo-Saxon, Italian—even Russian off the record with an engineering student from the Crimea.

In the American linguistic consciousness of 1908, the Far East was nonexistent despite its hundreds of millions of Chinese, Japanese, Koreans, Indo-Chinese, and Siamese speaking the tongues of Babel. To be sure, one could always obtain instruction in Hebrew, but that was "because it proved the Bible." I might have known, but did not, and few did, that two elderly aliens, an Englishman and a German, were, in half secrecy, like alchemists of old, imparting some knowledge of the Chinese language to a handful of American students at California and Columbia Universities. The one, Professor John Fryer at Berkeley, was a former English missionary and Chinese government translator. He occupied a chair of Chinese at Berkeley, named for the distinguished scientist Agassiz. This professorship had been endowed by California's State Senator Tompkins with valuable lands now within the city of Oakland. Such an unexpected gesture was, the Senator stated in the deed of gift, in view of increasing business with the Orient, and for the purpose of training Americans in the Chinese language in order to get rid of dishonest native interpreters. At Columbia, General Horace Carpentier had similarly established a chair of Chinese in memory of his faithful servitor Dean Lung. There Professor Friedrich Hirth, long in Sir Robert Hart's Custom's service in China, was continuing life-long researches in Chinese grammar, history, and art.

Thus unheralded, the foundations had been laid for the study of that land across the Pacific which had absorbed the flower of American talent for generations. The New England Everetts, the Bacons, the Forbes were men who in commerce knew their China well; innumerable others, S. Wells Williams, W.A.P. Martin, Arthur Smith, Chauncey Goodrich, could not be surpassed in knowledge of China, its people, its language, philosophy, religions, and literature. Fortunately, that remarkable missionary, diplomat, and scholar, the Rev. S. Wells Williams was ultimately selected for the chair of Oriental history at Yale University. *The Middle Kingdom,* his *magnum opus* remained the standard work on China, its history and culture, for several generations; and it formed the foundation of a similar encyclopaedic work by a successor, Professor Kenneth Scott Latourette.

American sinology—the systematized study of the Chinese language, literature, laws, and history, as the dictionaries define this word—was in danger of being converted into the dry-as-dust scholasticism which infected some of the European schools, though fortunately not all of them. China could not be treated as a civilization as dead as that of the Mayans of jungle-covered Yucatan, or its abundant recorded literature studied like the cuneiform inscriptions on the sunbaked bricks of ancient Assyria. The fetish of a certain type of scholarship animating the work of the Sanskritists must not be permitted to stifle Chinese studies in America. It was a satisfaction to play some part in combating this threatened blight.

In the academic year 1927–28 I had the personal satisfaction of offering introductory courses at my own alma mater on the history of the Far East, and on the political relations of the Western Powers to Japan and China. Thus, for the first time since its organization in 1817, and despite the fact that its most noted president, James Burrill Angell, had served as American envoy to China, the great University of Michigan took cognizance in its academic curriculum of the vast insular and continental world in the Western Pacific and beyond. The seeds sown then have continued to be abundantly watered. Within a year I was called to the University of California where a vigorous "full-dress" department of Chinese and Japanese studies had flourished for some years. Here my first American acquaintance on China's soil, Edward T. Williams, Agassiz Professor of Chinese, had distinguished himself in productive sinology, as he had previously in the American diplomatic service.

Interest in America, I found, had been transferred from an almost exclusive popular absorption in missionary activity in China and Japan, to considerations of the historic and cultural aspects of these countries. The new American school of sinology bade fair in scholarly productiveness to overtake the older European schools. Scores of American students came yearly to enroll in Chinese and Japanese language classes in our universities. Hundreds came to the general lecture courses on Far Eastern history, politics, and art. Eminent European and Chinese scholars were invited to lecture on the Far East in American institutions of learning. Funds of the foundations, which previously went almost exclusively to philanthropic enterprise in the Orient, now began to flow into channels of scientific investigation and for the underwriting of promising students.

Some may raise the question of the value of investigations into the early literature and thought of China. The answer is obvious. No nation has enjoyed a longer and more continuous racial existence than the Chinese. The vast sum of the experience of the greatest ethnic *bloc* on the globe has been recorded in written characters from the time of the inscribed tortoise shells and the highly wrought bronzes of a dozen centuries before the Christian era. Ancient Chinese literature contains deep spiritual utterances of value to us today. Here are the earliest recorded thoughts of humanity on perennial economic, political, philosophical, and religious problems. Aside from these fields, China has made valuable contributions in medicine and agriculture. We can no longer ignore the origins and development of a civilization which continued after several thousand years to dominate in Japan, China, and most of East Asia. No force will make for better mutual understanding than that the West shall know the East. A determining development of our age may be not the current of Western thought and practice, which for the past century set in so strongly from the Occident to the Orient; but the shift in cultural exchanges which may proceed from the ancient civilizations of East Asia to the relatively new societies of Europe and America. The profound impression made in America by the philosophy of living advanced by Lin Yu-t'ang is an evidence of this new cultural current from ancient East to West.

In the year 1927 I had believed myself, if not a "sinologist," at least a fairly attentive student of things Chinese for almost 20 years—since the time when in 1908 I arrived at Peking and had sat with a dozing Chinese pundit to learn the "tones," the monosyllabic words and the stereotyped phrases, and the ideographic symbols representing them. I had read the usual books beginning with S. Wells Williams' compendium, *The Middle Kingdom;* I had occasionally looked up an item in Herbert Giles' *Biographical Dictionary,* supplemented by Samuel Coulings' *Encyclopaedia Sinica.* Of course I had thumbed over Sir Walter Hillier's revised Wade's

Chinese language primer known to generations of Consular and Customs service students, the *Tzu Erh Chi;* I had used Stent's *Colloquial Dictionary,* and Soothill's *"4000 Characters."* In fact I believed that I had acquainted myself with all the basic authorities.

In the intervening years in America and Europe from my departure from China in early 1927 to my return in 1932, I had opportunities to become far better acquainted with the record of the racial experience, the history, and with the mind, the philosophical thought, of the Chinese people, than in all preceding twenty years of my stay over there. This was made possible by the astonishing development of facilities for Chinese studies in America. At the Library of Congress is to be found one of the greatest collections of works printed in Chinese in any centre of the world. Similarly at Columbia, the University of California, Harvard, and at the Institute for Advanced Studies at Princeton, great libraries of Chinese books are available to the student. Some of these works were printed from wood-blocks in the tenth century, four hundred years before Gutenberg "invented" the art of printing in Europe. Thus the *drang nach Osten* which carried me across the Pacific in 1908, had reversed itself within two decades. I returned to the West to complete and perfect my study of the East. This comprised five years of teaching and research in the Universities of Michigan and California, culminating in the degree Doctor of Literature and Philosophy at the Sinological Institute of the University of Leyden in collaboration with its distinguished director, Professor J. J. L. Duyvendak.

Streamlined Dragon

"I CANNOT see why you want to leave the academic quiet of an American university campus for the uncertainties of present-day China," wrote Frederick A. Cleveland, fifth Associate Chief Inspector of the Salt Revenue Administration. This was in April of 1932 immediately following a six weeks bombardment of Shanghai by the Japanese; I had been in America for five years. Dr. Cleveland so spoke in the course of transmitting to me the invitation of the Minister of Finance, Mr. T. V. Soong, to reenter the salt revenue service as Chief Foreign Secretary. Headquarters now were no longer at the old Capital, Peking, or even at Nanking the new, but conveniently situated at the great financial centre of China, Shanghai, alongside the powerful foreign and native banks.

Did Nicolo and Maffeo Polo delay upon the Great Khan's invitation to return to Cathay? They knew the way thither was long and dangerous, for they had already twice crossed the Pamirs over the Central Asian plateau, "the roof of the world." Too, Kublai would grow old, and there might be revolutions by "the little people who talked through their noses," and perhaps family dissensions among the descendants of Genghis that would make their sojourn uncomfortable and unsafe. Nevertheless the two elder Polos, this time accompanied by young Marco, started out once more

190

from Venice on that morning of 1271 A.D.... I sailed from San Francisco in July, 1932.

What had been the changes in China in the intervening half decade? First I found the personnel list of my old service, the Salt Revenue Administration, like the alumni roster of an American university. The Chinese chiefs of departments and heads of bureaus all held the American Ph.D. degree or at least an M.A.! An experienced, technically trained Chinese staff had been gradually recruited during the twenty-three years' existence of the Inspectorate. "Accountants," such as my old traveling companion Mr. Fu, had long ago been paid off; the mandarin-type of "Transportation Officer" and "Salt Commissioner" had, too, disappeared, together with their posts. On the other hand, the foreign staff had become less numerous but more selective, and were contributing improvements in budgetary, fiscal, and accounting methods or were serving as technical experts and co-administrators. Their continued participation in the administration served further to strengthen the position of China's foreign loans pledged on the salt tax. Frederick Cleveland, the foreign Chief Inspector, was one of the veteran budgetary experts of America. Resembling Sir Richard Dane in an enormous capacity for work, and in ripeness of experience, Cleveland was contributing to the Salt Administration scientific systems of accounting and auditing, which had neither been possible or perhaps desirable in our earlier days of improvisation and rule-of-thumb methods. When we began the reorganization task with Sir Richard Dane in 1913 and 1914, it was a question whether we could raise enough revenue from salt to pay the service of the loans.

A few months before my return in August, 1932, Nationalist China had put on a preliminary bout with mighty Japan at Shanghai. The Nipponese forces had remained in possession of the field; the valorous 19th Route Army had retired. Yet most observers considered it a draw. The modern Chinese soldier gained in this; he had stood up against an invading power, for the first time since the 1840's, for a reassuring length of time. There had been no panicky flight at the first attack. To be sure, in some foreign circles it was held that the Cantonese troops of General T'sai T'ing-kai had really had the rich International Settlement as their aim; the doughty Japanese had saved it! Moreover, Generalissimo Chiang K'ai-shek had remained strangely aloof. Japan was too formidable for China to engage as yet in the opinion of this close student of the Island Empire's military and naval power. A generation before, wise old Li Hung-chang's policy had been, "avoid dangerous collisions with foreign powers."

The ruins of war-battered Chapei, the section of Shanghai north of the International Settlement in which a million and a half Chinese lived, had scarcely left off smoking when I landed at the great city by the Yellow Sea. Gaunt roofless walls stood north of the Soochow Creek. On January 28 when the bombardment began, these now silent areas had housed a teeming population; innumerable factories, large and small, had bid fair to

191

make Shanghai, a city of three and a half millions, the industrial centre of East Asia.

The foreign concessions had escaped all damage, except a paralyzing disturbance of their enormous import-export business. A solid front of banking, insurance, and shipping-office buildings rose along the Bund. Their foundations went down to enormous pile-reinforced concrete masses veritably floating in the bottomless Yangtze delta silt. Beyond was Nanking Road, lined with shops vending silks and silverwares, choice Kin-hua hams, and Hangchow teas.

Out at the clanging tramway crossing of Chekiang and Nanking Roads, the city's "42nd and Broadway," rose many-storied department stores, organized by families of Christian, Australian-born Chinese. In these most modern emporia, every product of the globe could be obtained. Farther out, lay the Race Course, where, seventy years before, the scanty foreign community, reinforced by British and French blue-jackets, drove back in the bloody battle of Muddy Flat the marauding T'ai-p'ings. Now, its greens furnished sports of every variety for Shanghai's foreign citizens, as well as the excitements of betting on the "cash-sweeps" or "pari-mutual" for thousands of Chinese racing enthusiasts. Overlooking the great concourse was the new Park Hotel, the ultimate word in modern hostelries, its sky-terrace thronged nightly with gay dining and dancing parties of European and Chinese socialites.

Still beyond, at old St. George's, was *The Paramount,* patronized alike by highest Nanking dignitaries and all social Shanghai. The Cathay and Metropole Hotels, "Ciros," (all built with Sassoon funds apprehensively transferred from restive India) and those lesser *foyers* of hospitality and pleasure, Del Monte's, Faron's, and so down the gamut to Rue Chu-pao-san, "Blood Alley," the roistering world of sailor and soldier, gave Shanghai its valid claim as the gayest city of the world. Exclusive clubs, the *Shanghai, American, Çercle Sportif, Country,* and *Columbia* provided recreation for the feudal barons (and their families) of a unique European societal organization which ruled politically, commercially, and financially the lesser Occidentals and the swarming Chinese millions.

No more Chinese than alien-dominated New York is typically American, Shanghai drew from and ministered to the vast opaque hinterland. Even here the virus of modernity was infecting age-old economic and social structures. Railways were being feverishly built; every waterway, even the smallest, was being penetrated by small diesel launches. Motor-roads were rapidly radiating in all directions. We drove over the Shanghai-Hangchow road, newly opened on the National fête day, tenth of the tenth month of the twenty-first year of the Republic (1932). Much of its two hundred miles topped the great earthen dykes which for centuries had held back hurricane-whipped salt waves of Hangchow Bay from the rich Chekiang rice-paddies. Here and there we passed monoliths set up on the sea-wall in honor of Ming generals who had triumphantly repulsed six-

192

teenth century Japanese corsairs. Fifty miles beyond Hangchow motor cars could reach as far as "the Peaks of Heaven's Eyes," T'ien-mu Shan, lofty hills whereon the devout Buddhists of a thousand and more years ago had erected temples among giant cryptomerias. Far within the real China, Detroit *chassis* with crudely built bus-bodies were transporting the population and their goods in regions as far as the Great Bend of the Yellow River in Shen-kan or along the Tibetan marches of western Szechuan.

And there was Nanking, the shiny new capital immured in a vast encirclement of towered walls so ancient that even its diligent Jesuit chronicler Father Gaillard, could not trace their origins. Here had reigned that Emperor who, in A.D. 527, welcomed the first of the Indian patriarchs and induced the Emperor to become a simple devotee of Buddha. Eight and a half centuries later, Chu Yuan-chang, with his generals, drove the effete descendants of Genghis and Kublai back to their native Mongolia, and established his "Brilliant" Ming Capital here. Beatified as Hung Wu, founder of a three hundred year dynasty, (1368–1694), he still mouldered in a neglected tomb on Purple Mountain. Emulating Lenin's tomb at the Kremlin, Sun Yat-sens's followers had placed his glass-encased body in a mausoleum on the same hill-side near Hung Wu's. Nearby a scientifically proportioned "fifth-century" pagoda, in twentieth-century reinforced concrete, pierced the sky with nine up-curving roofs. On the mountain top a fabulously expensive astronomical observatory catered to the age-old Chinese obsession in celestial phenomena.

Within Nanking, the city's magnificent distances were being spanned by broad highways. So vast is the circumference of the Ming walls that little clumps of village hovels had been the only urban evidences in most of it. To the south was growing up, around the Bell Tower and near the American-founded university, a business centre, with stores, shops, and jerry-built hotels and cinemas. Gorgeous new structures imitated the Imperial palaces of Peking with blue and yellow glazed roof tiles, brilliant multicolored cornices, and vermilion-lacquered columns. Solid brick walls of many storeys, steel-framed windows, electric lights, modern plumbing, and heating, adapted old thirteenth century architect Li Ming-chung's aesthetics to modern office utilitarianism. These structurally syncretic but immensely impressive edifices were the new federal buildings of a city-planned Far Eastern Washington. Major l'Enfant would have gazed in wonderment at this streamlining of a city as old as Carthage.

*   *   *

Social life in New Nanking now shone with a brilliancy emulating the capitals of the West. The isolation of the Manchu Court of 1908 gave way to a degree of "mixing" that was breaking down all older barriers of racial prejudice. Leaders of the government had become adepts in Western usages, from long acquaintance with America and Europe. The ultra-modern Metropole Hotel formed a *foyer* for international gatherings where

193

a well-known American agronomist might be seen dancing in fancy-dress Roman toga with an exquisite Chinese lady in the role of Emperor Ming Huang's tragic favorite, Yang Kuei-fei. Sun Yat-sen's marble mausoleum and old Ming Emperor Hung Wu's red brick tomb on Purple Mountain are both in sight of the Nanking golf course where ambassadors played their eighteen holes with cabinet ministers.

In the newly completed American Embassy, Councilor Willys Ruggles Peck celebrated the thirtieth anniversary of his entry into the American Foreign Service. The Old Student Interpreters Mess foregathers once more, Peck, Johnson, Gale, and, in spirit, the others—some of those left from the youthful crowd of three decades before, now at various posts throughout China, or in Washington bureaus, or long outside the service. Julean Arnold is also there, Nestor of the language students. Too the "Student Interrupters" of 1910, Alice Jones Peck, Lady Chatelaine of the party, ever gracious hostess, and Annie Heron Gale are there. These two look at one another with women's deep understanding of the years between—of life in many parts of Asia, of difficult decisions in an often uncharted world.

Dr. Kung, K'ung Hsiang-hsi, with patronymic of China's ancient sage Confucius, is at the celebrant's dinner. Stout, baldish, the broad features of the Minister of Finance remind one that after all there had been a Hebrew infusion in North China, the forgotten colony at K'ai-feng-fu. It was from the North that China's famous bankers came and so did Dr. Kung. He is one of the dynastic brothers-in-law, affiliated through his wife with the Soong, a triumvirate of brothers, and a trinity of sisters. His Oberlin College training, both in the Shansi mission school and in Ohio, was superimposed upon a Confucianistic outlook on life and public finance. This enables him, in a constant rivalry, to out-manoeuvre his infinitely more clever, but Western-minded brother-in-law, "T. V." Soong, in the struggle for control of the National treasury. The contest particularly centres about the profitable salt trade and its taxation. Rising at table, the Minister pays an eloquent and touching tribute to our host's father, the late Dr. Albert Peck, pioneer medical missionary. When the speaker as a young Chinese had landed at Seattle on his first voyage to America, His Excellency relates, Dr. Peck had taken the bewildered youth in charge and had sent him comforted on his final transcontinental journey. How often that story of a kindly American protector could be repeated by Chinese in high places!

My brilliant and versatile Chinese friend, "C.T.," is no longer as young as he once was. My mind returns to the Ann Arbor sorority house-party of June, 1908, to the breathless meeting in the sanctuary of the Wagons-Lits Hotel at Peking at the moment of President Yuan's parliamentary purge in 1913, to the eloquent advocacy of his country's rights at the Washington Conference in 1922. He has been Ambassador, and is now Minister of Foreign Affairs. Through the years Dr. Cheng-t'ing Thomas

194

Wang had risen, as has ever been the opportunity in democratic China, to undreamed-of-heights in the service of his country.

"Confidential information has just reached me that Japanese troops are about to occupy a site at the mouth of the Pei-ho, below Tientsin," whispered Dr. Kung, as he drew me into a corner at Willys Peck's party. "I would like you to go up and find out if they are setting up a landing-field. The area includes some of the best salt pans along the North China coast," continued the Minister of Finance.

I took the train next day North to Peking. No longer, in 1936, did the Peking cart, the "covered wagon" of Imperial days, rumble over the rough macadam road-ways, as I had seen them in 1908. Asphalt pavements and electric street-cars provided transportation. One drove everywhere now by American motor car, even into the erstwhile sacrosanct precincts of the Forbidden City, thrown open to all who came. Alas, the glory had departed; the Palaces resounded with emptiness.

Tientsin, where twenty-eight years before I had first seen North China, had become a huge trading emporium, its narrow river winding to the sea crowded with shipping. The dazzling mounds of white salt, which we had seen from the train windows as we came up from T'ang-ku to Tientsin, were rapidly disappearing into the holds of Japanese freighters, for shipment to the chemical factories on the Inland Sea. The Japanese army intrigue was extending down through that ancient corridor of invasion, Shan-hai-kuan, into the plains of North China. They had staked out a site on the salt lands, perfectly suited for aeroplanes to drop down onto from across the Yellow Sea. Japanese Consul General Horinouchi professed, in reply to my enquiries, to have no knowledge about the Army's plans regarding the site. But, he added meaningfully, things could be done up here in North China without asking permission of the government at Nanking.

The familiar mustard-and-red of Japanese army uniforms was in evidence everywhere, the same as I had seen them a quarter of a century before in Korea. In the background were surly, khaki-clad Chinese soldiers; General Sung Che-yuan, their commander, wavered between his traditional dislike for the carpet-bagging southerners of Generalissimo Chiang K'ai-shek's nationalists, and fear of the frankly predatory Islanders. General Sung must have experienced the dilemma of old Wu San-kuei at the Mountain-and-Sea Barrier when he let in the Manchu hordes against victorious rebel Li Tzu-ch'eng. At Nankai University in the suburbs of Tientsin, the intellectuals of China, direct descendants of the ancient Confucian *literati,* chattered and wrote in impotent ragings against the invaders —who, unlike the ignorant Europeans, read with complete understanding the Chinese ideographs in which this animus was expressed.

The business of the Salt Administration also took me to less familiar South China. Britain's flourishing Crown Colony on the mountain-peak island of Hongkong, with Kow-Lung on the mainland, faces the area dominated by Canton, great southern metropolis. The teeming millions of the

195

Pearl River delta had found that salt, landed free of tax in British territory on the Kow-Loon mainland, might be bootlegged into China at attractive profits. The Cantonese are the shrewd and daring operators of China. To stop the leakage at Hongkong would mean millions to the Treasury.

I had not seen Canton since my overland trip by way of Central China in 1916. From a glorified "China-town" of those days, the famed City of Rams had now taken on a strangely modernized appearance. Along its Bund skirting the Pearl River, rose modern hotels, the Customs House, Post Office, and the office-buildings of the shipping companies. Within the city the Military Governor in the great Auditorium erected to the ever-vernal memory of Sun Yat-sen, gave a farewell dinner for an old friend of my Peking days, Sir Herbert Phillips, British Consul General, upon his promotion to Shanghai.

Beyond Canton City lay modern suburban homes. At the Aviation Club I was taken to an American University Club dinner-dance, with several hundred participants singing well remembered college songs and making the rafters ring with old alma mater's respective cheers with all the gusto of vividly remembered campus days. Lingnan University, creation of able American teachers, had the lecture halls of its broad campus crowded with eager students. Least changed was Shameen, site of the "factories" where Europeans and Americans carried on a restricted trade with the local "Cohong" merchants in the early nineteenth century. This artificial isle still insulated the Occidental community from the swarming city. In tall cool buildings of the old "compradoric" style, with deep, shady verandahs, the leisurely business of import, export, and banking exchange continued to be transacted in the grand manner of the clipper ship era.

Sir Andrew Caldecott, the Governor of Hongkong, received me as he sat in Council with the Colonial Secretary, the Colonial Treasurer, and the Secretary for Chinese Affairs. With the support of the District Director of Salt Revenue for Kuangtung Province, also an American, I had just explained to His Excellency that by levying a relatively light tax on salt, a handsome revenue could be derived for the Colony and a gesture of good-will extended to the Chinese government by putting an end to smuggling untaxed salt over the Kowloon border. (I could not but smile to myself when I recalled how I was repeating the role of that ancient statistician, old Kuan Chung, who described the rich possibilities of a salt tax to the Prince of Ch'i in the seventh century B.C.!)

"As this concerns the taxation of a food-stuff, I shall have to refer your proposal to His Majesty's Colonial Secretary at London," observed Sir Andrew. "This does not mean that your proposal is not acceptable in principle," the Governor added.

I privately knew that the prospects of augmented income to the Colony would be decidedly welcome. A careful examination of the colonial budget had disclosed increasing annual deficits owing to the mounting commit-

196

ments for pensions, and because of the fall in the gold value of the silver dollars in which Hongkong's taxes were collected.

I prefaced my remarks that morning with respectful congratulations. The *Hongkong Post* had informed us in its breakfast-table edition that the King was pleased to appoint Sir Andrew, upon promotion, to be governor of the rich but turbulent island of Ceylon.

"I am not sure I want it," acknowledged Sir Andrew, between puffs of his pipe.

This distinguished colonial administrator of Britain was not entirely unfamiliar to me. Bruce Lockhart in his illuminating *Return to Malaya*, relates how as a youthful rubber planter he had known an energetic young District Commissioner up in the Straits Settlements named Andrew Caldecott. This young Englishman ruled his district, organized and played with his native football team, and performed on the piano, with equal versatility. Inevitably he rose to be Colonial Secretary, the actual administrator always, at Singapore. I now met him on his way further up, midway between the Hongkong and Ceylon governorships. He sat at the head of the big eliptical table in the Council Room, a sturdy British figure of a vigorous man of sixty, puffing and relighting a black briar, pronouncing in plain but telling English his opinions on the business at hand. He listened attentively to his Councilors, but he did not hesitate to remind them sharply where they were wrong.

*　　*　　*

"I have two letters which I would ask you to take to Mr. T. V. Soong, who will arrive at Yokohama by the next trans-Pacific steamer" Mr. Chu, my Chinese colleague, had said when he heard I was taking my vacation in Japan in the summer of 1933. One succumbs completely to the China-coast heat by August.

"I wish you would hand these letters to Mr. Soong before anyone else sees him. One letter I give you unsealed; you may read it if you like. The other hand only to him, or destroy. If you succeed in placing it personally in his hands, cable me the one word *Delivered*."

I had left Shanghai four days previously to join my wife at Unzen, high up in the cool, pine-clad mountains of Japan's southern island. I had thus gone on to Yokohama instead of landing at Nagasaki for the journey up to Unzen. Upon discreetly informing the agent of the American steamship line of the confidential nature of my mission, he had taken me to see the Yokohama harbor master.

"This gentleman wishes to meet his sick wife and children by very first tender out to the incoming San Francisco steamer next Wednesday." The marine superintendent of the steamship line, beside whom I stood, spoke by way of mere formula to the Yokohama harbor master. The latter's face was as inscrutable as a carved ivory *netzuki*. But his black, beadlike eyes shifted enquiringly from one of us to the other. After a suspicious pause, "All right," he said laconically.

I had several days to spare before I was to make my early morning visit to the steamer in Yokohama harbor. The letters I kept snugly in my inside coat-pocket. I took a train up to Karuizawa, mountain summer resort, favored by missionaries and Tokyo diplomats alike. There I had outdoor grilled steaks with the Edwin L. Nevilles. . . . In a walk and talk, "The Duke" and I skirted, cautiously, the base of treacherous Mount Asama, which every now and then envelops daring climbers in deadly volcanic gasses. I was still to make the ascent of extinct Fuji's symmetrical cone, as well as smoking Aso-san, two others of Japan's volcanoes.

At length the day arrived. I was up in the grey dawn and out on a launch that closely followed the yellow flag of the quarantine tug. The passengers had already gathered in the smoking-room for passport inspection. Mr. Soong was there. I nodded to him across the heads of the crowd. He recognized me—had we not sat in our respective offices, he as Minister of Finance in the seized Russo-Asiatic Bank, and I in the immobilized Salt Revenue Building, in the early days of the "Nationalist" revolution at Hankow in 1926? We descended to Mr. Soong's stateroom. After he had locked the door, I handed him the letters. With a sharp glance at their contents, he tore them savagely to bits.

"Can I be of any further service," I asked "T.V." He turned on his heel and looked gloomily out the porthole to where the dreadnaught *Mutso* lay. At the moment His Majesty the Emperor of Japan ascended the red-and-white draped gang-way to inspect his most powerful battleship. A fleet of vessels, stretching as far as the horizon, broke out the Rising-sun flag for the Imperial review. Mr. Soong, brother-in-law of Generalissimo Chiang K'ai-shek of China, did not go ashore that day. The secret letter warned him that he would immediately be placed under duress to sign an agreement derogatory to his country's interests.

* * *

Our chairman for the monthly Shanghai University Club tiffin, was Dr. Yen, outstanding in the field of medicine. His eminence lay in his discovery of the snail as carrier of that scourge of his native Central China, "Yangtze fever," *schistosomiasis*. More recently he had been responsible for the erection of the model hospital beyond the French Concession border. He was now obviously thinking over the phrases with which to introduce the celebrated American tennis "pro."

Several hundred members crowded the tiffin room of the American Club in the metropolitan delta city, and still more were pouring in. All were eager to see, and listen to, the guest-speaker, "Big Bill" Tilden, whose prowess at the net was a matter of discriminating appreciation to his Chinese and American auditors alike. An oil portrait of George Washington hung over the massive fireplace. Ambassador, Judge, Consul General

198

and other chieftains of the American and Chinese official, commercial and educational community sat at the long head table.

From my place beside Dr. John C. Ferguson, dean of us all and notable for his years in education, business, and scholarship in China, I scrutinized the urbane features of Ambassador Johnson. After all the years intervening since the Mess days at Peking in 1908 there was little change. His was the career *par excellence* of the Student Interpreter, trained in the language and customs of the country. I watched, too, the sharp-cut profile of Consul General Clarence Gauss. In the years before, all three of us had been youngsters on Consul General Amos P. Wilder's staff in the musty old American Consular building, back of the Japanese shipping company's "godowns," along a street devoted to ship-chandlers and sailors' grog-shops. Gauss exemplified the efficient present-day foreign service officer equally qualified, it is believed, for duty in any quarter of the globe. Possibly by reason of not learning Chinese and thus saturating himself with the psychology of the alien people to whom he was accredited, he had preserved an aloofness which had its advantages in the maintenance of his country's interests. His next assignment was to be as America's first envoy to the Commonwealth of Australia.

The Chairman's shining eye-glasses and his well cut business suit gave him an air of marked distinction. I noticed his features soften as his eyes roved over the groups at larger and smaller tables, Chinese and Americans, chatting noisily in specially recalled American collegiate vernacular. His thoughts were doubtless traveling back to his father, who a bare generation ago, as a minor secretary in the Peking Board of Foreign Affairs, because of his gifts of speaking an uncouth beyond-the-seas tongue, was now and then permitted to consort, but only on official occasions to be sure, with Legation people—his father who had spent his school days in a Connecticut town in the home of the Congregationalist minister...

His reverie was abruptly terminated. With the sudden whine of swooping aeroplanes, the crash of bombs along the Bund, and the excited bark of answering anti-aircraft guns, the word spread; Chinese planes from Lunghwa aerodrome were bombing the *Izumo,* flagship of the Imperial Japanese Navy as she lay in the Whangpoo.

It was Saturday, August 14, 1937. Another era had ended. A half forgotten notion of "Manifest Destiny" had overleaped the Pacific to stalk the Asiatic mainland in olive-drab uniform, Japan's immutable policy to control China.

Retreat from China

SURROUNDED BY FAMILIAR brass-bound chests and celadons of distant Korea, I sat down to write a banker friend in Shanghai. It was on "Boxing Day," the day after Christmas, 1937, a fog-darkened morning in the drawing room of the old stone house fronting on St. James' Square at Bath. Uncle Jim had spent an extraordinarily happy ten last years in this

199

favored watering place of Beau Brummel. Other shades of England's literary past had been about him. Charles Dickens had lived in this house, near to the famous "Pump Room," where *The Old Curiosity Shop* with pathetic little Nell had been imagined. In it he had conceived those beloved characters whose pathos and humor had inspired Uncle Jim's own *Korean Sketches,* quaint Korean types, Dr. Quak and Mr. Moon; Puffschnauber, the "outdoor" Customs man in remote Wonsan with his Japanese wife, Kosie, and a resultant Eurasian family; "Fireblower," the missionary zealot.

I had been going through the literary relics of a scholar whose industry for forty years had been prodigious. Translations from Korean novels, historical *excerpta,* biographies of noted *literati* and statesmen of the Hermit Kingdom, intricate comparative chronological charts, whereby one could see at a glance what was transpiring in East Asia in Nebuchadnezzar's time. Much of this material had already seen publication. Over the years there had been the many books, learned and popular, from the ponderous Chinese-Korean-English dictionary to delightful folklore; there had been countless fugitive articles and monographs in the Royal Asiatic Society journals, in the *North China Herald* of Shanghai. They had reached as far even as *Victoria,* Dresden technical publication of the printing art, which had reproduced Gale's famous collection of "pre-Gutenberg" moveable bronze type cast in Korea, in 1307.

"Dear Charles," I wrote: "We left Shanghai when the bombing of the city was at its height on August 19. My leaves of absence—this time after full five years away from America—seem to coincide, as in 1927, with political cataclysms. We followed the Suez route, touching at those romantic ports of the East—Hongkong, Manila, Singapore, Penang, Colombo, Bombay. Britain's boasted air and naval base at the southern tip of Malaya was being hastily developed against contingencies. Brief visits in Egypt and Greece followed, and since reaching Italy, we have been in daily, almost hourly, touch with occurrences in China. That land has for the moment displaced in interest most other foreign news in Continental and British newspapers.

"Here in England the situation in the Far East is viewed with special dissatisfaction, despite the fact that in some commercial lines it has its brighter aspects. Jardine's and Butterfield's, the two major British shipping concerns operating in China waters, surprisingly enough, are reaping a harvest on the "closed" Yangtze and in coastwise operations. And Lancashire cotton mills cannot view with too great regret the destruction of both Japanese and Chinese spindles at Shanghai, and the absorption of their Island competitor in the vast piece-goods trade, in an exhausting war.

"On the other hand old China residents I have seen express concern for their holdings in China in view of their banks' commitments in the heavily damaged areas of industrial Shanghai. And the progressive destruction of great cities between Shanghai and Nanking, and what *will*

200

happen in all likelihood to Hankow and Canton, cannot but have disastrous effects on China trade. I think of the present situation in terms of the T'ai-p'ing Rebellion when vast areas of China in the middle of the last century were devastated and whole populations decimated.

"My long delayed furlough came when we could do little more than maintain the *status quo*—if that. To set aside reserve funds, both in Chinese and foreign currencies, for the continued operation of the Salt Revenue service; to distribute our employees so as to carry on if upcountry connections with Shanghai were broken, to return when those on duty would require relief—that was about all one could do.

"In London I have had special opportunities to sound opinion on the Far East. I found Sir Frederick Leith-Ross, Chief Adviser to H.B.M. Treasury, seated next us on the Calais-Dover steamer. You recall that Sir Frederick, a hard-headed Scotsman, came out to Shanghai in 1935 to advise the Ministry of Finance on the establishment of a managed currency system controlled by a central reserve bank. I arranged to phone him at his office, 'Whitehall 1234,' at the Treasury for an appointment. On the following Monday we discussed the China situation over tea. Sir Frederick placed great confidence in Chiang K'ai-shek as the most promising person to bring China out of her present difficulties.

"Earlier at Paris, I had seen Dr. Stanley Hornbeck, our outstanding technical authority on the Far East, Political Advisor to the State Department. He had just returned from Brussels. I myself had planned to attend the Conference assembled at the Belgian capital pursuant of the provisions of the Nine Power Treaty guaranteeing the *status quo* in China. As soon as we reached Italy I had notified the Chinese Ambassador to France, Dr. V. K. Wellington Koo, that I would be available; he replied, thanking me for my offer, and stating that he would be pleased to see me when I reached Paris.

"We accordingly moved along slowly in the direction of Brussels but the Conference suddenly wound up *sine die*. When I saw Stanley at the Hotel Bristol where the American Delegation stopped in Paris, I found that depressing colds had attacked the members of the Delegation from Mr. Norman Davis down. They were thus unable to accept the invitation to lunch at the Chinese Embassy, which Dr. Koo had asked me to transmit Nevertheless, I gained further notion of the reasons for the failure of the Conference. Japan fearful of another of those periodical "interventions" which as in 1894 deprived her of the fruits of conquest in South Manchuria, had flatly refused to attend. But the future, it could be forecast, would be pregnant with incidents such as we have just witnessed on December 12th in the bombing of the U.S.S. *Panay* by Japanese planes on the Yangtze, which might well produce international 'interventions' which no conference at this period could. It was obviously premature to expect the combatants, locked in a life and death struggle, to allow the battle to be called off by outsiders.

201

"To revert to my recent activities in London, they have been varied. I lunched at the City Club. We were served by red-liveried waiters in knee-breeches and buckled shoes! Viscount Ishii, Japan's astute diplomat of the equivocal "Lansing-Ishii Agreement," is in London on a special mission. At a small private reception I talked somewhat warily with the world known statesman. White haired, with fine distinguished features, soft spoken, and retiring, he seems to have little zest in his present occupations. Other persons who had long had important connections with the Far East, particularly with Japan, were present. Among these were Sir Charles Addis, former Chairman of the Hongkong & Shanghai Banking Corporation, Sir Eric Crowe, one time British Commercial Councillor at Tokyo, and Charles V. Sale, Governor of the Hudson Bay Company, with long business associations with Japan, and others. All deeply regret the newly developed animosity of the Japanese to England.

"These folk are of the opinion that Japan can carry on financially, at least through the war period, by means of the various expedients to which governments now resort; and, of course, they appreciate the ability of the Japanese for self-sacrifice and privation, historically displayed in the course of several extreme national efforts. But for Theodore Roosevelt's intervention, and American financial aid, Japan would have bankrupted herself in the war with Russia in 1894–95. More generally I find the opinion prevailing that the Chinese will continue the war until the Japanese are exhausted. One old China hand frankly put it that both parties to the struggle would emerge exhausted, to the advantage of onlookers. He admitted that this was a cynical view; and I added that it would mean protracted chaos and unlimited destruction in China.

"I met many erstwhile residents of Shanghai at the Thatched House Club. Here old-timers from the Orient are likely to turn up. We arranged a table with one of Shanghai's erstwhile *taipans* and owner of a famous string of racing ponies, and a former Commissioner in the Chinese Maritime Customs Service.

"Sir John Brennan of the Foreign Office, lately Consul General at Shanghai, was in the lounge; we had a brief conversation. At the Overseas Trade Department I talked with Mr. Ottewill, for many years a Consul in China; and just across Old Queen Street at No. 36, I discovered the 'Non-Resident Secretary' at London of the Chinese Maritime Customs, J. H. MacCoun. My friendship with this witty and shrewd Irishman had begun at Peking in 1908.

"In Paris at the formal luncheon given by the Wellington Koo's at the Chinese Embassy, many celebrities were present. These included the French Minister of Colonies, the Vice Minister, a Governor General of Indo-China, and others. Among the latter was Mr. Ch'en Kung-po, one of the left-wing leaders in the Nationalist government at Hankow in 1926–27; he later served as Minister of Industry and was now in 1937 a sort of special emissary to European governments. I recalled our previous

202

associations at Hankow. Mr. Ch'en had just conferred with Premier Mussolini and his son-in-law Count Galleazzo Ciano, Italy's Foreign Minister, our recent fellow citizen when he was at Shanghai as Italian minister to China and lecturer on international law at one of the Chinese universities. You remember the stir among our ladies to call on Edda Mussolini Ciano to see the newly arrived *bambino,* Il Duce's first grandchild. Mr. Ch'en had likewise conferred with the French Vice Premier, Leon Blum. His next mission was to take him to London.

"A small and quite black person present with curly hair unusual for a Chinese, I ultimately identified as Eugene Ch'en's son. We had lately seen him about Shanghai a good deal since his return from a protracted sojourn at Moscow. His father, Eugene Ch'en, you recall as that clever journalist, Oxford graduate of West Indian provenience, Foreign Minister in the Wu-han 'Soviet' government of 1927. Though holding portfolios in several ephemeral revolutionary governments, Eugene Ch'en once admitted to me that he knew no Chinese and could not read a state document in his government's official language!

"At the University Club in Paris I met the Minister of Education, M. Jean Zay, and a retired American diplomat who has earned undying fame in the foreign service as the 'originator' of the practice of leaving a despatch long enough on his desk so as to make action unnecessary. Metternich, I believe much earlier held some such method as ideal in diplomatic practice. At the American Church on Thanksgiving Day, Ambassador Bullitt—with whom I had dined at Consul General Cunningham's home at Shanghai the previous year—had as his guests the Duke and Duchess of Windsor. The lady made a very smart appearance, as we observed her from a nearby pew. Her Grace is a connection of Mrs. 'Georgie' Barnett and once spent some time in Peking as her guest. The Duke appeared more animated than when I had last seen him at the Imperial cherry-blossom garden party at Tokyo in 1922, when some of my clothing and the baggage of the Prince's suite were alike consumed in the burning of the old Imperial Hotel.

"We observed an air of gloom at Geneva; all seemed to feel that the great institution sponsored by President Wilson and promptly disowned by his government, had reached a critical phase in its existence. I found old China friends: Howard Bucknell, formerly in the China service, has been assigned to Geneva as Consular observer. Our sometime Harvard representative in the Peking Legation of 1908–9, Leland Harrison, is now American Minister at Berne. Nellie Oiesen Tullis is serving as director of the *Maison Internationale des Etudiants.* She is the brilliant daughter of my companion of many walks on the Kuling hills of years before. The only important American connected with the League, though not in an official capacity, is sponsored by the Rockefeller foundation.

"We had tea with the Herbert Chatleys just outside London a few days ago. Dr. Chatley retired last spring as engineer-in-chief of the Huangpoo

203

Conservancy Board and is now devoting himself to his researches in early Chinese writings on astronomy, a field in which he is widely known. He still receives a retainer from the Chinese government as consultant in connection with the construction of another mammoth dredger for the Yangtze River bar, which is under construction in Germany. Its predecessor was seized by the Japanese and immobilized, while the Yangtze bar continued to silt up. *Nonsense.*

"Through a characteristic fog, we motored to Bristol on Christmas afternoon to drop in on Dr. and Mrs. Evan Morgan, well known for many years in China in the Christian Literature Society. I took over the editorship of the *Journal* of the North China Branch of the Royal Asiatic Society from Dr. Morgan in 1932. Both he and Herbert Chatley have been presidents of the venerable Society founded in 1859 by an American pioneer missionary and sinologue, the Rev. Elijah C. Bridgeman. The headquarters of the Society housing its library of rare books and its museum is on the original Crown land grant of Shanghai. The roster of the Society's officers is a distinguished one, including such names as George F. Seward, brother of the Secretary of State and U. S. Consul at Shanghai, the first American Minister to Peking, Anson Burlingame; F. B. Forbes of the early Boston family trading to China; Friedrich Hirth, later Professor of Chinese at Columbia University; Henri Cordier, the French sinologue and bibliographer; John C. Ferguson, American educator and sinologue; and Florence Ayscough, felicitous translator of the delightful poetry of China.

"After Christmas here, we return to London and sail on the 31st for New York—after five and half years' absence from America. Doubtless I shall find American interest in China as a field for present investment at a discount! As Julean Arnold, our energetic Commercial Attaché, said to me before I left Shanghai, 'This is no time for trade promotion!' Curiously everything is at the crest of the wave in Great Britain, good business everywhere; while so far as we can learn the United States is in an economic funk.

"Munitions making accounts for much of the prosperity over here. Certainly England gives the appearance of greater stability and solid wealth than any of the countries we have been through from Suez on. Italy is putting up a front but must be in a very uncertain financial state. France of course is rich enough, despite the general shabbiness of everything. We had hoped to get into Germany, but just out of the East we have had enough of this European weather; we have scarcely seen the sun since leaving Switzerland.

"My last letters from Shanghai were dated about mid-November, since which time much of importance has occurred, particularly Japanese interference with Chinese government organs in the Settlement and French Concession. I take it there was quite a *hejira* of Chinese officialdom to Nanking. There has been a complete 'black-out' of news in England since

204

Friday as all newspapers have suspended publication over the holidays. We may pick up something over the radio tonight.

"The vigorous policy which has developed toward Japan by Great Britain and the United States growing out of the recent Japanese attacks upon their naval vessels on the Yangtze may serve to restore the almost entirely lost prestige of the two countries in Oriental affairs."

Fate of a Nation

THE DAY OF MY RETURN to China continued to be put off. The salt administration, from olden times, has formed a certain barometer of China's political and economic weal or woe. Gradually, the Administration was driven back from the principal ports, the river valleys, the railways, and from the large interior cities. It finally centred with the refugee government itself at Chungking. From here it controlled outright the salt revenues of Szechuan, Yunnan, Shensi, and the Northwest, with less certain collections from the clandestine transport of salt in the partly occupied regions.

Extraordinary ingenuity was disclosed in supplying the hinterland population with this essential of life. From under the very guns of the Japanese, huge quantities of salt were carried from the sea-coast into the interior. Until Canton was occupied, the railway northward brought shipments across the divide into Central China. Reenacted were the daring exploits of salt-runners in the days of the Yangtze valley salt famine caused by the T'ai-p'ing rebels.

In North China, the invaders had as a "fifth column" their own Japanese nationals, already serving in the Salt Administration. Backed by the army, these erstwhile employees of the Chinese government took over control, maintaining the form of the original administration with Chinese collaborators and Japanese operatives. The term "north" included the whole area occupied by the Japanese Army with headquarters at Tientsin; this meant the great salt and revenue producing regions of Changlu, Shantung, Shansi, and North Kiangsu. In the south the salt officers of the Nanking regime had no "foreign" colleagues as provided in the original Loan agreement arrangements, but there were "secretaries" and "advisers," exclusively Japanese, more powerful than their puppet chiefs.

The rich Shanghai trade, providing salt and "soy" sauce for millions, had been a merchant monopoly, closely supervised by the official *Gabelle*. This now became the prize of warring groups: Chinese merchants and Japanese military. The store houses were seized. The former monopolists suffered immense losses. A new Salt Administration, "bogus" the loyalists termed it, was formed by the Nanking "puppet" regime. It was a hollow mockery. It achieved nothing; it exercised no control over the remote salt works on the sea-coasts; it had no influence with reputable traders. It evolved no program, and failed to collect a single cent of revenue in the proper sense of the word. Despite the disintegration of the regular service by reason of wholesale dismissals and retirements of its officers, few of the old staff joined the new administration of the "reformed government."

Nevertheless the salt administration of China must carry on. Its revenues are essential to the support of the state, which in turn is responsible for an adequate supply of this necessity of life. There is *no* substitute for salt. From the time of Kuan, statistician-financier of the State of Ch'i in the seventh century B.C., there has ever been a salt tax in China. At the change of a dynasty it has invariably fallen into confusion, to revive in the hands of vigorous new administrators. Foreign loans are secured on these revenues forming a further reason for their perpetuation. Service, to be sure, on the Anglo-French, the Hu-Kuang, the "Crisp," the Reorganization (actually paid in recent years from Customs funds) loans ceased in 1938. The depleted revenues of the refugee government at Chungking could no longer sustain the strain of payment. The "New Order" in East Asia ignored China's erstwhile foreign financial commitments.

*　　*　　*

The lure of China, the still unanswered enigma of the Far East, found me again, as thirty years and more before, a voyager on the well known way—the day's stop-over on "Robinson Crusoe's Island," clouds over verdure-covered, sleeping volcanoes, and beaches up which the warm salt combers forever rolled; from the steamer's deck, the endless spaces of the balmy Pacific, with only a lonely sea-bird in sight, hundreds of miles from the nearest land; and finally old Fuji's summit glimpsed through early-morning mists, just as Commodore Biddle in 1844, as Commodore Perry in 1853, as Consul Townsend Harris in 1856, and as I saw it in 1908, when each reached, for the first time, the Mikado's kingdom:

"Kyoto, August 26, 1939

"I am renewing our 1936 vacation trip when we came down from Lake Yamanaka by backdoor. We took, you recall, the express over the Japanese Alps, down the picturesque Kiso-kawa Gorge onto the Yamato Plain, and ended by staying a night at the busy town of Nagoya. This time, however, I have come direct from Tokyo. It was only the final section from Nagoya to Kyoto that we did then. Our train passed through Otsu where we had the *unagi-meshi,* those delicious fried eels from Lake Biwa. Today I had a *bento,* as good as ever, with hot rice, omelet and other serve-yourself condiments in the neat wooden box. And so I am here in this, the oldest cultural centre and early capital of Japan. As the *President Pierce* does not sail from Kobe for Shanghai until early Monday, I shall have all day tomorrow in Kyoto.

"Naturally, I have been interested to see how Japan looked, on the surface at least, after two years of exhausting war. So when we entered Yokohama Harbor, I was up before six. Certainly the blue sea, the green cliffs of 'Mississippi Bay' (named for one of Commodore Perry's ships anchored here on July 8, 1853), and old Fuji raising its symmetrical cone

206

above the fleecy mists of early morn, gave no hint of the harsh distresses of a reckless overseas adventure from which the land and its people are suffering. It has been a brilliant day, with great cloud-heaps on the mountains characteristic of Japan. We have been told that everything appears shabby and run-down in Japan; but Yokohama, entirely rebuilt since the destructive earthquake of 1923, looked little changed, since last I saw it in 1933.

"Taking the electric train for Tokyo, I saw on all the crowded station-platforms only two possible veterans of the China war, with bandaged heads, and scarcely any soldiers at all. No troop trains were visible on the trip. The disastrous venture on the mainland is not made more evident to the people than necessary. But from an American teacher who shared my seat from Nagoya to Osaka (she had just come down from Karuizawa and gave me from her lunch-box a most delicious peach), I heard there are whole blocks of buildings housing the wounded, and constant processions of the ashes of the dead carried home to the little Shinto cemeteries.

"At Tokyo of course I made the Imperial Hotel my headquarters. This is the achievement of the distinguished Chicago architect, Frank Lloyd Wright. It alone of most large buildings withstood the earthquake of 1923. I found my banker friend, from whom I expected to get information, in America on vacation.

"Very few young able-bodied men were to be seen working in the towns and villages—all boys or old men, but numbers of women were in the rice-fields. This was a day devoted to some ritual of the paddy. At sundown lights were set out in the fields, making a pretty sight over the fresh green.

"After catching up a bit on the newspapers (although we have had a very generous Radio News Sheet on the *Pierce*), I hired a motor car to have a look about the capital. Tokyo now, as you recall, has its many fine buildings, with spacious boulevards. But to me the medieval walls of the palace, the wide moats, the picturesque gates through which one gets glimpses of carefully swept avenues, and the palace roofs just visible among the gnarled pines, contain the charm of the Tokugawa Yeddo Shoguns. Even here in the capital there was no visible signs of warlike bustle. The Emperor quietly returned to his castle today from his summer residence. Doubtless Hitler's and Stalin's *rapprochement* had something to do with curtailment of the Imperial holidays!

"Once on the train, I had my luncheon, foreign style, in the diner, as the fast 'Sakura' express sped westward. All along were the usual lovely vistas of sea and mountain. In addition to nature's charm is the quaint work of man, villages and towns of thatched and tiled houses. But set out in the midst of rice fields are smoking modern factories, cement plants, chemical works, etc. indicating the amazing diversified activity of the people, and the limited space in which they carry it on. Japan cannot complain now of unemployment problems with admittedly a million and

207

more soldiers on the mainland and tens of thousands of camp-followers, traders, and laborers, keeping up with military campaigns the equally effective economic invasion.

"The eight-hour train ride has been through the most charming part of Japan. I wondered why it appeared so unfamiliar until I recalled that I have hitherto traveled over this section by night, reserving the day-light ride for the run along the picturesque Inland Sea from Kobe to the straits of Shimonoseki.

"What an industrious people they are! Everybody is busy. They are like ants or bees in their concentrated effort. And today there is a great to-do about a big air-plane, the *Nippon,* which with much ceremony is starting a round-the-world, 'good-will' flight, visiting twenty countries or more. It flies to Alaska, the United States, South America, Europe, Arabia, India, and home—if it escapes disaster. Perhaps all this fuss about it in the papers, with innumerable photographs of the plane, its crew, and its sponsors—mostly high personages in business, government and finance, is to distract attention from the disturbing news of the German-Soviet non-aggression pact. The Japanese just can't make out why Adolph Hitler dropped them for their hereditary enemy Russia. They are rethinking their international position, and it almost looks as if Japan would have to join up with the 'Democracies' now!"

"On board S.S. *President Pierce,*
August 26.

"Returning to the excellently managed Kyoto Hotel by 5 P.M., I took the elevator to the roof-garden to enjoy a flaming sunset over the surrounding hills. Later I had fried prawns at the *tempura-bar. Neisan* cooked the delicious crustaceans over a *hibachi* and then dropped them with her nimble chopsticks into a small shallow basket before me. Everything is done according to rule, as in the tea ceremony or flower arrangement. How extraordinary it is that this people can be so charming, courtesy itself, and then display such ferocious qualities towards their neighbors the Chinese on the mainland. The paradox is true of all Orientals—and apparently of Occidentals as well. Why draw invidious and meaningless distinctions?

"At 8:22 that evening I took the electric express down to Kobe, past the glaring neon-lights of Osaka, Japan's chief manufacturing and exporting city. All these towns of the Yamato Plain are energized from the hydro-electric plants of the nearby water-shed. From station to steamer I picked up a box of delicious native-grown peaches, pears, green grapes and apples, which I now have in the steamer's ice-box for use in Shanghai, where indulgence in fresh fruit is virtually *verboten.*

"Not leaving until ten this morning, we have come right out into a tropical typhoon, which is hurling itself against Japan with terrific force. One of the war-time built '535's,' the big steamer, lightened of its heavy

208

cargo of pig-lead, scrap-iron and raw cotton, discharged in Japan ports, is bobbing about. I have just tried out my 'Kodachrome' movie-films in bright sunlight and hope to have some good views of a typhoon at sea. We are not going through the Inland Sea, with its scenic but treacherous channel, but to the east of Kyushu island and then directly across the Yellow Sea to Shanghai."

"August 30.

"Whew! Since leaving Kobe we have been in "dirty weather." It has been blowing "great guns," with seas mountain high. We have a full passenger list; U. S. navy people, bound for Shanghai on the *President Harrison,* were transferred to this ship at Kobe; and of course the usual end-of-August vacationers are returning from Japan to steamy Shanghai.

"Last night the ship rolled and pitched furiously. At 1 A.M. my wardrobe trunk, standing open on end, came down with a crash—no damage but quite startling to me and McCauley, a sun-tanned young Englishman, who shares my cabin. Then, although we were up on the boat deck, water came through the port and soaked his bed. I escaped the deluge. At the same time a number of passengers still lingering in the smoking saloon— it was so hot in the cabins with closed portholes that many people were still up or trying to sleep in the social rooms—were swept with tables and chairs across the room and several received hurts. Recollections came to me of Joseph Conrad's exciting yarn—Chinese coolies locked between decks during a hurricane, the chests containing their carefully saved dollars breaking open, the Chinamen frantically chasing the rolling dollars back and forth with every lurch of the ship!

"This morning the passengers were not allowed on deck and they looked dismal enough seated about the social rooms. By 3 P.M. we entered the turbid, but welcome, estuary of the Yangtze in the shelter of the Saddle Islands. The sea has greatly moderated. I have had no trouble at all, a seasoned sailor boasting my ninth trans-Pacific crossing. My only concern was to keep in bed, especially when about 4 a.m. this morning the ship's course was altered and we did some heavy wallowing."

"Shanghai Club
September 2, 1939

"Arriving a day late on account of the typhoon, I still found my reservation good at the Shanghai Club. So far as I can see, the city looks about the same, if more crowded. It is a hive of activity. The war-damage was all in the remote factory district. But armed police and military squads are at strategic corners ready to go into action at a moment's notice. I have of course not as yet been around to observe much.

"Behind all the unrest and dislocation, there remain still the familiar features of life in China. Here at the Club the servants are efficient, smiling, unobtrusive. In the great dining room, which looks out onto the crowded shipping of the Whangpoo, I recognize "boys" who waited on me thirty years ago. A ten-thousand-ton cruiser of the "Shire" class, flying the Union Jack, is tied to the "senior buoys" off the Bund. Before her is the magnificent ultra-modern U.S.S. *Augusta,* flying the flag of Admiral Hart, Commander-in-chief of the American Asiatic Fleet. These powerful naval craft give a sense of confidence and security to us Americans and Britishers so far from home.

"September 3.

"This is my fourth day in Shanghai. Everybody looks the strain of the past months. It has been impossible for most people to leave town for a brief respite from the summer's heat. All Shanghai is in a turmoil over the European crisis, just as in August 1914 when I was also here. Shipping is badly disorganized. The British and French garrisons are expected to be withdrawn. Then the Japanese will have everything to themselves. The International Settlement and French Concession will be helpless, unless the American government takes a strong stand. Possibly a settlement will come quickly in Europe, but not likely, for the 'fat is in the fire.'

"My last letters were posted on the Canadian Pacific liner, the *Empress of Japan* scheduled to sail on Monday at 10 A.M. Owing to the declaration of war, all Britain's ships in port were temporarily held up by orders of the Admirality; but the *Empress* is at last away and, after setting ashore all Japan-bound passengers, she is off hot-foot across the Pacific, no stops *en route.* I am reminded of the confusion here at the outbreak of World War I in 1914. Now as then, British and French residents expect to be called up and the whole tragic business reenacted. There is almost a sense of boredom at the thought of another long war with all its ghastly losses. This time Germany, it is expected, will see a lot of destruction of her own cities from the greatly improved air-arms of the allies—something she scarcely experienced in 1914–18.

"The question is, what is Japan going to do; *something* without doubt! With the probable withdrawal of British and French forces, Japan can move in as she pleases. Report has it that a further two battalions of U. S. Marines are on the way out. It is also rumored that Japan, Soviet-Russia, Germany, and Italy, are forming a new 'Axis.' That would point to a determined intention to raid Britain's Far Eastern empire and divide it among the 'have-not' powers.

"For $40 in American travelers cheques I have bought Chinese $555, or about Chinese $14 for U.S. $1, a little over 7 cents for a Chinese dollar. Until the war inflation set in after 1937, the Chinese dollar was worth 29½ cents in American money. Consular, Marine, and Navy people here paid in U. S. dollars, are 'on the crest of the wave.' One Marine captain and his wife, here in the Cathay Mansions, are paying Ch. $1,000 a month for commodious bed and sitting-rooms *and* all meals. This is about U. S. $70 a month! But of course people on Chinese dollar incomes are in a bad way."

"I rode in a ricksha to the General Post Office today, crossing Honan Road Bridge on which there was no Japanese sentry. East of the Post Office, North Kiangse Road was blocked off by barbed-wire entanglements. It was thus necessary to take a ricksha back, across Honan Road Bridge again, then to follow the Soochow Road embankment to Garden Bridge. Here I left my ricksha and joined the throng crossing the bridge— pedestrians, rickshas, motor-cars, trucks, in endless stream. The way led first past British Highlander sentries, barbed-wire barricades, and then Japanese sentries. I had watched Chinese pedestrians crossing the Kiangse Road Bridge. Each must doff his hat and bow as he passed the Nipponese guard; many were momentarily stopped, as on the Garden Bridge, but the sentries seemed listless and perfunctory in their duty.

"I looked up Hallett Abend, the seasoned and realistic correspondent of the New York *Times,* who is still living in the magnificent new Broadway Mansions building. He has new land-lords, the former British owners having sold out to Japanese, but his long-term lease, with rent payable in Chinese dollars, provides him with a luxurious pent-house at an extraordinarily reasonable sum when calculated in American money. Abend took me on the terrace to view the broken walls and gutted buildings, which stretched for miles to the north towards Chapei and the railway station, and eastward through the factory district of Yangtze-poo.

"It was through this congested district that the desperate struggle between the Chinese troops and the Japanese landing parties raged for days. I remembered the drone of the planes, the explosion of bombs and the pillars of fire and smoke hanging over this vast area in that fateful August, 1937.

"Walking back across the bridge, I entered the Garden at the junction of Soochow Creek and the Whangpoo River. The Creek as of old, was a huddle of sampans, cargo-boats, and small steamers, leaving only a narrow lane for moving traffic. Enjoying the Garden, open to all upon payment of a small fee, were Chinese, Indians (Sikhs), children, and native nursemaids. The Whangpoo foreshore has been shut off by barbed-wire fences 8 or 10 feet high, leaving some 15 yards of jetty for loading and unloading cargo. A large British steamer—its name painted out—was being worked alongside the pontoons.

"The Bund I found entirely devoted to shipping. The fine greensward of old had disappeared; heavy trucks were tearing about over it. A large storage 'godown' had been erected of bamboo and matting in front of 'Jardine's' office building. The whole of the open park and walks have been enclosed in a high bamboo fence as far as the Customs jetties. Rearing its fine architectural lines far up into the sky and taking its place among other handsome and substantial buildings along Shanghai's famous water front (comparable to New York's 'Battery'), is the new Bank of China building. Construction has stopped midway with its Chinese sponsors scattered from Hongkong to Chungking. The exterior of the impressive tower is completed, but the lower facade is covered with the contractor's bamboo shrouding, and the whole pile bears witness to the paralyzing hand of war on civilian enterprise.

"Now much of China lies in ruins after this 'trial by arms' with powerful Japan. China's miseries have been so various and complete—her floods, her famines, her plagues, her bandits, her civil wars—that it has been piling Pelion on Ossa to add the grevious tale of modern mechanized war to it all. The air-arm of Japan has reached out to every Chinese city almost as far as the Tibetan border. The unexpected resistance which China has put up, has brought home to the world the spiritual and material resourcefulness of her people, based on a philosophy of life older than that of any existing people. Too, time, vast spaces stretching to the Central Asian ranges, and a man-power as countless as the sands of the sea, will continue to make conquest elude the invader.

"The centre of it all is Shanghai, an agglomeration of three and a half million souls, a seething mass of humanity. Today it is as I first saw it thirty years ago, with modern 'gadgets' added. Streets swarm with pedestrians, hawkers, wheelbarrow-coolies sweating as they push along cargo of all kinds; motor-trucks ('lorries' out here) piled high with boxes and bales; busses, mostly 'two-deckers' as on New York's Fifth Avenue, crammed with passengers; motor-cars driven by Chinese chauffeurs with apparent disregard of all traffic rules. Open shops line the streets; sales of fruits, edibles, hats, clothing, proceed briskly. Dimly through the shadowed gates of concrete block-houses, people may be seen pledging, redeeming, buying all sorts of articles. The pawn-shop is the poor man's bank in China.

"With darkness, colored neon-lights flare across the city's skyline. Here and there, from the Bund back for miles, modern skyscrapers rear up loftily above the sea of grey-tiled roofs. Up-to-date hotels and apartment houses, built chiefly with foreign capital, raise their sixteen or more stories, with roof-gardens, pent-houses and apartments as luxurious as those on Manhattan's Park Avenue. By night gay Shanghai throng the sky-terrace of the Park Hotel, Shanghai's swank hostelry, with dancing to crooning orchestras; gaze languorously at exotic floor-shows; sip champagne; and then go to 'Farren's,' 'The Pelican,' or 'Del Monte's,' where tired-eyed Russian hostesses begrudge the men their jeweled women companions whose presence deprives them of exiguous dancing fees. Later a stop in for a final "doch-and-doris" on the spacious verandah of the *Çercle Sportif* in Frenchtown or in the cooler breezes around the dancing floor on the roof. A procession of the notables of the world pass through this 'cross-roads of the universe.'

"Equally elaborate cabarets cater to Shanghai's gilded native youth. Denationalized, these ignore the sanguine struggle carried on by their heroic countrymen in the far interior. Ousted from their haunts at Canton,

212

the *fan-tan* operators have established the 'Bad Lands' here, under protection of the new 'puppet' governments. That versatile Missouri journalist, J. B. Powell, invited me to go slumming in this odorous region. I declined. It furnishes the native 'mosquito press,' our 'tabloids,' with too many murder plots.

"There is the Shanghai Club, which as every round-the-world tourist knows, boasts the longest and best equipped bar in the world. At noon Shanghai's British business world, with a sprinkling of Americans and others, sips its 'Q.C.', a mild gin-and-bitters; and discusses 'exchange,' shipping and rubber stocks. At 4:30 the Domino Room fills with dignified merchants and officials for afternoon tea, while they scan the *Illustrated London News,* the *Bystander* and those other home-side pictorials with invariable photos of Royalty and the aristocracy at the Ascot races, at Wimbledon tennis matches, and Sandringham garden parties. Save for the inevitable hum of conversation from the cavernous bar, the rotunda and reading rooms preserve all the quiet and decorum of a London Club. It is England in a beleaguered medieval city, surrounded by chaos, at the ends of the earth."

* * *

"Along the dark side-streets and just behind the million-dollar American Club, on Honan and Kiangse roads, where shouts and clatter of milling humanity resound all through the bright day, there is the stillness of death. The shops which cater in all things to the native populace, have put up their shutters. Only here and there a shaft of light gleams through.

"On the sidewalks, in the dark doorways, lie forms, some on bits of matting, some on the bare stone pavement. Torsos covered with a few shreds of cotton cloth, with naked legs and bare arms, are stretched out in the sleep of exhaustion and misery. This is basic China. A poverty, a destitution which cannot be equaled in any part of the Western world, inconceivable, inevitable. In China neither Dante nor Doré would have needed their macabre imaginations. They could have had stark reality."

"On board *S. S. President Coolidge,*
Shanghai, November 23.

"My last glimpse of Shanghai is from the boat deck of the liner *President Coolidge,* the finest of America's trans-Pacific fleet. It has been raining—typical Shanghai weather—but the moon is now shining from out scudding clouds. Lights twinkle here and there across the River in Pootung, 'East-of-the-Whangpoo,' a no-man's land of guerillas and Japanese raiders. The glow from the great city in the distance, lights up the sky even under the brilliant moon. We are down river tied to buoys, ready to cast off. A large crowd had waved us farewell at the Customs jetty in the early afternoon.

"The harbor, fifth of the world, is dead save for small Japanese and native craft. With no outgoing cargo the Blue Funnel, the British-India,

213

the Shire and those other semi-tramp steamers are no longer swinging at the buoys. Even the busy little motor-ferries, in which the progressive municipal administration took so much pride, have been suppressed by the Japanese. The invaders have seized all public properties outside the foreign controlled Settlements and Concession; and, of course, the up-river districts are closed to foreign traffic. The familiar Yangtze river steamers are tied up alongside darkened wharfs. Nothing goes up or comes down river except on Japanese 'transports.' Big 'squeezes' must be paid to move anything at all. But in the far interior of China already a vast transformation is under way. The trek of millions from the brutality of the Samurai Sword into the promised land of free China—those rich but primitive provinces of the west, Szechuan, Yunnan, and even Sinkiang as it borders on the U. S. S. R., is accelerating China's modernization. Those skills and techniques brought in from the Occident in the past century have been available only in the coastal 'treaty-ports' or along the riverine highways."

Report from Chungking

ON THE SUNDAY FOLLOWING the disaster in the Hawaiians, I walked with my old friend of China coast days, Admiral Chester W. Nimitz. As we stepped out of his "Q" Street apartment, the Chief of Naval Operations, "deeply humiliated," indicated in characteristic sailor's phrase the tragic extent of our losses.

"We've got no shot left in our lockers," he sighed.

The Admiral had been sorrowfully scanning the Pearl Harbor casualty lists. Even Freckle's tail drooped, as the Admiral's invariable companion, his sprightly cocker, nosed the bolls of the trees dispiritedly.

That evening our telephone rang. It was Katherine Nimitz.

"Father is packing like hell," her excited voice told us over the wire.

Admiral Nimitz was hurriedly readying to set out, in civies and on a commercial plane, to play his historic role in the Western Pacific, commander of the greatest armada of all time, and to share with General Douglas MacArthur the most far-flung amphibian command ever known.

As we walked along listlessly that Sunday afternoon, I recalled a brief insight I had just had into "intelligence" as developed by the fighting forces. On December 6 Admiral Nimitz had introduced me to Captain James Roosevelt, U.S.M.C. as one long experienced in the Far East and particularly in China. The affable "Jimmy" was at the moment serving as aide to Colonel William Donovan in the organization and staffing of the newly created Office of the Coordinator of Information. This was the progenitor of the celebrated "cloak and dagger" intelligence gathering organ, the later Office of Strategic Services. The previous summer I had been brought in from Northwestern University to serve with former Vice Governor of the Philippines, J. Ralston Hayden, as Far East consultant. My ultimate assignment was to be to that city so familiar to me for thirty

214

years or more, Shanghai, the Far Eastern center of international intrigue. Here I was to improvise an underground apparatus that would report even if I was removed from the scene. I would necessarily be associated with naval intelligence.

Captain Roosevelt took me along to meet Captain Allen G. Kirk, Chief of the Navy's intelligence division, O.N.I. Captain Kirk greeted me kindly enough. He was just settling into his office, after a year's term as U. S. Naval Attaché in London.

"I want you to meet our officer in charge of Far East intelligence work," directed Captain Kirk. "You and he are old China hands and ought to get on well together."

Conducted to an adjacent room, I was presented to an officer in commander's uniform who sat at a desk littered with papers, with telephones continually going. I recognized a naval officer whom I had met on the China station some years before, as well as a Marine officer and one or two others, including some civilian acquaintances, all occupying desks in the room. It struck me that I was in a gathering of old time Shanghai acquaintances.

"Well, what do you know about naval matters?" commenced the Commander in a rasping voice. I could see he was a very harassed man. At the abrupt question my former acquaintances in the room showed startled interest at their office head's bluntness. They knew that I at least could claim an intimate acquaintance with the Far East in general and certainly China in particular, and that in the Shanghai community I had enjoyed a fairly authoritative status.

Before I could formulate a reply, the Commander continued.

"Can you distinguish between the different types of fighting ships? What do you know about torpedoes.. ?"

At that moment one of the desk phones buzzed insistently.

"Yes, Admiral," his voice took on a well modulated tone. "Our best information is the Imperial Japanese fleet is steaming south along the Indo-China coast."

The next day a Japanese fleet came down from the north behind a cold front and struck at Pearl Harbor. I cancelled my reservations for the trans-Pacific crossing.

*   *   *

Some weeks later a bright January morning of 1942 in wartime Washington had begun for me with an urgent telephone message from Colonel Willard G. Wyman to come to the War Department by ten o'clock. The Colonel, a handsome dynamic man of forty, was my liason with General Joseph Stilwell's party. We were all under orders to get out to West China. In place of flying across the Pacific to arrange my intelligence set-up at Shanghai, I was now scheduled to take plane to Brazil, cross the South Atlantic, on through Central Africa south of the Sahara, and around the

215

world's middle *via* India till I reached Chungking. Luckily my original departure *via* the Pacific on December tenth had not been set for a week earlier. For somewhere on a mid-ocean islet, at Manila or Hongkong I would have been picked up by the Japanese to spend the remainder of the war years, if I had survived, in one of their noisome detention camps. Many of my old China colleagues did, some to live and some to die.

I entered the designated room in the temporary War Department building on Constitution Avenue a little before ten, where several army officers were already gathered. Their manner indicated something important in the wind.

"General Stilwell," announced Colonel Wyman, addressing the tall, hawk-beaked, weatherbeaten officer with the two stars of a major general on his shoulder straps, "You ought to know Doctor Esson Gale. You're both old China hands."

The General shifted his long, ivory cigarette holder between his steel-trap lips. His cold blue eyes scanned me as we made a brief handshake. I don't recall the General uttering any sound however. I was in turn introduced to two other general officers, several colonels and the most junior, a major. Without further delay, our party passed into a large, rather badly lighted room. All took seats along the inner wall, thus facing the light from the windows.

As we filed in and took our chairs, an officer seated at a large roller-top desk swung briskly around and faced us. My immediate impression, almost with the force of a shock, was that of a man of strikingly agreeable personality, a dynamo of energy, and one who could penetrate to the essence of things with the least possible fuss and delay. I only caught the name, *General Eisenhower,* doubtless on the understanding that all knew the Army's Deputy Chief of Staff for Plans. As a mere civilian, the name of the future Commander of the Allied Forces in Europe meant nothing to my ignorance at that time!

"When you reach Chungking, Doctor," the General admonished, but with a disarming smile that removed anything he said from the asperity of a command, *"tell our people out there they might as well come home if they can't get on with the Chinese and their Generalissimo."*

"And," the General went on, "please reassure General John McGruder that his replacement by General Stilwell," nodding to the silent, austere, cigarette-smoking officer, "means no dissatisfaction with his three years' command of the United States forces in China. It is simply that we have other plans for him, and that General Stilwell will take over a wider area of responsibility—the Burma, India, China theatre. I anticipate, Doctor" —General Eisenhower seemed to be well briefed about me and my plans —"that you will reach Chungking at least two weeks earlier than General Stilwell and his party. I hope then that you will find it possible to talk with McGruder before General Stillwell sees him."

216

General Eisenhower gave special meaning to this last remark. I could see that he was a peacemaker.

Actually I was delayed a week and more at blacked out Cairo after my trans-Africa flight. Rommel's desert armies were coming closer and the Egyptian capital was full of turbulent Anzacs on leave. The terrace of Shepheard's Hotel was daily crowded with dust-stained officers. All civilian airplanes to the Far East were downed or destroyed by the Japanese advance into South East Asia. Singapore's "impregnable" naval base had fallen by the time our aircraft had crossed the South Atlantic to the West African coast. At length General Stilwell caught up with me at Cairo and we all went on to India together. General McGruder was already at Calcutta to meet us, flying over from Chungking. I thus belatedly delivered General Eisenhower's message after Stilwell and McGruder had met. I judged from General McGruder's manner of receiving my belated message that the meeting had not been too cordial.

The picture comes back to me. The tall, spare figure of "Vinegar" Joe Stilwell in khaki shorts and an old Spanish-American War sombrero, yellowed by the fever of the Burma jungles where he had taken "a hell of a licking," flailing his arms like a North China salt water windmill as he exercised on the flat roof of the American Military Mission headquarters. As the bitter war years marched on, the disagreement between the allied Chieftains, Chiang Kai-shek and Stilwell, reached the peak of acrimony, paralysing the war effort in Southwest Asia. General Eisenhower, with prophetic insight, had admonished me *"Tell our people out there they might as well come home if they can't get on with the Chinese and their Generalissimo!"* It was the old story of Horatio Lay, of Thomas Wade, of the American general Burgevine, of Francis Aglen. If they couldn't get on with the Chinese they might as well come home. This was the underlying principle of success or failure in the cooperation of the Western world with China.

I left Dum Dum airport on the outskirts of Calcutta at 2 P.M. on the seventh of March. In a Douglas D.C. 2 equipped with uncomfortable bucket seats, we rose over the alternate hills and jungles of Assam and Burma. We could look down into the deep gorges of the great Salween, Mekong, and Irrawaddy Rivers as they flowed within a few miles of each other on the "roof of the world." Passing over Mandalay and its pagodas, we refueled at Lashio, head of the Burma road, just as the sun set.

As our plane settled down on the sand spit in the Yangtze comprising the airport, Chungking's lights blazed defiantly, symbolizing China's unconquerable spirit, in contrast to Cairo's and Calcutta's cautious blackouts. China's wartime capital turned out to be a most astonishing mixture of impressive scenery, gaping, bombed-out edifices and the persistence of human beings in carrying on under the most adverse circumstances. Japanese bombers had turned a great city for the first time into a shambles. Here was concentrated most of the people I had known so well at Shanghai and Nanking. Rather than to yield, the talent of the country, especially represented by a brilliant group of Western-trained Chinese, was refugeeing in this remote and primitive area of China's Far West.

Once more the Salt Administration bulked large in my affairs. My old associates came to my aid with the loan of an ancient Ford. With its cracked windows and windshield, its bulging tires and sagging springs, it proved the most luxurious equipage I ever rode in. After trudging for weeks afoot over the muddy streets, or riding in precariously carried sedan chairs or pulled along in ramshackle rickshas. I could now make official calls in comfort and dignity. Though most of its foreign officers were gone, I found the Salt Administration the dominating, modernizing factor in all this region. It was building the roads, and constructing the river dams and the bridges. It was running hospitals, orphanages, and schools. The staff, comprising some of the best trained and most experienced officers in the government, had been retained on the old civil service basis which we had established.

I dined one evening *en famille* with my old chief Dr. H. H. Kung. The Minister of Finance and Director General of the Salt Administration, and his charming American educated wife provided a meal somewhat luxurious for the stipulated economies of wartime, but austere enough compared to the lush days of the pre-war era down in the coastal cities. Dr. Kung, with Oberlin and Yale degrees, discoursed in his excellent English about his achievements as Minister of Finance over nine progressive years. He took a justifiable pride in the unprecedented feat of balancing China's budget in fateful 1937. As China's representative to King George VI's coronation in that year he had met many important personages. He was, for example, invited to meet Mussolini by Count Galleazzo Ciano whom he had known when the latter was Italian Minister to China. As relations between England and Italy were not cordial at that time, due to the Abyssinian war, and as Dr. Kung's mission was to be exclusively devoted to the coronation, he felt it inappropriate to meet other chiefs of state while still en route. He adroitly avoided the embarrassment by making an appointment with an eminent specialist at Prague for a medical check-up.

Arriving in London, Dr. Kung continued, he sought to be peacemaker by improving relations between Great Britain and Italy. In a talk with Foreign Secretary Anthony Eden he raised this question.

"We have no objection to maintaining good relations with Italy provided Mussolini does not pursue his ambition of reviving the Roman Empire," was Eden's comment.

Upon his return to Rome, Ciano asked Dr. Kung what Eden's attitude was. This was embarrassing, but finally Dr. Kung repeated what Eden had said.

When he saw Chamberlain, he proposed a Pacific Conference to head off the impending war.

"You will have to persuade the man in the street before anything can be done," was Chamberlain's reply. Dr. Kung thought that this was anything but constructive, for actually the British public was ahead of the government in its appreciation of the Far Eastern situation. On the other hand, he later observed that the American public was lagging behind President Roosevelt.

Dr. Kung then related a typical Chinese story illustrative of the European situation as he had found it. A tiger treed a monkey. The monkey sat on a limb but was so frightened when he looked down on the snarling, ferocious beast below that he covered his eyes with his hands instead of grasping the limb on which he was safely perched. Seeing this, the tiger swished his great tail against the trunk and so shook the monkey down into his jaws. This was Chamberlain and his appeasement policy at the outbreak of the European war!

The story of his talk with Hitler was dramatic. He described how Hitler's eyes blazed with hatred as he spoke of Russian communism and he gave every indication that he would attack Russia first. Was he merely acting, speculated Dr. Kung, since he attacked France first?

In America Dr. Kung told of meeting the President and his mother at Hyde Park. Dr. Kung professed great admiration for President Roosevelt's profound acquaintance with world affairs, which enabled him to foresee the international cataclysm. He noted that his admiration for the President was fully shared by Generalissimo Chiang K'ai-shek.

Shortly afterwards I met the Chinese chief of state. It was at a reception by Generalissimo and Madame Chiang K'ai-shek on United Nations Day at the new Foreign Office, built on an eminence looking out over the broad Yangtze and to the mountains beyond. The "exalted couple" appeared in due course and walked about, nodding and saying a word or two to each guest. As had been frequently remarked by those who have met him, Generalissimo Chiang has an engaging personality, with curiously farseeing eyes. He speaks no English but in his wife he has a superb interpreter. She, of course, is charm itself, mixed with a quiet tinge of superiority. Madame Chiang wore a tight-fitting Chinese gown with broad stripes alternately light and dark blue running horizontally. A handsome diamond brooch, two wings with a wheel joining them, was clasped on her left shoulder. This she told me was her insignia as Colonel of the American Volunteer Flyers. Later as I spoke with Madame on the verandah she complained that she had "three gray hairs" from her arduous work on the Airplane Commission. But, since she had resigned that position, she had no more.

Wartime Chungking I found a microcosm of talent and distinction. The press of the world was represented. The journalistic fraternity, however, proved at times something of a nuisance for if they couldn't find out all about you and your business they started inventing and that got people into trouble. They particularly resented being housed in a sort of ghetto, the thatched-roof press compound buildings improvised after the heavy bombings. They were also irked by Vice Minister of Information Hollington K. Tong who restricted their news items to official handouts. The bad press which came to plague the Nationalist government in after years appears to have had its origins at this time.

At one memorable press dinner, Edgar Snow, bell wether of the pro-Communist scriveners and Tong, mouthpiece of his Nationalist leader Chiang K'ai-shek, sat opposite each other. Both were alumni of the University of Missouri's famous school of journalism. They continued to exchange wary ideological blows, while Mademoiselle Eve Curie, visiting Chungking at the time, listened with attention and some amusement.

In my own intelligence reporting I was obliged to transmit everything by special code through the American embassy, supplying our Ambassador, Clarence Gauss, with paraphrases of my messages. His Excellency, well known for his chronic cynicism, never hesitated to express his disbelief in the verisimilitude of code message to paraphrase! At the time, all attention was concentrated in our war theatre on the precarious Burma situation. The Chinese were critical of the British for running away or so promptly surrendering, as they regarded it. They had become very outspoken about American war material being directed to British needs and little or nothing to China. This appeared unreasonable as vast quantities of American supplies had gone as far as India but couldn't get further. Lend-lease goods were either destroyed or captured in Burma, much of which would have reached China had the Burma Road been efficiently managed.

As my mission to Chungking neared its end, a onetime colleague in the Salt Administration invited me to accompany a party to the famed salt wells of West China. Our cavalcade left by car for a well-planned program of sight-seeing at the town of Tzuliutsing—"Self-flowing-wells." I had heard of this extraordinary place with its "derricks" for raising the brine from deep bored wells scattered over the hills and valleys, with bamboo pipelines through which the brine flowed by gravity from well to boiling shed, all affording the exact appearance from a distance of the skyline of a California oil field. Instead of steel the derricks are fabricated of enormous bamboo poles lashed together, each upright column bound strongly around with bamboo strips. Though rising forty or more feet high, little or no metal is used in the construction of these ancient prototypes of the American oil derrick. We examined with great curiosity the ingenious pipelines, again made of bamboo tubes five or six inches in diameter, wrapped tightly with strips of the same material and sealed at all joints with watertight cement.

A colorful ceremony marked the official occasion of our visit, the opening of three locks on the Yenching River to help in the transport of salt by water. The solid masonry locks let salt boats through a "midget Panama Canal," as one of the University of Michigan trained engineers wittily termed it. A ribbon was cut by a pretty Chinese girl, a bottle of Chinese wine broken, and a fleet of fully laden salt boats made their way for the first time through this modern engineering achievement two thousand miles inside China.

Here, too, in remote West China, as in my old district of the Central Yangtze Province, the salt merchants proved to be affluent and hospitable. We were their guests at a picturesque, walled hill top town where they had their homes. As elsewhere in China and Manchuria the wealthy entrepreneurs were taking due precautions for their safety. A feast was served for our party in a lovely villa with a magnificent panorama of the distant plain below. The quality of the viands was characteristic. There was choice fruit grown on the top of the hill, wine thirty years aged, and all sorts of delicacies including the mushrooms and tender wood fungus ("silver ears") for which this province is famous and which were always to be found on every gourmet's table throughout the empire.

Before returning to Chungking we must have a glimpse of the most celebrated of China's Five Sacred Mountains, Omei-shan. The trip across country, ever westward, presented a succession of the scenes associated with the typical Chinese landscape, thatched roof villages, feathery bamboo groves, hewn stone honorary archways, temples picturesquely ensconced on steep hillsides and almost hidden by luxurious groves, and soaring above all on lofty eminences, towering nine-storied pagodas, the hoary cathedrals of Eastern Asia. My disappointment at the bleak and bare appearance of North China at my first arrival in 1908 was at last banished in these charming scenes.

Our chair coolies carried us up the mountain's rugged pilgrim steps, passing through avenues of trees of every conceivable variety. Mount Omei appeared a veritable botanist's paradise. Giant "madonna lilies" glowed among the bamboos. A final ascent through lichened pines brought us to our journey's end, the "Golden Pinnacle." Here on the mountain top two miles above sea level were unpainted wooden temples, in the best of which we took up our quarters. My own room looked out directly over an enormous abyss.

I stood for a moment on the spot, fenced off with an iron chain, where as the sun declined in the west, I saw my own enormous shadow on the white mists below. The devout pilgrim, seeing his own reflection, imagines this to be the veritable image of the Buddha. In pious exaltation, he throws himself down into the All-Merciful's arms! We were lucky both that night and the next morning with visibility perfect. As the sun rose, the Great Snow Mountain of the far Tibetan marches glistened pearly white. It was Minyakonka we could see, 150 miles away on the horizon, 25,000 feet high, a huge horn shaped summit, with other shining snow-covered peaks on either side.

My last days in Chungking, or for that matter in China, were busy beyond description, with all the work of winding up my affairs. And again as so many times in the torrid summers of the Yangtze valley, I melted in

221

the humidity of a hundred degree heat. Friends of "three dynasties" of China days came to bid me farewell. At daybreak my plane took off from the sand spit in the River. We speedily rose to 18,000 feet to cross "The Hump." I was bidding farewell to a Cycle of Cathay.

Epilogue—China Then and Now

THROUGHOUT this personal narrative, I am an observer and often a participant in many wars and revolutions. Foreign residents of China regarded most of these as minor annoyances in an otherwise agreeable existence in the somewhat comic Celestial Kingdom. I have told of my share in the first (1911) and the second (1913) revolutions in the American Company of the Shanghai Volunteer Defense Force. Through the "Era of the Warlords" (1915 to 1926), I dealt personally in the business of the Salt Administration with these truculent and avaricious chieftains. At the culmination of the Nationalist revolution at Hankow in 1927, I was one of the foreign residents who along with my fellow British and American "bourgois" became targets for the Chinese communists and their Russian co-conspirators, the while certain American fellow-travelers lurked in the background. Nevertheless despite armed uprisings and civil commotions, China until 1937 was comparatively safe for our business and residence. Chiang K'ai-shek had promptly ended the bloody excesses of the left wing Nationalists after the consolidation of his government in 1927.

Not until Japan's ambitious program for "The Greater East Asia Co-prosperity Sphere" did the complete breakdown come. Under the treaties between China and the Western nations, conditions had been stabilized for many years. The system peculiarly suited to the conditions of China at the time—treaty ports for foreign business and residence, and the international operation of China's principal governmental services—made life agreeable not only to foreigners but promoted immensely the development of China itself. The regime headed by Chiang K'ai-shek proved the most progressive China had ever experienced. Dr. Yung Wing's seemingly frustrated educational mission to America of the 1870's had eventuated in a vast number of Western-trained Chinese predominating in government and in business.

As I stood on the sidelines in the great international seaport of Shanghai at the outbreak of the First World War in August 1914, and again in 1939 at the moment of a second declaration of war by Great Britain, I could little foresee how these cosmic cataclysms would destroy the mechanisms which had served us for so long in providing peace, security and relative prosperity to China, and which had been of substantial benefit to the Chinese people themselves. Under Japanese attack first, then by reason of the postwar struggle culminating in the disastrous domination of entire continental China by the Communists, all the old safeguards were removed, extraterritoriality protection for foreign residents against the vagaries of Chinese justice, treaty ports providing effective municipal

222

governments. China under the nominal headship of ideologist Mao Tzu-tung is little more than a satellite of the Kremlin. This has resulted in the disintegration of the vast international trading fabric, and has drastically reduced China's overseas food supplies, her former huge volume of im-ports and exports and has thrown back her modern organization which had been proceeding apace. Vast disillusionment has ensued in the achievement of real political and agrarian reforms so glibly promised by her subverters.

Once again, as so often in the past, the eyes of the world focus on the erstwhile Hermit Kingdom, misnamed *Chosen* by the Koreans themselves, "Land of Morning Calm." Here the war is hot between the Communist and the democratic-capitalistic world while the miserable Korean people bear the brunt of it. At the close of the nineteenth century, Korea was the arena of bitter rivalry between China, the traditional suzereign, Russia al-ways expanding east and southward in Asia, and the Island Empire Japan anxious for its safety in the "dagger thrust at its heart," as it viewed the Korean peninsula in the hands of a hostile power. This struggle was for the time being settled by the Russo-Japanese War of 1904–1905. Japan was granted virtually a free hand in all South Manchuria. Korea was an-nexed shortly after I saw Prince Ito and the puppet Korean "Emperor" at the Seoul railway station one frosty winter morning in 1909. The Kuriles Islands and the southern half of Sagalien Peninsula were ceded to Japan. Thus Japan built up an impregnable land and sea barrier against Russian aggression in the Far East. Despite victory by the United States and her Western European allies, the tragic secret treaty made at Yalta between the astute and experienced Stalin and the enfeebled President Roosevelt (Churchill having already left the Conference), handed back to Russian control or influence the vast territories which her ambition had once gained. Japan's counterbalance to Russia in East Asia was now removed.

The present near monopoly of power by Russia in East Asia is of spe-cial interest in historical retrospect. From the time the first Portuguese navigator, Ferdinand Andrade, arrived at Canton in 1517, it was the es-tablished policy of the Chinese government, then the Manchu monarchy, to keep all Europeans at bay. The British sent two unsuccessful missions to Peking in an attempt to open up diplomatic and regulated trading re-lations. The Russians had in Peking already for many years their cele-brated "Mission." While this representative agency was not active, it was always on hand to conduct whatever negotiations might be necessary be-tween Russia and the Chinese court. Other nations were obliged to work through distant Canton with unreliable Chinese officials as intermediaries. The mandarins in South China were under strict obligation to keep the foreigners, that is non-Russians, from proceeding north to establish them-selves at the Capital. It was only the wars of 1838–1842, 1858–1860 and other forms of pressure that enabled other powers than Russia to set up diplomatic relations directly with the central Chinese government.

223

Viewing the present situation, China's international intercourse is thus returned to the position of the early nineteenth century and before. Today, Soviet Russia is in full diplomatic relationship with the Chinese (Communist) government. Most other powers are excluded. The British have attempted to rectify their position, just as in the late eighteenth and early nineteenth centuries, they tried to establish working connections, but equally without success.

In the years from the opening of Canton and other treaty ports to foreign trade, Americans have followed a cooperative policy with China. Their merchants have not been aggressive. Missionaries and teachers have gone to China at their own expense and established churches, hospitals, as well as many educational institutions of the American pattern. Thousands of Chinese have benefited from these benevolent activities.

American diplomacy towards China has suffered from failure to consider the lessons of the past. Department of State records disclose that after the Boxer "rebellion" in China, Russia adopted an extremely aggressive attitude. She excluded, or attempted to do so, all interests from Manchuria save her own. A "cold war" developed between American and Russian representatives in that area of China down to the Russo-Japanese war. This latter conflict threw the Bear back to North Manchuria and ultimately to its own Siberian territories.

When in 1942 I saw Chiang K'ai-shek and his people driven to the West China frontier but still holding out against a remorseless enemy, the United States was aiding Nationalist China in a somewhat bad-tempered, half-hearted way. I watched fearfully the disintegration of our friendship with the Chinese nation at a most crucial period in history. It is a sorry story which needs no repeating. I could not but continually recall General Eisenhower's warning to Americans in China "If you can't get along with the Chinese you might as well come home." The traditional cooperation between China and America has now been completely blacked out. In its place a most virulent anti-American propaganda issues forth from Peking.

It is easy to trace the origins of the present animosity against the historic friends of China, the American people. By the close of the War subtle forces were doing all in their power to disparage and destroy the reputation and morale of Chiang K'ai-shek and the Nationalist government, the people of China on our side. Over the United States, newspapers, magazines and books poured forth vilifications and charges. To be sure, those of us who knew our China could admit its deplorable societal, economic and political conditions, ineluctable to over populated Asiatic countries. India with two centuries of British rule falls below even the debased living standards of the Chinese populace. By this powerful propaganda, Americans were made to forget that Chinese morale had suffered greatly after years of exhausting warfare, much of it fought without allies. Forgotten were the corrupt and oppressive days of our own carpet-bagging politicians after our protracted Civil War.

224

Most important, America did not heed the repeated warnings of Chiang K'ai-shek that the future threat was Communism, not only to China, but to the whole free Western world. For this the great Chinese leader was taunted with being concerned more with the Communist menace to his government, than with winning the war. The event demonstrated the realism of Chiang's thinking. Obviously the war with Japan had to be won by the well-equipped western allies and not by the demoralized armies of impoverished China. The nation must consider its position at the close of the war with the menace of a Soviet-backed revolt readying to be launched against it. Nevertheless American official policy was even geared to force Chiang to take into his government the rebel Communist element.

The Chinese Nationalist leader's prophesy has been tragically confirmed. In a few swift months of bloody battle, the so-called "simple agrarian reformers" (the Chinese Communists), supplied by Russia with captured Japanese and American war material, with able Soviet staff assistance, drove the friendly government of China to its last refuge, the Island of Formosa. Here it waits either destruction by the overwhelming forces of the Russian-directed Communists, or revival as effective allies of the United Nations in the desperate and never-ending struggle with Russian imperialism, by whatever name, in the Far East.